WILLIAM CAMPBELL

HERE'S

Creative solutions for Ireland's economic and social problems

HOW

A Brandon Paperback Original

First published in 2010 by Brandon
an imprint of Mount Eagle Publications
Dingle, Co. Kerry, Ireland, and
Unit 3, Olympia Trading Estate, Coburg Road, London N22 6TZ, England

ISBN 9780863224270

2 4 6 8 10 9 7 5 3 1

Cover design: Anú Design
Typesetting by Red Barn Publishing, Skeagh, Skibbereen

www.brandonbooks.com

Contents

Introduction 7

Sit in the Theatre and Learn about Rules...........................11

Seven Things to Do in a Week...20

The Uncivil Service 21

Preventing Corruption 31

Bankrupt Banks 33

NAMA...43

Stamp Duty 47

Screen Scraping 49

Postcodes..52

Remember Everybody 56

Cartels and Congested Markets 58

Food and Agriculture...66

Culture..76

The Irish Language 82

Space for Children 85

Broadcast Media 90

Broadband and Telecoms 99

Burglar Alarms 103

Energy...105

The Army 112

Education and Science..113

Vehicle Registration Tax 128

Bankruptcy and Debt 130

The Workless Class...133

Travellers...141

Benefits 145

Local Services 147

Waste Problems 152

Planning...157

New Housing Agency 173

Local Authorities 177

Electoral Reform...181

Major Financial Crime 189

Quangos 195

New Alliances..198

The Health of the Nation...203

Illegal Drugs..216

Cigarette Taxes 220

Gay Rights..223

Justice 225

Crime...238

Judging the Judges 247

Transport...253

Conclusion..268

Notes 269

Introduction

This book is a collection of suggestions on how to make Ireland a better place – happier, healthier, more just – and more prosperous – but it's not just a simple list. The ideas are designed to work in complement with each other, and they are guided by the principles of lateral thinking and rationally examining the best solutions to problems. International topics that are outside the power of Irish people to change are excluded from consideration, and no doubt many good things that can be done within Ireland have been missed. If you think of something, please visit the website associated with this book, **www.HeresHow.ie** and submit your idea. You are also welcome to give your opinions – for or against – on all the issues in this book.

Niccolò Machiavelli wrote in *The Prince* in 1513 that advocates of reform will always face unreasonable resistance, no matter how good their proposals. Many of the ideas in this book are sure to provoke the opposition of vested interests, and of people who just disagree. Overcoming this opposition is also outside the scope of the book – these are the ideas; how to persuade people to implement them is a book for someone else to write.

This book is an attempt to come up with solutions based on reason and evidence, rather than ideology. Almost every fact in the book is sourced, but rather than wasting trees printing hundreds of footnotes, you can find them online. The great majority of references are of web links to newspapers, academic websites and other sources, so clicking on them online is also easier for the reader. You can find them at **www.HeresHow.ie**. Also on the website is a free bonus chapter which you can download.

Ireland in 2010
Ireland is in deep trouble. We went into an economic depression in 2009.[1] In April 2009 the ESRI predicted an economic contraction of 14 per cent by 2010,[2] but we are already beyond that point because GDP dropped 7.1 per cent during the last quarter of 2008[3] and by more in the first quarter of 2009.[4] Unemployment shot up from 4.5 per cent to 12.5 per cent by the end of 2009.[5][6] We have the world's highest gross external debt at 811 per cent of GDP.[7] We are very close to national bankruptcy. But this book is not a response to the economic crisis which ended the Celtic Tiger. It offers solutions to long-term structural problems that have existed, in some cases, for generations. However, many of these problems contribute to our immediate difficulties, so the crisis makes solving them more urgent.

Rip-off Republic

From groceries to mobile phones, there is a huge disparity between prices in Ireland and those in neighbouring countries. Because Ireland is a small and isolated island, there is often little competition between suppliers, giving them opportunity to gouge the market with little incentive to reduce costs. This effect is magnified because even competitive suppliers must pay, and pass on to customers, prices for supplies they buy from uncompetitive sectors.

Public Sector Inefficiency

Despite denials from trade unions, nobody who has dealt with the public sector – the civil service, local authorities, state agencies – will imagine that the taxpayer is getting good value for money. Public sector trade unions point to the 2008 OECD report which says that Ireland has the third smallest total public expenditure as a proportion of GDP of any OECD country.[8] This is true but irrelevant; anything at all, measured as a proportion of Ireland's GDP, is meaningless, because:

- Almost all other OECD countries have large military budgets, which count as public spending, artificially inflating their figure; Ireland does not.

- Thanks to immigration and other demographics, Ireland's dependency ratio is far lower than other developed countries, and this gives a much lower requirement for public services such as health care and education.[9]

- Ireland's GDP is artificially swollen by the transfer pricing of multinationals, who shift profits to Irish subsidiaries to avail of low tax rates, which is no indication of real economic activity in Ireland.[‡]

- The OECD report was compiled at the very height of Ireland's Celtic Tiger GDP, which has fallen rapidly since.

Even if none of these points above was valid, simply measuring the size of the public sector gives no indication of the value for money achieved and is no proof that good performance in some areas of the system is not masking great inefficiencies elsewhere.

Corruption

In recent years credible accusations of serious crime have been made against politicians such as Charles Haughey and Michael Lowry, as well as bishops, bankers, businessmen and judges whose names are omitted on legal advice (see **Libel** on page 97). Not a single one of these has stood trial.

The damage from corruption is not confined to the billions stolen from the public purse or from consumers. The perception at home and abroad that

---

[‡] According to the Finfacts website, SanDisk's Irish operation, with just eight staff, posted a profit of €762 million in 2007.

corruption is tolerated is even more damaging than the corruption itself. It deters foreign investment and reduces the willingness to trade with Ireland. If you doubt that, ask yourself what you did the last time you got a business proposal from Nigeria.

Poor Enforcement

Aside from corruption, there is a culture of non-compliance in Ireland. Everything from littering to speeding to tax evasion imposes much greater costs on society than any benefit to the rule breaker, but there is a tolerance of non-compliance at all levels. There is huge scope to improve these and many other areas, at very little cost and with great benefits to society.

Cultural Weakening

The internal and international standing of Ireland's culture is, generally, good, but there is no reason to imagine that this will continue without careful nurturing.

It's Not All Bad

There is good news. We have serious problems, but they can be solved. For all its flaws, Ireland is still a country to be proud of. We score highly in almost every international ranking index; out of almost two hundred countries on the planet, we are ranked twelfth on the Democracy index,[10] eighth on the Education index,[11] fifth in the Human Development Index,[21,‡] and by a wide margin we are number one on the Quality of Life index.[13,§]

And that is not the good news. The good news is this: we score highly despite a wide range of serious problems; those problems have solutions. If we tackle and solve those problems we can prosper – socially and economically – like never before. We can lead the world.

A Coincidence

At roughly the same time that the Celtic Tiger boom imploded, the world economy went into a serious recession, and many said that Ireland's problems were caused by this recession. They are wrong. While Ireland's internal economy tanked, this had nothing to do with international problems. In 2009, while other countries were slashing production, Ireland's exports *increased* by almost €3bn over the previous year, and profits in multinationals accordingly shot up by more than €1bn.[14] Miraculously, the international recession passed Ireland by. All our problems are internal and

---

‡   This measures a combination of life expectancy, literacy, educational attainment, and GDP per capita.

§   These figures are trailing indexes, so no doubt we will dip somewhat given the depth of the economic crisis, but nevertheless our scores are impressive.

of our own making. This is good news too: if we are responsible for our own problems, the solutions are in our own hands too.

Sit in the Theatre and Learn about Rules

Rules benefit society. If we stand in the theatre, we get a better view, at the cost of the person behind us, so she may stand too, to restore her view. Pretty soon, everyone in the theatre is standing – we all have much the same view as when we were all sitting, and we all have tired legs. So society has a rule that in the theatre, we sit.

The rule is never enforced, because it doesn't have to be. Its benefits are obvious; the cost of the rule (not getting a better view) and the benefit (not getting tired legs) are evenly distributed, with the exception of the people in the front row, and they don't need to be told that they would suffer serious social consequences if they disregarded the rule.

Not every rule is like this – some rules have clear winners and losers, and without enforcement the losers are not motivated to obey them; but I accept that I must pay for my shopping, because I expect protection from those who would steal from me. A rule that costs me in the short term can have long-term benefits. But there are some areas where the rules are not working in Ireland today.

A rule with one consistent loser and another consistent winner is clearly unfair. Extreme examples such as apartheid can expect consistent challenge, but even minor injustices cause problems of non-compliance. Rules should be just.

Plastic Bags

A few years ago, Ireland led the world in one small issue. Plastic bags are environmentally destructive. Used for 15 minutes to bring the shopping home, they take 15 million years to degrade in landfills. Irish people used hundreds of millions of them per year. Miraculously, when on 4 March 2002 they were asked to pay a 15c‡ environmental levy for each bag,[15] they discovered that they didn't need nearly so many. The use of plastic bags dropped by more than 92 per cent.[16]

How could people have thought that they needed 13 times more plastic bags than they really did? The answer is that they didn't think about it at all. If something is free, no rational person will worry too much about its cost. So the first principle is this:

1. If you want to achieve efficiency, make a connection between cost and use.

---

‡   Later increased to 44c

The cost of "free" bags was internalised in the cost of the goods in the supermarket. However, the real cost of a plastic bag is not its manufacture, but its disposal. Storing one plastic bag in a landfill for a year doesn't cost much, but multiply it by 15 million and the cost becomes real. The consumer paid this cost because it was imposed on society as a whole and the consumer is part of that society. Before the levy, anyone reusing plastic bags would have their saving diluted in a sea of wastefulness. When the cost was individualised, consumers changed their behaviour, so here's another principle:

2.   People react more to a personal cost than a socialised one.

The plastic bag levy internalised a cost and encouraged rational use of a resource. It is a positive example of how motivation changes behaviour. There is, however, no shortage of negative examples.

Burglar Alarms
Think back to the last time you heard a burglar alarm. What did you do? Most people do nothing, and with good reason. A Garda source confirms that more than 99 per cent of times, the property or vehicle is secure when the alarm goes off. At the time of writing, the Golden Pages website lists 543 firms who fit burglar alarms in Ireland. How can there be so many businesses fitting such unreliable equipment? The answer is motivation, or lack of it. Owners of alarm systems benefit from the monitoring provided by their neighbours. They pay nothing for this monitoring, therefore they have no motivation to use it carefully; they suffer no cost if the alarm goes off when it shouldn't, and no inconvenience either, because they are always away when the alarm is armed.

Suppliers of alarms feel no pressure from their customers to make reliable systems, and because they can only compete on price, they would be unwise to impose the extra cost of making the system reliable on their customers.

Long-suffering neighbours quickly learn that most alarms are false alarms and don't react, so society is left with blaring alarms and little security benefit. When everybody is behaving rationally and things are still going wrong, it is time to change the motivation. This demonstrates some important principles:

3.   People are often selfish, but usually rational.

4.   People are usually careful with their money, and will react quickly if they do not receive value.

5.   When others are paying, they are not so careful.

See page 103 for a proposal about better burglar alarms.

The Credit Card Principle

If you have plastic, you'll understand. It just doesn't feel the same as handing over cold hard cash. When making the decision about a purchase, the more distance you can put between yourself and the cost, the easier the cost seems.

Retailers have to pay credit card companies a margin of 2 to 6 per cent for the privilege of using their system, on top of set-up charges. They accept losing the margin, because they know that the increase in sales will more than compensate. This principle is:

6.   People react more to an immediate cost than to a delayed one.

This principle can be put to use; society may want to promote one type of spending over another. Without coercing people, it is possible to encourage good behaviour by attaching the cost more immediately to one item than another. And that brings us to socialism.

An Idea with a Great Future behind It

"To each," Marx said, "according to his needs; from each according to his ability." Which would be great. The problem is persuading each to give according to his or her ability and to refrain from taking more than their needs. The international recession has sparked claims from the extreme left that what they like to call "late capitalism" is failing and their revolution is just around the corner, as it was during the recessions of the 1980s and 1970s. Nevertheless, it seems clear that even without Stalinist repression, communism is doomed to have serious economic difficulties because, just like with plastic bags, people tend to be wasteful of resources when they are not paying for them directly.

Also, it is obvious that people tend to discipline themselves to work more productively when they have a personal stake in the profits. When the profit of a greater effort is diluted in the laziness of the rest of society, human nature dictates that people will not make the same effort. Another principle:

7.   Many people enjoy their work, but don't enjoy it as much as they enjoy not working.

And a big one:

8.   Sometimes there may be a reason to socialise the cost of a product or service, but without such a reason, the presumption should be that people may earn, keep and spend their own money.

Communism also failed because of complexity. It wasn't a bad idea for its time – 1867 – when the Rockefellers, Carnegies, Vanderbilts and other robber barons decided what industries to locate where in smoke-filled rooms with no regard for anything but their own enrichment. It was reasonable to assume that the people's ministers of oil, coal and steel could make the same decisions with the interests of the people at heart. But the economy became vastly more complex in the last century, and it seems like the complexity will only grow.

The history of government-run industries is not glorious, and even the most committed socialist wouldn't claim that the government could be good at running industries like manufacturing mobile camera-phones, DVD players or iPods, websites like Google Maps or Facebook, or even supplying fruit smoothies or cappuccinos. The old criticism about people knowing more and more about less and less is actually what allows people to devote the huge talent of humanity to fabulous new inventions. New industries succeed because tiny, highly specialised groups dedicate everything to them, and hit the jackpot if they come up good, although most fail.

It is impossible for the government to continue to control as large a proportion of the economy as it once did. This is not only because the government in particular is poor at the job, but also because no organisation could possibly manage that level of complexity. The best that a government can hope for is to create conditions to allow the economy to thrive and carry out a small but vital list of tasks that the private sector cannot achieve.

If you doubt the difference in innovation between nationalised industries and new-economy upstarts, compare Eircom to Skype. Skype, which provides video and telephone calls over the internet, was founded in 2003. It has a total worldwide staff of 500[17] and provided 23.6 billion minutes of computer-to-computer calls in the first quarter of 2009, a rate that is growing at about 60 per cent per year. They also provided 2.9 billion minutes of calls to regular telephones.[18]

Eircom, with the highest line rental charges in the world,[19] employs more than 6,000 people, 12 times the number employed by Skype. Eircom's voice traffic in Q1 2009 was 4.7 billion minutes, a decline of 8.5 per cent.[20] Big, old-style organisations, even when they are privatised, simply cannot innovate or use innovation the way that smart, motivated entrepreneurs can. And you don't get anything bigger, or older-style, than governments, therefore:

9.   Governments should do as little as possible, as well as possible.

Money is Not the Only Cost
Money doesn't just mean money. Human beings are willing to pay money for a wide variety of things: property, stocks and shares and other things that tend to appreciate, food and clothing that is consumed or depreciates, but also for intangibles such as holidays, a window cleaner, charity or a coin given to a toddler to put in a busker's hat.

People are willing to trade money for status, friendship or quality of life, and sometimes willing to trade these things for money. Some will say that no amount of money could match some of life's pleasures. But if you don't account for non-financial assets, they are often just valued at zero. It is an imperfect analogy, but what is referred to here as a "cost" is anything one is willing to pay money to avoid, and a "benefit" is anything one is willing to pay money to acquire.

Principles

When applied to most of the problems of Irish society today, the principles here suggest solutions that would improve our country. Here are some more:

   10. When the wrong person does the job, don't expect good results...

   11. Because if they are not incentivised to succeed, they probably won't.

In some cases when a job is being done badly, the solution is to motivate the person doing the job to improve, but this can be very difficult. Sometimes the solution is not to give motivation to the person with the job, but to give the job to the person with the motivation. Above all, it is important to make sure that the person best able to succeed has both the job and the motivation.

   12. Injustice is bad for society.

   13. When there is an inequality of power between parties to a dispute, society should ensure that everyone enjoys equal justice.

Injustice is Bad

Perhaps only the last two principles would be disputed. In the name of progress, some may argue, we have to trample on some toes. Authoritarian governments say that the rights of the individual sometimes have to be sacrificed for the good of society. Bullies have always been good at self-justification. The best rebuttal of this argument comes from the American comic writer PJ O'Rourke. In his book *Eat the Rich*, he compared two socialist countries, Sweden and Tanzania, with two capitalist ones, the United States and post-communist Albania.

Swedes have a high standard of living, with excellent social services and low crime. Tanzania is not only poor, but rapidly getting poorer. The USA, while suffering from much inequality, is a hugely successful economy, but Albania since communism is a basket-case. O'Rourke argued that, as long as you stick to the rules, it doesn't really matter what the rules are. In Sweden, laws are enforced equally – the most senior member of society can expect the same fine for littering as the most humble. Everyone pays their taxes, so no one is at a disadvantage for being honest. In Tanzania, the other socialist country, bribery and corruption are the order of the day.

Equally in the USA, compliance is expected. Doubtless there are problems, but the criminals who ran Enron and WorldCom are in jail. Albania, nominally capitalist, is really a kleptocracy like Tanzania. No one bothers working, because if you earn anything, it will be stolen. And if you're in the mafia, why bother working when you can steal with impunity?

In a theoretical perfect economy, every individual seeks the most rewarding career, and every employer finds the best employee; this means that every person is working to the best of their ability, and society is at its most productive. Now, move one member of our perfect economy into a job that they are not best qualified for. It means that the job won't be done as well as it might, which costs society productivity, and the best-qualified person their rightful job. Every bit of pull, every wink, every nod and every stroke drags down productivity in society.

- The employer loses the talents of the best-qualified worker.

- The talented worker loses their rightful job.

- But what about the dullard who gets paid for a job they don't deserve? Doesn't the injustice benefit them?

It might, if there was only *one* dullard. Even the well-connected dullards have to live in a society where being a well-connected dullard gets you the best job. The cost to the dullard of living in this society outweighs the benefits of being well connected. If you want proof, just look at the brightest and the best that Albania has to offer. You'll find them sweeping the streets (or walking the streets) in any major western city and paying their mafia handsomely for the privilege of being people-trafficked to do so. They will risk life and limb to swap being rich in a poor country for being poor in a rich country.

Money and Wealth

They seem like the same thing – an individual who has a lot of money is wealthy, but for a society it is different. Spain demonstrated this spectacularly. In the time of Columbus, Spain was the pre-eminent European power. Then gold and silver from the New World began to flood Spain's economy to such an extent that galleons with chests full of Spanish doubloons still reverberate in popular culture. Far from getting richer, Spain entered a long decline that continued until the end of the colonial era. The Spanish crown defaulted on its debt 14 times between 1557 and 1696.[21] Economists even have a name for this effect: resource curse. The gold and silver did allow them to buy some resources from other European countries, but it deterred reform and economic development in their own country.

For an individual, money is wealth which can be used to outbid other members of society for goods and services. The whole of society cannot outbid itself, so money is not wealth on a national scale. For a society, wealth means producing more goods and services that are of use to that society. The more efficiently we produce those goods and services, the wealthier we are. Wealth is efficiency.

Wealth is Efficiency

In 1811, the weaver Ned Ludd and his followers were so outraged by the advent of the power loom that they violently destroyed the new technology that was competing with them.[22] But they were wrong; the purpose of weaving is to provide cloth for customers, not jobs for weavers. We could have banned the telephone to keep telegraph operators employed; we could ban DVDs to preserve jobs in VHS factories. The Chinese phone company is indeed trying to ban Skype to preserve its own revenue,[23] but all that is achieved is a delay in the flow of the benefits of efficiency to society.

The more that businesses innovate, modernise and become more efficient, the more that we will benefit, even those of us who lose out in the short term. This is not to say that businesses may not become too big or powerful; they will, and they will use every trick in the book to make more profits, to avoid regulation and competition, and to take short-cuts to profits that don't involve having to innovate, modernise and become more efficient. It is the function of government to set limits on the behaviour of business and to make sure that they behave well. The guiding principle of this is that the purpose of regulation should be to benefit society. The regulation of taxi numbers was not, and the regulation of pubs, pharmacies, radio stations and many other businesses is not designed to protect society; it is designed to protect uncompetitive operators, at the expense of society.

Tax if You Must

All taxation reduces the number of potential businesses which are viable. A business is a risk, and entrepreneurs will not take that risk unless they believe the rewards will justify the risk. Direct taxes – on wages or profits – reduce the reward if the business succeeds. Increase the indirect taxes and you reduce the amount of money in the market to make the business successful. Every time that taxes tick up, they pass the point at which many businesses are viable, reducing competition for customers.

But the state must levy taxes to pay for the services that the private sector cannot provide, or provide well. The balance to strike is to provide for these services as efficiently as possible; we must tax enough to provide those services, without raising taxes so high as to make work unattractive, leaving ourselves in a spiral of ever fewer businesses and employees paying ever more taxes.

On one side of this see-saw, Ireland does relatively well. Irish taxes are low, by developed world standards, although there is one problem; an absence of property taxes means that the tax base is narrow and taxation is skewed towards income and sales, rewarding old money and punishing those who generate new wealth.

On the side of efficient delivery, Ireland fails badly, with huge amounts of waste in the public sector. We gave a billion-euro budget to the job-training agency Fás when just 80,000 people were on the dole, €12,500 for each jobseeker per year. Excess at the top gets a lot of attention, and it must be tackled, but so must waste and low productivity at every level of the Irish public sector. This book proposes many ways to improve this.

The Case for Regulation

Freedom is good. People may not always make the best decisions for themselves, but that is not the threshold for deciding whether they should be allowed to make those decisions. The threshold is this: can it be shown that taking away their freedom would lead to better decisions? Humans are fallible, and it is easy to point out mistakes people make in their lives. Governments are also made of humans, and just as fallible. However, governments are not as motivated to make good decisions as the people directly affected.

The presumption must always be in favour of individual liberty – the standard of proving the need for government regulation in any sphere is high, but it can be met. In his 1968 essay *The Tragedy of the Commons*, Garrett Hardin argued[24] that sometimes the sum of individual interests in society are not the interests of society as a whole. Hardin used the example of shepherds who share common grazing land where they are all entitled to let their animals graze.

Each shepherd is motivated by self-interest to put as many animals as possible on the common, even though this destroys the grazing. The shepherd receives all of the benefits from the additional animals, but the damage to the common is shared by the entire group. If all shepherds make this individually rational decision, the common is destroyed and they all suffer. However, if a wise authority fairly limits the number of animals allowed by each shepherd and enforces the rule strictly, all the shepherds benefit from the indefinite use of the land. The argument can be applied to everything from overfishing to pollution, but does not overcome the problem that many governments fail to produce good regulations.

Thaler and Sunstein, in their 2008 book *Nudge*,[25] give detailed recommendations on how regulations and other government interventions can be made work better by nudging people, without forcing them to do anything against their will. Several ideas in this book owe inspiration to them.

Seven Things to Do in a Week

Some problems will take years, maybe decades to work out, but there are plenty of improvements that we can effect in a very short time. Here are seven things that we can do in seven days.

1. Change prison food and reduce reoffending by a quarter – see page 241.

2. Require publicans to serve the full pint that customers pay for – see page 63.

3. Start eliminating toxic waste from batteries, litter from ATM receipts and other pollution – see page 152.

4. Speed up the broadband roll-out by penalising rather than rewarding Eircom for failure – see page 99.

5. Use social pressure to encourage people to sort their recyclables correctly – see page 155.

6. Make switching bank accounts easy by getting the new financial regulator (proposed on page 39) to implement the proposals to encourage competition on page 64.

7. Stop the drain of €500m per year from taxpayers' pockets caused by cigarette smuggling – see page 222.

The Uncivil Service

The woman behind the window was scrutinising every document, and finally she thought she got a hit. "You don't have the ... ah ..." she trailed off as she realised I had given her all the paperwork for her to issue my driving licence. Her face clearly betrayed her disappointment. I had already been sent packing once from the motor tax office, the person behind the window shoving my paperwork back at me. This time I had everything. She rolled her eyes and gathered up the documents, and I paid for the privilege.

It isn't a dingy office. The floor and walls in the bright, newly built Smithfield office are polished marble, with almost 100 wooden seats in fixed rows for the public to wait for their number to be called. The high counter where the staff sit behind a glass partition is old-style civil service though, and they have added their stamp in other ways. Poorly photocopied translations of the forms into immigrant languages are sloppily sellotaped to the marble walls. And there is a queuing system – please take a number. I did, and quickly calculated that I could write off most of the afternoon.

I went to the Spar shop around the corner and found three staff – half the number that worked on the counters at the motor tax office – serving the customers as they came in. The three, all immigrants, kept up a humorous banter between each other and the customers. Between sandwich making, lotto tickets and newspaper returns, their job was no less complex than that of the motor tax office.

They stood for their entire working day, greeted every customer with a smile and helped an older woman to input the code for the mobile phone credit she had bought. And they didn't have 100 seats installed for waiting customers. Yet they are paid between a quarter and a third of a typical civil servant. Wages in the private sector are nothing to aspire to; the real issue is productivity levels in the civil service.

Most European countries pay their civil servants significantly less than private sector workers. In 2009, the Central Statistics Office's National Employment Survey showed that the average hourly wage for Irish civil servants was 48 per cent higher than the average hourly wage for the private sector, and the gap could not be explained by age, experience or qualifications. Public sector jobs matched to equivalent jobs, with equally educated and experienced staff, in the private sector paid up to 76 per cent more. The smallest public sector bonus that existed was 25 per cent.[26]

This happened because, after benchmarking, public sector wages started out well ahead, and when the depression bit, private sector wages came crashing down, but public sector wages were still increasing in 2008, going up by 2.9 per cent that year,[27] mostly through what are called "increments", pay rises which public servants quietly get for longevity in the job, which are in addition to cost-of-living increases. The public sector pay cuts announced in the December 2009 budget are at least partly offset by these increments which are still being paid.[28]

Public sector trade unions justified the hugely expensive benchmarking process by claiming that they were entitled to have their wages adjusted to reflect changes in private sector wages, although since the process was excluded from the Freedom of Information Act, it is impossible to gauge whether the calculations were realistic. They don't seem to appreciate the irony that they are now apoplectic because their wages are partly following the downward trend of the private sector salaries, a principle that they insisted on when it favoured them.

Aside from this injustice, there are spectacular abuses in the civil service. Civil servants are given 30 minutes paid leave every payday to cash their cheques, even though they are paid by electronic transfer directly into their bank accounts.[29] Some get extra unofficial paid leave to attend Punchestown Races and other events.[30] You couldn't make it up.

The author is personally familiar with a section in a government department that holds a staff quiz every Friday morning, followed by a pub lunch from which few, if any, staff return. They are working a four-day week while being paid for five days.

The Unions

The earliest trade unions were established in Britain by seamen to prevent black men from becoming sailors.[31] More recent trade unionists have been active in opposing racism and have taken a deep interest in social justice. The basic conflict remains, however, between promoting the interests of members by improving society, or by doing so at the expense of non-union workers.

Some employers maintain the fiction that each of their employees freely enters into a contract as an equal with them. They will not accept unions "interfering" in a discussion on pay and work practices between what, they say, are two equal parties. The notion that there is an equality of power between a billionaire airline boss and a 20-year-old on the minimum wage is too daft to debate. The employer writes the contract, sets the work practices, decides the pay rates, hires and fires. The employee has two choices: take it or leave it. The employer wouldn't dream of writing employment contracts without high-powered professional advice, not to mention the PR specialists who contrive the "we're all equal here" line for the boss to present to the media.

In such a situation, it would be foolish for an employee not to seek the support and advice of their more experienced peers. Trade unions can be proud of the work that they have done in many industries. But trade unions are powerful structures, and it would be unreasonable to expect the people who run them – human beings, after all – not to try to maintain their power and position. While the fair distribution of the fruits of the economy may remain a lofty goal, it must be tempting to take the shortcut to prosperity by simply getting a better deal than non-union workers.

The computer used to write this work was made in Limerick by Dell. Dell employed about 3,000 people in Ireland through the boom, and was staggeringly productive, at one point accounting for 7.8 per cent of all of Ireland's exports. So 0.00167 per cent of Ireland's workers produced 7.8 per cent of our exports – or to put it another way each of Dell's workers produced more than 45 times the exports of the average Irish worker. Ireland's 3,695[32] prisoners are guarded by 3,426[33] prison officers – we have almost as many prison officers as prisoners, every one of whom is a member of the IPOA union. Those prison officers earned an average €80,000 each in 2008, the wage bill having shot up by 40 per cent in the preceding four years.[34] They take an average of 24 days – more than a month – sick leave each per year.[35]

In contrast, Britain has a ratio of 3.25 prisoners[36] to each prison officer.[37] While Britain's prison system is hardly a model of a liberal, reforming organisation, it is difficult to see any benefits from having so many more prison officers per prisoner in Ireland. (For more on this issue, see **Drugs in Prisons** on page 236.)

The vast disparity between work rates, work practices and pay rates between the public and private sectors – or more precisely the protected and unprotected sectors – is unjust. Membership of this privileged caste has become almost coterminous with trade union membership,[38] and Irish trade unions are returning to their roots, protecting the privilege of their well-fed members with no interest in the welfare of less well-connected and less politically powerful members of society.

These less fortunate workers are paying a real price for the good times of their unionised public-sector colleagues. In 2009 the government spent €58bn, €25bn more than it collected in tax,[39] money which was borrowed and added to the national debt and must be paid back with interest, hobbling the economy for years into the future. That is €473m per week.

Every working day in 2009, every one of the 1.2m remaining private sector workers got another day older and €78 deeper in debt.

Public sector wages make up more than €20bn per year of government spending,[40]so there is no prospect of reducing government spending without reducing the public sector pay bill. However, public sector representatives have another answer to the problem. "Tax the fat cats" is a refrain from union leaders like David Begg,[41] who also sits on the board of the spectacularly incompetent Central Bank (see **Never Again** on page 36). There is no need to cut spending, they say, just increase taxes on the super rich.

This is a total failure to understand the scale of the issue. Trinity economist Constantin Gurdgiev has pointed out that the total wealth of the Irish component of the 2008 *Sunday Times* rich list would only cover government spending for about five months. Given that much of the wealth was in property and shares, which have since collapsed in value, and other difficulties in collecting the taxes, the amount of money available if Ireland's rich were left naked and starving by the roadside would cover government spending for about eight weeks.[42] Then what?

Perhaps go after more ordinary high-earners, those on €100,000 or more per year. Vincent Brown has suggested increasing the tax take from them from an average of 33 per cent to 43 per cent (a 30 per cent increase in their tax bill), claiming that this would yield €3.2bn in extra tax take.[43] His calculations are utterly wrong, because he ignores the fact that such a tax increase would cause a flight of high-earners (the rich are mobile), motivate others to earn less and depress the tax take further by taking money out of the Irish economy. But even if €3.2bn was possible, it would barely dent our €24.6bn deficit; and the €100,000-plus families would include many public servants, such as a Garda married to a nurse, who are already livid about modest reductions in their wages.

While the money to be earned in the public sector may be good, that doesn't mean that it's a great place to work. It's not. The lack of work to do in many areas, and the dysfunctional nature of so many employees, leads to very unhealthy workplaces. Bullying and other employment cases are normally kept quiet by combining payouts with gagging clauses, but some stories are so spectacular that they leak out. One senior civil servant was left idle for five years, after complaining about bullying by a colleague. He was required to attend his office every day, but was given nothing to do other than read the paper and play on the internet.

The €80,000-a-year employee took a complaint to the Equality Tribunal, complaining of this situation and was awarded a further €40,000 to compensate him for the stress of the situation. His employers had to be ordered to find him meaningful work to do.[44]

Work rates in the public service are often at a level unheard of in the private sector. The Money Advice and Budgeting Services (MABS), a government service to advise people with personal finance problems, were allocated 19 new staff by the Department of Social and Family Affairs in August 2009, to cope with the demand for services from the worsening economic conditions.[45] A month later it was revealed that MABS staff dealt with an average of just nine clients each per month. The department protested that MABS also takes phone enquiries – about six phone calls per month for each staff member.[46]

Call centres, allowing customers to do everything from book concert tickets to repair their computers with the assistance of someone at the other end of the line, are typical of the new economy. While the number of calls an agent takes or makes depends on the service provided, 60 calls per day is the norm,[47] and many jobs require agents to handle 100 or more calls per day.[48] [49] Even allowing for differences in the types of work done, there is clearly a vast disparity in the work rates between many public and private sector jobs.

Good News – You're Fired!
How did the culture of bullying, low work-rates, laziness and lack of consumer focus take hold in the public service? The answer lies in the hiring and firing practices of the public service.

Rarely is getting fired presented as good news. The Eighties' ethic that job losses are bad news, often approaching tragic proportions, has raised its head again since the end of the boom. But whether someone works for the public or the private sector, throwing them out of a job can be good news, even for the person getting the P45.

People enter the work force at the latest after they complete university, often much earlier. On the day they enter the work force, they may have learnt a lot, but inevitably, many people enter the workforce with unrealistic expectations.

A colleague tells of interviewing a 22-year-old graduate for an entry position in a large central Dublin office during the boom. Before answering a single question, the applicant announced to the interview panel that he wanted to know where his car-parking place would be; he wouldn't be happy if his parking place was in a different building. Another new employee insisted forcefully that her statutory entitlement was in addition to the holidays mentioned in her contract, and threatened legal action if she wasn't given nine weeks' paid holidays per year.

These may sound comical, and such attitudes are unlikely to last long during a deep recession, but moving into the workforce is one of the least talked-about transitions in a person's life. Go to the self-help section of any bookshop, and you will find an avalanche of books on what to do when having a baby. Books about finding a partner in life are not far behind. Search for books on how to behave in your first job; you won't find many. Unrealistic expectations can easily slip through in the interview process.

Young people joining the workforce are sometimes surprised to learn that they are expected to show up on time and work all day, perhaps wearing clothes that they don't like, and not use telephones or stationery for their private interests; the employers won't listen to them often, and even if they get heard, their advice will rarely be followed; and working to all the rules only earns them the absence of being hassled by their boss.

There will be three reactions to this life-changing experience. A young person may have other life experiences that alert them to accept what is coming and be prepared; or they may come unprepared but recognise that they have to shape up. However, student life can be narcissistic, and this will lead at least some to believe that everyone is wrong except them. They may lecture their employers on how to change the workplace to suit them; they may get argumentative; they may refuse to meet expected work rates; they may get resentful and threaten employers with real or imagined ways to enforce what they see as their rights. And, particularly when eager applicants are plentiful, they may get fired.

Ways and Means
There are many euphemisms for getting fired. It is now routine for companies to include a probationary period of six months or more in a contract, effectively classing as temporary a position that is intended to become permanent. The employer reviews performance at the end of the period, and if the new worker isn't up to scratch, their contract is "not renewed".

But the informal route is far more common. The new employee is called in, told that things aren't working out, and it would be best if they resigned rather than be fired. All this is no bad thing. Not even for the person who is fired. If a person entering the workforce does not quickly develop realistic expectations of what having a job means, they are unlikely to prosper. When all else fails, getting fired is an effective way of providing feedback to a new worker that their ideas need changing.

It is unlikely to do their career much damage. Getting fired from several briefly held jobs is easy to disguise on a young person's CV, but it will communicate to them how they can expect to behave if they want to keep their next job. After a couple of lessons learnt, the aspirant employee settles into a career. It is a maturing process that has probably happened to more people than are prepared to admit it.

Hitting an Anvil

One thing can happen which will stop this process, with the ringing whack of Tom rushing headlong into Jerry's anvil – getting a job in the public sector, where the boom never ends. People just don't get fired. The Department of Education has admitted that in the four years up to 2005, out of the 50,000 teachers they employ, one was fired. That's an annual rate of one-in-200,000. So, in an average school with 20 teachers, you expect one to get the sack once every 10,000 years. Our teachers may be good, but they are not that good. This pattern is typical of government jobs. There is an unwritten rule that in the public sector, nobody ever gets sacked. Why?

The Process Interrupted

It would be a bad situation if public sector employees did not benefit from the same maturing process that many private sector workers go through. But the real effect is worse than this. Much worse. Not only do public sector employees lack feedback about acceptable work rates and practices, the process has the effect of sucking the most incompetent, the least mature and the laziest workers into the public sector.

If the recruitment process is equally expert in the public and private sectors, both sectors will initially recruit an equal proportion of unsuitable workers. The unsuitable workers in the public sector stay put, but those in the private sector get short shrift and end up back in the job market, where they will again eventually be recruited, by either the public or private sector. The more incompetent, stubborn and unsuitable the employee, the more they will go through this cycle; and they will keep going through the cycle until they learn – or until they get a public sector job.

And it gets worse: a feckless employee who has gone through the cycle a few times will quickly recognise that the public sector is an easier number and, once in, will be unlikely to go of their own accord. Hardworking and diligent workers initially recruited to the public sector often realise that their talents will be better recognised elsewhere and leave. So the ban on firing public sector workers not only fails to deal with the bad; it repels the best, it attracts the worst and deters improvement. Scrap it.

Disruption

The public sector needs disruption. Stability is the friend of vested interests. The decentralisation plan, announced by then Finance Minister Charlie McCreevy, implemented by Tom Parlon, was a huge missed opportunity. The proposed pace of decentralisation was daft from the outset; there was never any prospect of moving so many people so quickly. Moving the Legal Aid Board to Cahirciveen,[50] in the heart of the then Justice Minister's constituency, typified the backslapping jobbery of the plan. Some of the details of the proposal were so stupid that it is difficult to believe that they were made seriously.

The Probation Service was moved to Navan,[51] despite the fact that the distribution of crime in Ireland more than justified the Probation Service being based in Dublin. When it was reported that not a single probation officer was willing to go, it was suggested that untrained civil servants from other areas who were willing to make the move would take the probation officers' jobs in Navan, and the probation officers would take up other civil service roles in Dublin.[52] All of the institutional memory, all of the experience and all of the knowledge of the probation officers would be lost.

Probably this plan would not seem so ridiculous if applied to most areas of the civil service. Civil servants move from one department to another quite regularly. But can anyone imagine a technician moving from a pharmaceutical company to a software company so easily, and without any loss of status or pay? This demonstrates how little real skill exists in many areas of the civil service. You can only understand how this proposal was made if you know how little politicians expect of civil servants.

The Changing Workplace
Times change. Technology moves on. When credit cards were introduced, they were used with a roller machine; the retailer manually wrote out the transaction and other details on a three-page booklet and carefully put it, along with the credit card, into the machine. When the roller passed over the booklet, the embossed name and number on the card was transferred to its carbon paper pages. One page of the booklet became the receipt, another was the retailer's record, and a third was sent to the credit card company for processing.

The processing was done by thousands of data-entry employees around the world, who spent their time reading the amounts, credit card numbers and retailer details from the grubby slips and typing them into a computer, which produced the bills, which were then posted to customers. The customer would then bring the bill to their bank and pay it. All this is gone.

Now retailers' checkouts and websites are connected directly to the bank. The customer enters their pin number to confirm a sale, and the data is transferred directly to the bank's computer, which deducts the amount automatically from the customer's bank account. There is no human intervention; it is totally automatic. All of those data-entry jobs are gone, and that makes us all better off – even the people who did those jobs. The reason for it is this: wealth is efficiency.

If society must no longer pay people to do unnecessary jobs – typing in the details of millions of credit card receipts, chasing TV licence evaders, printing and posting airline tickets – then the productive talents of those people will be put to use for something that actually benefits society.

Technological changes have come to governmental areas as well. Any employer will be familiar with the Revenue Online Service (ROS), through which almost all PAYE, PRSI, VAT, Corporation and other tax returns are now made. The system is clunky and poorly designed, but it is a vast improvement on the endless paper trail that those taxes generated for businesses before. Third-party software is available that calculates the amounts to be typed in and generates the files to be uploaded. Tax liabilities are then collected automatically by direct debit. Irish companies can now do all their reporting without using one sheet of paper.

Car owners will be familiar with **www.motortax.ie**, which replaces a previously difficult and time-consuming process with an automated website for paying car tax (proposals for further improving this are on page 257).

However, new technology is implemented very differently in the public and private sectors. In the private sector, technology makes companies more efficient, reducing costs to the customers and making society wealthier. In Ireland's public sector, this just hasn't happened. Technology has been introduced in many areas in recent decades, but the number of people employed has increased.

Decentralisation

Pick a town. A nice town – somewhere you would like to live. There are a few criteria. Decent transport links are important, but so is a theatre, a few good restaurants, an attractive shopping centre. In short, somewhere you would like to walk around, rather than a retail park of prefabricated outlets. There are lots of reasons you might like to live there, but the biggest reason is because your friends might also like to live there. Dublin has swollen at an astonishing rate. Whether you come from Portlaoise or Poland, aside from the attraction of employment, the fact that there are many people who are or could be in your social network is a crucial deciding factor on where to live and work.

The National Spatial Strategy (NSS)[53] recognised this. The reason that towns outside Dublin were failing to attract people was that they were all trying to develop. The NSS recommended selecting a few towns that would be developed intensively and could generate the critical mass required to attract people and industries. Outside Dublin, the NSS chose Cork, Limerick/Shannon, Galway and Waterford as existing gateways, and designated four new national-level gateways – the towns of Dundalk and Sligo and the linked towns of Letterkenny/Derry and the midland towns of Athlone, Tullamore and Mullingar.

Of course, every local authority, backbench TD and minister whose town wasn't earmarked for development insisted that they be included, and the result was the opposite from that intended. What little development there is in Ireland outside Dublin is smeared so thinly that it covers every townland in every electoral area and cannot attract the twenty- and thirty-somethings who would bring the jobs, the spending, the commerce and the development that would make Ireland a multi-centred country. Parlon and McCreevy's decentralisation plan could have been fine-tuned to match the NSS – provide employment in half-a-dozen key towns by moving in a large number of government employees, but it had nothing to do with anything other than jobs for the boys.

Throughout this book, there are recommendations for new government agencies and offices, many of which replace the functions of existing workers. All of these should be established in the national-level gateways identified by the NSS. They should be in modern office buildings and have modern private sector work practices and productivity rates.

The jobs should be open to all applicants. For example, creating a single national planning agency (page 168) will, of course, mean that there are likely to be redundancies around the country in local planning departments, and it would be sensible to consider applications from staff leaving those departments, particularly since such a transfer would save the state a redundancy payment. However, the decision should be based solely on who is the best person for the job.

Civil servants whose functions have disappeared because of reorganisation, new technology or any other reason, and who have not successfully applied for a job elsewhere in the system should be made redundant, just as would happen to any private sector worker.

Preventing Corruption

Ireland has a systemic problem with corruption, separate from the poor enforcement of the law. In many areas of public life, jobs, contracts and advancement can be gained by means other than meritocratic competition. This invites corruption.

If a private individual can become rich overnight by having a farm designated as development land, by limiting the number of a taxi-plates, by receiving exclusive licences to run telephone companies or radio stations, or by any way other than using talent, effort and learning, there will inevitably be corruption. When politicians or public officials of relatively humble means have the power to choose a successful applicant who will make a huge amount of money, it is unreasonable to imagine that this money will not find its way back into the decision-making process. The true fault here is not corrupt businesspeople, politicians or public servants. The fault is the system.

The value in state-issued licences belongs to the state and should never be given to a private individual. Regardless of the morality of the issue, the practicalities are disastrous. Sometimes there is a factor which limits the supply of a value-yielding resource; sometimes there isn't. The factor might be the limit of bandwidth on the radio dial or the existence of suitable sites for development as housing.

In the case where there is no external limiting factor – as with pub or taxi licences – there is no justification for creating a government-imposed one. The licence should be given to anyone who meets the criteria for application; and the criteria should be set only to ensure orderly conduct of the market. Where there is a limiting factor, the increase in value should go entirely to the state. The Kenny Report[54] attempted to do this for rezoned land. All licences that cannot be given to an infinite number of applicants, such as FM radio stations, should be auctioned to the highest bidder, for periods long enough to provide a stable service but short enough to allow for any shifts in value that may happen over time.

This will ensure that the taxpayer gets the full market value of the licence which the state is giving, and it will also make transparent the process of allocating those licences. Most importantly, it will eliminate the possibility of gaining a licence by bribing an official into judging one applicant as more worthy than another.

Opinions and Facts

Scientists have a great word: *falsifiable*. To qualify as a scientific test, something must, amongst other things, be capable of being falsified. This means that, when you think something is true, you must imagine that it is not true and work out how you would prove that it is not true. If a false assertion could never be proven false, then no scientist could ever refute somebody making that assertion. Therefore all scientific assertions must be capable of being proved false to be accepted.

"Mary Smith lives at 21 High Street" is a falsifiable statement, because we can go and check. "21 High Street is imbued with Mary Smith's spirit" is not falsifiable, because nothing could possibly exist to prove to somebody that it is false.

Government regulation too often relies on vague terms where officials say that they "feel" something is "adequate" or "sufficient". Even when they are wrong, nobody can ever prove that the official doesn't feel that. Except in the most exceptional cases, all official decisions should be made on published criteria, and all decisions should be reasoned and falsifiable.

Bankrupt Banks

The banks are bust, and that is a big problem. Without a shred of sympathy for the bankers, we still need banks for the economy. Banks trade in money; they take it in from depositors and lend it out in mortgages, credit cards, business loans and other products, making money on the margin. Lack of consumer credit can have serious implications for the economy, but lack of business loans is a catastrophe. A typical business must pay its staff, rent and suppliers long before it gets payment from customers, so without revolving credit, even many profitable businesses would need to close down.

Banks long ago discovered a trick that allows them to increase their profits: money they lend out is quickly spent and deposited back in the system, so they can afford to lend out far more than they actually have in deposits, certain in the knowledge that the extra money will come straight back into their system. Inevitably the temptation is to constantly increase this ratio of deposits to lending (called leverage). The greater the leverage, the greater the risk that some event will trigger enough depositors to ask for their money back that the bank will run out of cash. A bank without cash is a very unpopular bank and will soon discover that nobody will give it money, and everybody will want their money back, leading to instant collapse unless someone even bigger – a bigger bank, or a government – rescues them.

Banks lend large amounts to each other, to make up for differences in deposit and lending patterns, so one bank collapsing would quickly lead to all the others following.

For this reason governments regulate banks, making complex rules about ratios of deposits to loans in different types of business, depending on the risk of the lending. The regulators are there to prevent human greed overtaking common sense. Since the 1990s a fashion for "light-touch" regulation swept the world. Like an adolescent desperate for acceptance laughing too loudly at a joke he doesn't understand, Ireland over-eagerly tried to keep up with this fad and barely enforced the level of regulation that existed. The *New York Times* called Dublin's International Financial Services Centre (IFSC) the "Wild West",[55] because the non-existent regulation was attracting the worst of the financial industry.

Around the world, motivated by the huge instant profits of pretending that risky loans were safe, the banks lied to the uninterested regulators, lied to their shareholders and lied to each other about business they were passing on.

Internal dynamics in the banks made this worse. Dealmakers in the banks took ever bigger risks. The bank paid more for riskier deals, because the bank made more money, but when these deals went wrong, they could hardly recoup the billions lost from the trader, even if that trader had received a million-euro bonus in previous years. The banks motivated their traders to always look at the figure and never look at the risk, and the traders responded to this motivation.

This did not happen everywhere. In Spain[56] and Canada[57] particularly, the regulators kept a tight rein on their banks, which were relatively untouched by the international crisis, leaving them in a strong position. At the height of the crisis, Spanish bank Santander bought out the British institution Abbey National for a song.[58]

Irish banks were the most eager to lend money against hugely inflated property prices and claim that this was low-risk, and they imploded accordingly. We are now in an extraordinary situation. The government – the taxpayer – owns a large stake in all major banks, and owns Anglo Irish Bank outright. It had no choice; if any Irish bank had gone bust (a certainty without intervention), they would all have imploded, and Ireland would have faced far more than just 15 per cent economic decline in six months. The taxpayer is paying €54bn to buy out property loans via NAMA, far more than the value of the assets backing those loans. This is more than €12,000 for each person in the country. We can't change the past, but we can change the future. There are four things that need to happen. We must:

- punish the guilty without mercy
- minimise the losses that the taxpayer has made on the bank guarantees
- create a banking regulatory system which ensures that we never face this situation again
- nationalise and then refloat the banks as viable, responsible facilitators of economic growth as soon as possible

Punish the Guilty

As revelations about political corruption broke in the mid-1990s, a debate grew on the appropriate punishment for political corruption. Some called for prison sentences, others pointed to the cost of imprisoning men who were growing old and seemed to pose no further threat to society. It just wasn't worth sending them to prison, we were told.

This couldn't have been more wrong. Even with the grossly bloated cost of our prisons, locking up the corrupt would have been worth every cent. As a matter of simple justice, it is important that serious criminals are seen to be punished regardless of what section of society they come from.

However, at a practical level, there is very good reason to believe that people at the top of the banking profession did what they did in the belief that the law would never be applied to them. If bishops, ministers, judges and captains of industry were spending their declining years sewing mailbags, it is likely that the perpetrators of our current scandals would have thought twice about their behaviour. Maybe, having thought twice, they might have gone ahead with their malfeasance anyway, but maybe not. The Gardaí are simply not equipped to prosecute these crimes, and Ireland needs a specialist unit to investigate and prosecute financial irregularity – see **Tackling Financial Crime** on page 193.

Minimise the Losses

In 2008, before the full extent of the banking crisis was appreciated, there was talk of the Central Bank encouraging the banks not to push too hard those developers who were getting into financial trouble. The rationale was that it was better not to push a developer to bankruptcy because it risked a ripple effect through the economy which might cause a recession.[59] So much for that.

At the time there may have been sense in the idea of not shoving the developers closer to the cliff's edge, but the developers and banks insisted on racing in that direction anyway. The cartel of builders and bankers was harmful enough through the boom, but they are of no value whatsoever today. They have done their worst. We should have no fear of them now.

The government has two contradictory pressures in its ownership of a huge chunk of the banking sector. Promoting competition between banks is good for the economy, reducing the banking costs for businesses; but the share price of the banks will be higher if they are allowed to operate a cartel and fleece their customers.

Between these two demands, there can be no competition. Ongoing economic competitiveness is far more important than a once-off gain for the taxpayer. The cosy cartels have had their day. The government cannot be trusted to own such a large chunk of the banking sector; nobody can be trusted with such a monopoly. We need competition in banking.

Once the toxic debts are cleared from retail banks, the government must appoint senior management of international standing, entirely independent in each bank. Their brief should be to return the banks to profitability in a regulated, competitive market, with a view to privatisation when stability has been restored to the market, making as much as money for the taxpayer as possible – see **Refloat the Banks** on page 40.

The author has personal experience of the reports on borrowing and lending that the banks are required to submit to financial regulators. These reports are emailed in Microsoft Excel spreadsheets extracted from the banks' databases. The regulator intends this reporting to ensure that rules about the size of deposits and loans are enforced, and to prevent banks from putting themselves at risk.

These reporting systems were frustrated by Seán FitzPatrick, the director of Anglo Irish Bank. He took highly irregular loans of more than €100m from Anglo, without bothering to inform either his shareholders or the regulator,[60] and now seems not bothered even to make interest payments.[61] Irish Nationwide Building Society kindly lent €228m in overnight money to Anglo to cover the hole in its accounts made by these loans and others on the dates that Anglo had to submit reports to the regulator.[62] But FitzPatrick actually complied with the pathetic reporting systems. A dishonest banker could simply submit false Microsoft Excel spreadsheets, and the regulator would have no way of spotting this. Equally, it is unacceptable that reports are made on dates known in advance, allowing questionable transactions to be hidden so easily.

Never Again

Before 1999, the Central Bank had two roles. It was responsible for regulating the banks, and for maintaining our currency. Then the Irish pound disappeared to be replaced by the euro, and the Central Bank fought to maintain its role as the financial regulator for fear it would have nothing to do. It was a clear example of the tendency of bureaucrats to prolong their employment beyond their usefulness. It wasn't looking good. The Central Bank had been the banking regulator for the entire period when Des Traynor at the private bank Guinness and Mahon (G&M) operated a tax-evasion scheme. Huge sums were defrauded from the taxpayer within a few hundred metres of the Central Bank headquarters.

As early as 1976, the Central Bank was aware that "considerable measures were being taken by G&M to ensure certain schemes would not become known to the Revenue". Central Bank officials were fully aware of the illegal back-to-back loans but were assured by Des Traynor that the activities would stop, and the Central Bank pursued the matter no further.[63] The practice continued, cheating taxpayers of hundreds of millions, for the next quarter of a century.

Guinness and Mahon existed for the superrich, but bogus non-resident accounts were held by tens of thousands of Ireland's more ordinary wealthy.[64] The accounts were supposed to be available only to people resident outside Ireland, with the funds exempt from deposit interest tax (DIRT); however, their main purpose was to hide untaxed income from the

Revenue. The commercial banks can hardly have failed to notice that the accounts were being held by Irish residents, particularly when they arranged for direct debits to pay telephone and electricity bills from them.[65] The focus in 2001, when the scandal became known, was on the evasion of DIRT; headlines spoke of "Call for DIRT dodgers to come forward",[66] and the *Sunday Business Post* even stated baldly that the accounts "were set up to evade Deposit Income Retention Tax".[67] This is simply false.

The tax-cheats with these accounts were certainly evading DIRT, but DIRT was only applied to the interest earned on the capital, not the capital itself. Many customers were running the accounts as though they were current accounts, which would not have earned any interest anyway. A far larger question was not the interest on the capital, or the tax on the interest on the capital, but the capital itself. The main purpose of the accounts was not to evade DIRT, but to hide untaxed income for those outside the PAYE system. Given that marginal tax rates were up to 70 per cent during the period and that the tax-free allowances of the holders were most likely consumed elsewhere, it was not the DIRT evaded that should have concerned the tax authorities.

The penalty for fraudulently filing a tax return is €125 plus twice the tax liability, in addition to the tax liability itself,[68] so the unpaid taxes and penalties were far in excess of the total deposits in the bogus accounts, not a fraction of the miserly interest. The banks, including the state-owned ACC bank, were colluding in stealing billions from the taxpayer. Unsatisfied with all this, National Irish Bank branches around the country also resorted to straightforward theft of money from customers' accounts.[69]

Not a single banker was prosecuted for any of these crimes, and not a single one of these gross, systematic, widespread frauds which operated for decades was successfully detected by the Central Bank. They were all discovered by investigative journalists. All this was not enough to convince the government of the day that the Central Bank was unfit to be the banking regulator, so they appointed a committee to advise the best way forward for banking regulation. The committee also told them that the Central Bank was unfit to be the banking regulator and advised moving the supervisory and regulatory functions to a new regulator.[70]

Under pressure from the well-connected bureaucrats eager to hang on to their prestige, their huge salaries and their expense accounts, the government ignored the evidence and created even more nests to feather, making the Financial Regulator and the Central Bank the constituent parts of the "Central Bank and Financial Services Authority of Ireland". According to the Financial Regulator's website:

> The structure combines two distinct component entities – the Central
> Bank and the Financial Regulator – each with its own particular set of
> responsibilities and each with its own specific governance structure...

> The roles are complementary and we enjoy the closest cooperation
> with our colleagues in the Central Bank. Indeed the recent and ongoing
> market turbulence has reinforced our view that prudential supervision,
> financial stability and consumer protection are inextricably linked so
> as to merit the combined approach to supervision that our structure
> demands.[71]

More committees, more board meetings, more expense accounts and more
jobs for the boys.[‡] During the Oireachtas hearings on the bogus non-resident
accounts, the word was put out in briefings to journalists that they were
justified in not pressing the banks too hard on stealing millions from their
customers, and billions from the taxpayers, because stability of the banks
was more important.

A secret internal report, leaked in October 2009, compared the Financial
Regulator to its international equivalents. The report found that it was one
of the most expensive in the world, with the taxpayer picking up most of
the tab, unlike other countries where the regulator is funded by the banks.
Ireland has fewer inspectors and "an over-emphasis on internal management
rather than reporting of core prudential, policy, market or outward-facing
activities".[72] Too many managers, not enough regulation.

The purpose of the Financial Regulator, according to their website, is:

- to help consumers to make informed decisions on their financial affairs
  in a safe and fair market; and

- to foster sound dynamic financial institutions in Ireland[73]

Of their two tasks, preventing risky business practices in banks was the one
that, according to themselves, they really cared about. Every bank they
regulated has needed billions in taxpayers' money to prevent their collapse,

---

‡   To give an understanding of the level of the bureaucracy here, on its website the
    Financial Regulator lists its committees and departments as the Authority, the
    Consumer Directorate, Prudential Directorate, Registry of Credit Unions, Consumer
    Information Department, Consumer Protection Codes Department, Domestic Credit
    Institutions Department, Financial Institutions and Funds Authorisation Department,
    International Credit Institutions Department, Insurance Supervision Department,
    Investment Service Provider Supervision Department, Legal and Enforcement
    Department, Markets Supervision Department, Planning and Finance Department,
    Registry of Credit Unions, Executive Board, Consumer Committee, Prudential
    Supervision Committee, Audit and Risk Management Committee, Budget and
    Remuneration Committee, Consultative Consumer Panel, Consultative Industry Panel,
    and the Credit Union Advisory Committee. Perhaps wisely, the Central Bank does not
    give out this information.

precisely because of risky lending. In an outrageous move in January 2009, Patrick Neary, the regulator's chief executive, was permitted to resign with payments and a pension worth many millions,[74] in circumstances that demanded his sacking at a minimum.

It is clear what the Financial Regulator does: nothing. It should be wound up and its entire staff fired. What the Central Bank does is not so clear. Before the launch of the euro in 1999, the Central Bank ran the national currency. Before 2003, it was responsible for financial regulation. What now is the purpose of the bunker that disfigures Dame Street? According to its website, the Central Bank is responsible for:

- contributing to the maintenance of price stability
- ensuring safe and reliable payment and settlement systems
- managing foreign exchange assets, on behalf of the European Central Bank[75]
- producing and distributing euro banknotes and coins

The small print mentions that the first three of these functions are carried out of "in conjunction" with the European Central Bank (ECB). "Contributing to price stability" means setting ECB interest rates for the entire eurozone. The Central Bank does not set this rate, the ECB does. The Central Bank is a branch office, whose only real function is printing banknotes to the design sent over from Frankfurt years ago. It is a glorified Prontaprint franchise.

The Central Bank needs an entire clean-out. For European law reasons, it probably cannot be abolished and reconstituted, but all the senior staff associated with its incompetence should be let go, and even at a junior level it appears seriously overstaffed. Moving its location (to much more modest premises) would also help change the culture and be an excellent opportunity to undo Sam Stephenson's architectural vandalism. Both the institution and the building should be demolished.

Financial Regulator

Greed, stupidity and incredibly bad regulation destroyed the Irish financial system. Unfortunately we can't do much about human greed and stupidity, but we can improve regulation. Matthew Elderfield, formerly head of financial regulation in Bermuda, took over as Head of Financial Supervision in the restructured Central Bank in January 2010.[76] This structure is deeply imperfect; the new regulator should start from a green-field situation rather than inheriting the structures and practices of his failed predecessor, financed by a levy on bank turnover, not the taxpayer.

At a minimum, Elderfield should appoint two deputies, one with in-depth knowledge of Irish banking, and one international. A non-Irish majority at the top is vital to make sure that small-town groupthink does not set in. The regulator should:

- maintain a list of permitted banking products and practices which banks may operate, with everything not on the list being prohibited

- have a general rule that banks may not do anything that would endanger either the financial security of the banking system, the security of customers' deposits or public faith in the banking system, regardless of whether it is specified in regulations or not

- require secure real-time access to all the banks' computer systems, giving them live visibility on every transaction in every bank

- require banks to have systems which record all telephone calls made by senior management, along the lines of systems used to monitor the dealings of share dealers, and the regulator should have live unmediated access to all the recordings

- require senior bank management to hold all their personal finances within the state in accounts notified to the regulator

- levy unlimited fines on senior managers personally for any breach of the rules, and collect payment from the notified accounts

- be entitled to make unannounced inspections at any bank, with access to all documents and levy unlimited fines against the banks

- investigate, with or without a complaint, and refer cases for prosecution directly to an organisation set up to investigate and prosecute major white-collar crime – see **Tackling Financial Crime** on 193.

- recruit at least 50 per cent of the regulatory staff at all levels from outside the Irish banking system

- forbid its employees from taking a job at any Irish bank, or any organisation associated with senior banking figures, or their subsidiaries, for ten years after they leave the employment of the regulator

Refloat the Banks

Elsewhere in this book, there is much about the dead hand of government regulation. With banking, excitement is not what we need. Staid, prudential financial services may be boring, but boring is what banks need to be. The banks should be nationalised (see **NAMA** on page 43), but they should not stay nationalised.

There is a role for competition in the banking market – small businesses have long complained about the bank charges that they face,[77] and there can be no doubt that Irish bank customers pay outrageous charges as a result of the lack of competition.[78] [79] If Irish banks do not return to operating competitively this will continue to be a burden on consumers.

The lack of competition was bad enough when each bank operated as a separate entity. Now that the state is at least the dominant shareholder in much of the banking market, there is scope for the situation to get worse. Even with the best of intentions, it is unreasonable to expect the state to act against its own interest, encouraging the banks that it owns to compete with each other, lowering the profits they may make.

When market conditions allow – which may not be for a number of years – the banks should be refloated on the stock markets, in the way of UK privatisations of the 1980s. Shares should be offered to a wide mix of large international investors and small shareholders, in a way that will secure the best price for the taxpayer, hopefully offsetting some of the losses suffered.

Reform before Privatisation
The time before privatisation must be put to good use. Firstly, in conjunction with the new financial regulator, all products and business practices of the banks must be audited, and the financial regulator must provide a list of what can continue and what must change. Practices not specifically permitted should be assumed to be prohibited. Items to look at here would include:

- novel financial products like mortgage-backed securities

These products started the worldwide credit crunch[80] because the banks' senior management, not to mention the regulators, had no notion of how they functioned or how risky they were, and more junior members of staff were allowed to take huge bonus-driven risks. The presumption must be that each banking product is prohibited until it is cleared by the regulator.

- poor data security

In 2008 a laptop computer was stolen from a Bank of Ireland employee which contained details of more than 30,000 customers.[81] Anyone with basic IT knowledge is aware that data can be accessed from a server over a secure connection, and the server kept in a physically secure location. Allowing such data to be taken out in such an insecure way is sloppy, which may indicate that other work practices are equally sloppy. The regulator should draw up detailed compulsory data security guidelines.

- programme for change

Banks should be required to draw up a detailed plan for complying with the regulations, with a timetable to achieve them before they are refloated. Regulators should enforce the timetable, and levy fines on the banks who fail to create and enforce adequate systems, and levy fines on individual managers who fail to prevent breaches of the work practices.

Except Anglo and Irish Nationwide. The other banks – AIB and Bank of Ireland in particular – have profitable and relatively efficient retail and commercial banking businesses. There is no evidence that Anglo Irish Bank or Irish Nationwide Building Society have anything to rescue. The EBS Building Society appears likely to take over Irish Nationwide, and this is probably the least worst solution.[82] The regulator should make a judgement whether, once the bad practices are removed, there remains a viable business in Anglo. It is likely that, once the sharp practice, the underhand dealing and the bankrolling of daft development plans is removed, there will be nothing left.

That's the regulator's call. If the conclusion is that any institution cannot return to being a viable independent bank, then it should be wound up immediately, with the bulk of the staff being made redundant, and the remaining business taken over by the two main banks, in roughly equal proportions.

In addition, the banking market needs to be regulated to make sure that there is adequate competition – see **Banking Competition** on page 64. Finally, separate from the regulator who looks after everyday business, Ireland needs a specialist financial police to prosecute major fraud and financial crimes – see page 193.

NAMA

The National Asset Management Agency (NAMA) Act of 2009[83] has created the world's largest property company,[84] with most of its property concentrated on one small island in the North Atlantic.

There are many idiotic concepts embedded in NAMA, but one of them leaps off the page. It will be an offence to communicate with NAMA "with the intention of influencing the making of a decision in relation to the performance of [its] functions".[85] This is a whole new type of stupid. In the lunatic asylum that is Irish government stupidity, this deserves a padded ward all to itself. The provision was probably made with good intentions, but it goes to the heart of what is wrong with NAMA as it stands. NAMA is giving away free money.

There are many instances where the Irish government has, in one way or another, given away free money cited in this book, from taxi licences to rezoning, and they all have one thing in common. They are all disasters, because the free money inevitably makes its way back into the decision-making process, so the officials deciding who should get the free money are utterly compromised. NAMA is the ultimate free money scheme. A €1,000 fine will not deter nods and winks in every bar, golf club and dinner party in the country when billions are at stake, and anyone who imagines otherwise should be kept well clear of sharp implements.

This problem goes to the heart of NAMA and its flaws. The stupid, greedy banks were permitted by the stupid, lazy regulator to lend stupid amounts to stupid property developers to build stupid developments that nobody was stupid enough to live in. The developers used credit from the banks to bid against each other, driving up property prices, and the banks took those inflated prices as the security on their loans. If you owe the bank a million you are in trouble, but if, like Seán Dunne who paid €379m for three hectares,[86] you owe the bank a billion, then the bank is in trouble.

Seán Dunne, however, is only the runner-up in the stupidity competition; he paid €133m per hectare. Jerry O'Reilly and David Courtney paid €35.9m for a tiny site, €206m per hectare. In normal times, if the borrower defaulted, the bank would repossess the property, but many properties are now close to worthless. Remember that the banks are lending far more money than they have on deposit, supposedly on the promise to the regulator that they have carefully checked out that this is very secure credit.

The banks' losses were so huge that, to avoid a run on deposits, the government had to promise depositors that, if the banks can't pay them back, then the taxpayer will. That prevented flight of deposits, but it didn't change the fact that the banks now had no money to lend to Irish businesses; indeed, their leverage was so high that they had to call in every overdraft they could to try to get it back to realistic ratios, causing a huge credit famine for Irish businesses, driving otherwise viable enterprises to the wall.

The solution, we are told, is NAMA. The government will buy all of the property speculation business from the Irish banks, who will then be free to provide us with commercial and retail banking services. Except they won't.

Remember that NAMA is not buying property, it is buying loan books – the right to the future repayments in exchange for cash now. But loans where the borrower can't make repayments aren't worth much, and if the security on that loan is depreciating rapidly, the loan is worth less again. NAMA proposes to pay €54bn for a loan book that it values at €47bn. There is a mountain of evidence that the loan book is not worth remotely near €47bn,[87] but even if it was, that would still mean €7bn of free money for the banks, from the taxpayer. To justify this, the government have cooked up a notion of "Long Term Economic Value" and even created the acronym LTEV to give it the ring of a well-known economic concept. It is nothing of the sort. Google indicates that the acronym did not appear on any website before 2009, with the full phrase only appearing shortly before.

The €7bn (in reality a lot more) of free money from NAMA has nothing to do with buying a loan book. It is simply being given to try to get the banks recapitalised, get their ratio of deposits to loans back to realistic levels. Finance Minister Brian Lenihan defended this in July 2009, saying that if NAMA only paid the market value of the loan book, this would not be enough to recapitalise the banks.[88] So the free money is a reward for the banks from the taxpayer for having lost so much money so stupidly; but the tragedy is that the country does need well-capitalised banks, and if nobody else will do it, then the government must recapitalise them.

But the money should not come for free. Loan books acquired by NAMA should be rigorously priced according to their value on the day of sale. All further money needed to recapitalise the banks should be paid for in bank shares. Because the money needed probably exceeds the share capital, this would mean that all the banks would be nationalised, which may irritate believers in free markets.

NAMA's Task

Much as it is hated, NAMA (or some NAMA-like structure) is required to manage, on behalf of the taxpayers, the vast assets and white elephants that are being offloaded from the banks. What should Ireland do with all that property? Firstly, we should take Mrs Beaton's advice and get hold of it. NAMA must take a detailed audit of:

- the non-compliant loans that are on the books of the banks
- who the borrowers are
- what the total assets of those borrowers are

Remember that NAMA is buying a loan book, not the properties themselves, although it is inevitable that they will have to take possession of properties in the many cases where the loans are in default. Many property speculators have multiple investments, and it is possible that some of these are the subject of mortgages that are being serviced – not all developments were a disaster. Where a loan is not being repaid, forfeiture of the property is not good enough if the value of the asset does not meet the outstanding loan. In such cases, NAMA must take ownership of property valued at the total amount of the outstanding loans *at prevailing values* or the total assets of the developer (mortgaged or unmortgaged), whichever is the greater. The assets of the developer should include property and anything else of value, in Ireland or abroad.

The possibility that high-risk developers could offload the nonperforming parts of their portfolio at gigantic cost to the state, while retaining the benefit from the more successful developments, would be an outrage that cannot be permitted. NAMA must be vigilant that, having overpaid for the loan book, it does not write off loans when there are assets available for seizure, or seize less than the full value of the loan being written off.

Depending on the nature of the property acquired, NAMA should assign it to different uses:

- undeveloped land should be set aside for new parks and playgrounds (see **Space for Children** on page 85)
- most completed and nearly completed housing developments should be handed over to a new state housing agency to end the housing lists (see **New Housing Agency** on page 173)
- other properties could be converted for state uses such as the bail hostels proposed on page 234
- some of the office space may be useful for government agencies
- some housing may be judged to be of long-term value, even if no buyers or renters are now in the market; such properties should be secured and mothballed, and placed on the market when that is viable
- sadly, the best thing to do with some of the dafter rural housing estates is to demolish them, and return the land to agricultural use; decaying ghost towns would attract vandalism and anti-social behaviour

Other creative uses for the land should be sought, and in December 2009 FKL Architects organised an exhibition of suggestions which included some sensible ideas, and dafter ones, such as creating a real "ghost town" using unoccupied estates to inter the dead.[89] Some of this smacks of bored architects desperate for something to do, but seeking creative ideas is a good strategy.

Stamp Duty

One way to make future property development more rational is to encourage liquidity in the market, so people can buy and sell easily when they need to. Stamp duty is a major barrier to this.

UK stamp duty on residential property ranges between 1 per cent for properties priced over GBP£175,000 and 4 per cent for properties over GBP£500,000.[‡] All properties priced below GBP£175,000,[90] or in large swathes of the country classed as disadvantaged, are entirely free of stamp duty.[91]

In Ireland, up to 1969, stamp duty was 2 per cent for properties up to IEP£6,000, and 3 per cent up to IEP£50,000, a gigantic sum at the time. Since then, the rates kept ratcheting up, with the top rate going to 5 per cent in 1973, 6 per cent in 1990 and 9 per cent in 1997,[92] following the first Bacon report.

Then came an orgy of adjustments, with changes made in 1998, 2000, January and December 2001, 2002, 2004 and 2007, moving rates up and down, and making and reversing adjustments to the tax treatment of rental properties. Most of the time the top rate was 9 per cent of the rocketing price of houses.

These changes were largely inspired by the three reports of economic consultant Peter Bacon, who caused great turbulence in the market before eventually returning rates to what they were before the implementation of his first set of recommendations.[93] The fall in property prices and transactions since 2008 have led to a collapse in the huge stamp duty receipts, which the state enjoyed during the boom.[94] [95]

The Tax Drug
Vast revenues went to the state from the combined effects of the very high rates of stamp duty, the very high house prices (pushing more properties into the higher rates) and the extraordinary number of property transactions during the boom. The effect was like a drug, where the exchequer became used to the rocketing income and others became dependent on the rocketing spending that it funded.

Accountants distinguish between current and capital income and spending;

---

‡ In a study of the asking prices for properties for sale on www.findaproperty.com, using Birmingham as an example, just one house in fifty would attract the top rate of stamp duty, and 80 per cent of houses would attract no stamp duty at all.

current spending is regular and ongoing, such as food bills or a company's salaries. Capital spending is for items that last for many years, such as a car or a building. An iron rule of accountancy is this: once-off capital income must not be used for current spending, because the income will stop, and the spending will not.

The current deficit is, in part, a result of the boom in current expenditure that was caused by the failure to recognise that stamp duty was capital income. There was no prospect of it continuing indefinitely, and it was foolish to create expectations that the spending which it funded would continue.

The Tax Damage

Stamp duty makes it expensive to move house. Mortgages (sensible ones, anyway) require you to repay the price of your house over about 25 years. To move, however, you must pay the state nearly one-tenth of the value of your house, along with all the legal and other transaction costs. This is a tax on taking up a new job; a tax on upsizing or downsizing your home to meet family needs; a tax on marriage break-up.

It is an unfair and capricious tax, forcing people to pay very different amounts that have no basis in reason or justice. People who were unlucky enough to buy closer to the peak of the market are further penalised by having to pay far more tax on an identical property bought at a more advantageous time. Illiquidity in the housing market creates illiquidity in the labour market, and this obstacle in the way of people taking up jobs is likely to slow any recovery in the economy.

- Stamp duty on all properties should be abolished.
- A sound policy-based property tax should be introduced.

Stamp duty is our only residential property tax, and this is irrational, because it focuses taxes entirely on work, unfairly favouring the already rich over people who work and create new wealth. The solution to this is the **Value Deficit Tax** (See page 162) and people and companies who paid stamp duty on a property which they now own should be permitted to reclaim that payment as a write-off against the new property tax.

Screen Scraping

Almost all innovations these days include some use of the internet, and one of the best is screen scraping. If you already know what screen scraping is, you can skip this section. If you don't, prepare to learn something new about the web. If you are not so hot on technology, take two aspirins before continuing.

An excellent introduction to screen scraping is **www.momondo.com**. Momondo is a Swedish-based website for finding flights, rental cars, hotels and other services. Put in your holiday dates and destination and the screen fills with the best deals on offer, from a wide variety of airlines and other companies. How do Momondo get all this data on their website? The answer is that they don't.

The information arriving on your screen is not contained in the Momondo website – that website is programmed to do a job for you. It takes the dates and destination which you input, and then logs into dozens of other websites for you, collecting the prices and other data from them, which presents it to you in a useful fashion. You can then book the best deal with a few clicks. Everybody benefits:

- You get the best deal without having to trawl through many websites.
- Airlines and car hire companies are motivated to allow data to be collected from their websites.
- Most of all, society benefits, by putting pressure on companies to be efficient and offer the options that customers want.
- The screen scrapers benefit, because they get to place advertising on their website, which generates revenue for them.

Some websites object to having their content presented on a third-party website. Ryanair took severe commercial and legal action against screen scrapers who allowed flight bookings to be made;[96] others actively encourage it. Screen scraping is relevant because it can be a powerful tool for consumers and citizens. Where governments and commercial organisations make data available, it should be on the web in a format that can be read easily by screen scrapers.

If citizens are entitled to information, shouldn't they just look it up on a standard website? No. In *Freakonomics*, the economists Levitt and Dubner demonstrated how creative analysis of data could turn up all sorts of interesting information. When high-stakes tests, on which teachers' salaries were based, were introduced in the US, there was a strong suspicion that teachers were allowing students to cheat, or were cheating on their behalf. Armed with access to computerised records of students' multiple-choice exam in Chicago, Levitt and Dubner decided to search for patterns that would tell them something. As summarised by an anonymous blogger:

> Levitt caught teachers by analyzing all the individual answers of every student in the Chicago public school system. What he found was that after students had turned in their tests, teachers were going through and changing their answers. Not every answer, mind you, but enough to boost scores. In his example, he shows how in a class of 22 students, at least 15 students had the same string of six correct answers. At first glance, this seems a little suspicious, especially since the string comes towards the end of the test, where the harder questions tend to be. Not only that, but several of the students who got these answers correct left at least four of the questions in the same section blank, showing they probably could not have answered the earlier questions correctly. To add to it, these were poor performing students who did not have strings of six answers correct anywhere else on the test. The students made huge leaps during this year, however, the next year they sank back down to their low level. Obviously something was amiss.[97]

Note that the city of Chicago got this valuable information for free. Data analysis is not most people's idea of a fun time, but there are some people willing to do it. Nobody knows what they will find until they look, but there are examples of spectacular successes. In the mid-1850s, long before computers, Dr John Snow mapped the deaths from an epidemic that was gripping London, believed to be caused by inhaling infected air. He realised that at the centre of the cluster of deaths was a water-pump that all the victims used. The authorities capped the well, the death rate dropped dramatically, and Snow had discovered the cause of cholera.[98]

Dr Snow operated without modern information technology that makes it much easier to organise vast amounts of data and spot much more subtle patterns. Nobody knows what we might find if all state data (anonymised where necessary) were made available to anyone interested in crunching it, but since the cost is almost nothing, just the possibility of useful results is enough.

Making government data available on the internet is recommended for specific cases in this book; however, the presumption should be that all data should be released like this unless there is a pressing need to do otherwise. This principle challenges deeply-ingrained practices in our civil service. Government bureaucracies around the world have the same tendencies, but change is coming. On his first day in office as president, Barack Obama signed an open government directive[99] which has led to the creation of a website where anyone can access census data.[100] However, this approach is too narrow in the data it releases, and too prescriptive in creating online applications to use, rather just giving out raw data.

In the UK, a project has been launched to make all possible government data available on the internet, with a particular focus on encouraging amateurs to come up with their own creative ways of analysing it.[101]

- Ireland should record all its government data in a standardised, format and make it freely available on the internet in a machine-readable format.

- Information that would breach the privacy of an individual should be anonymised, and an exception should be made for commercially sensitive data.

- Aside from these exceptions, all other data should be published as a matter of course.

- Where an exception is made, the reason for the exception, and the person making the decision, should be published.

- Government regulations which require the disclosure of private-sector data (everything from the price of petrol to the ingredients of food products) should be amended to include a requirement to make that data available on the internet in a machine-readable format.

Postcodes

Almost uniquely in developed economies, Ireland has no postcodes, yet. A proposal has been on the cards for years, and it has been announced that postcodes will be introduced in 2011.[102] An Post[103] and the Communication Workers' Union[104] have ferociously resisted this move, aware of its potential to allow competitors to enter the postal market.

Of all the addresses in Ireland, 40 per cent are non-unique,[105] which means a house that has precisely the same address of at least one other house. These addresses mostly occur in rural areas, where there is no street numbering, but are also common in towns and cities where there can be many streets or housing estates with identical names.

In the UK – including Northern Ireland – postcodes have a resolution of 26, meaning that no more than 26 residences have the same postcode. Typically, each side of a street will have a unique postcode, a small block of flats would have its own code, and a large block would have a different postcode for each floor. Because almost every dwelling has a street number, the combination of this number and postcode uniquely and reliably identifies each dwelling and business. The importance of postcodes to modern business will be apparent to any Irish person who phones a call centre which is more used to dealing with calls from the UK. Regardless of whether you want an insurance quote, a computer repaired or a concert ticket, the first detail they want is your postcode.

But if An Post is vigorously resisting postcodes, what do we need them for? Everything. Far more things than houses and businesses need postcodes. Since An Post is the only group who seem not to need them, let's not call them postcodes at all; let's call them **Unique Location Identifiers**, ULIs.

Good decisions require good information, and location is vitally important information in many decisions. The author's home address has more than 20 versions, which can be generated by changing part or all of the address into Irish or using different neighbourhood names. If minded to commit insurance fraud, dozens of different policies, all for apparently different addresses, could be taken out with little chance that insurance companies would recognise that they all related to the same house. Such fraud would be impossible if every house had one ULI. Multiple claims at the same address could be spotted instantly. Who else can use ULIs? What can be done with them?

- Calculate the flooding risk for a location

- Map the location of every crime, to spot patterns and aid detection – see page 232

- Map the occurrences of illnesses to allow the quick spotting of patterns that would aid prevention

- Assist the delivery of shopping, flowers or any number of online services

- Allow people to organise lift-sharing to work by matching close departure and arrival points

- Calculate the proximity of radio and TV transmitters

- Calculate the closest government offices or shops in a chain

- Calculate nearby dates on a dating website

- Organise street furniture and road sign maintenance work

- Organise utility maintenance crews

- Track mobile medical and screening services

- Tell a taxi or ambulance service exactly where to find you

- Tell courier services where to start and stop

- Allow the tax authorities to trace tax compliance for rented properties and primary residences

- Track car hire locations

- Allow people to buy and sell online to people in their locality

- Track TV licence compliance – see page 93

- Allow franchised businesses to precisely map the territory of their franchisees

- Track advertising billboards

- Prevent insurance fraud

- Prevent social welfare fraud

- Prevent money-laundering

- Prevent Companies Act offences

- Track criminal offenders who are ordered to live at a particular address

- Reduce conveyancing costs – see pages 163 and 174

- Allow tourists to find hotels, guest houses and attractions

- Track banks, ATMs, pharmacies, petrol stations, and other services using GPS navigation devices

- Match people with nearby allotments – see **Dig for Victory** on page 74

And that's only the start. Given the huge proportion of our economy that is dependent on the location of the supplier or the consumer or both, there is almost nothing that does not have the potential to benefit from ULIs.

Proposed System

Ireland needs postcodes with a resolution of one, but the proposed system would only identify areas rather than particular addresses, with a three-letter code to identify the town and three numbers to narrow down to a particular area, such as GAL123 in Galway or ATH123 in Athlone.[106] This severely limits the system's benefits because houses with non-unique addresses are most usually beside each other and are likely to also end up with an identical postcode.

Every location where goods or services are delivered should get its own unique ULI – homes and businesses, obviously, but also every field, bus and Luas stop, lamp post, post box, litter bin, electricity sub-station, manhole, mobile phone mast, telecoms box, billboard and pedestrian crossing.

The system announced by the Department of Communications can be easily adapted to improve its resolution. Adding just two alpha-numeric characters (excluding the letters O and I and the numbers 1 and 0) at the end will give 1024 unique combinations.[‡] An extra element of the postcode should be added, which should be as short as possible while guaranteeing there would be enough variation for every installation in the area, giving complete postcodes like GAL123QF and ATH1238T.

Roll Out

To roll out a complete postcode system, all that is needed is a once-off mapping exercise, followed by a postcard to each address informing them of their new ULI, and some free-media publicity. All government services, including Social Welfare and Revenue, should require the postcode of all applicants; firstly, they would need it to properly track their clients, but also to raise the level of public awareness.

On an ongoing basis, all that is needed is a website for forgetful people to enquire what their postcode is and to apply for postcodes for new structures. This may require a staff of two or three, but it is possible that it could be done entirely automatically.[107]

---

‡   The intended resolution is unclear, but it is likely it will be similar to that used in the UK, which allows a maximum of 26 residences per postcode. In this context 1,024 unique variations should be more than adequate, but if this is not enough, using three characters gives 32,768 combinations.

Privacy

Concern has been expressed, though not very clearly explained, that postcodes will lead to some unspecified breach of personal privacy, or to a surge in the amount of junk mail.[108] Since almost every other developed country has a method of uniquely identifying residences (by combining house numbers and postcodes) it would be remarkable if a negative effect existed that had not already been experienced in one of those countries. The fact that no such problem is cited demonstrates that it is not real.

The Data Protection Commissioner raised the issue that if, for example, research information about the prevalence of a particular disease was done by postcode, this could have the effect of identifying a particular house and thereby a particular person; and that this was sufficient reason to abandon the entire project of resolution-one postcodes.[109]

This is not credible. Detailed geographical analysis on disease rates is compiled using postcodes in almost every other country, without this negative outcome. In the UK, where house numbers and resolution-26 postcodes identify every property uniquely, the practice is to simply do such analysis by postcode without the house number. There is no reason why the Data Protection Commissioner could not develop a protocol whereby computer systems using postcodes for this type research would be designed to remove or not accept characters that identify unique properties, using the form GAL123 and ATH123.

Junk Mail

Contrary to fears, resolution-one postcodes give us the power to permanently end the problem of unwanted junk mail. All commercial mail should be required to carry a postcode, with a standard fine (say €200) for each item that does not, imposed by the Data Protection Commissioner. Consumers can then be allowed to give their preference on receiving junk mail and have that preference enforced. Here's how:

- Require commercial mailers to create and maintain a single website where people can input their postcode, to opt out of all (or a selection of) junk mail.
- When a preference is input, a confirmation is sent by letter to that address, with a confirmation code which must be input in the website to make the choice take effect.
- Householders could make up to three changes of preference per year.
- The list of opted-out postcodes (but no other data) should be available to commercial mailers.
- A standard fine (say €1,000) should be imposed for each item of junk mail sent to an opted-out postcode, by the Data Protection Commissioner.

Remember Everybody

If the state wants to deliver services efficiently to its citizens, a minimum requirement is for it to know who and where we are. "If you want to know how many people work here," a senior private sector source says, "don't bother asking HR – ask payroll; anyone who is missing from that list will let you know pretty fast."

The organisation that keeps an efficient list of almost all citizens in the country is Revenue. Your Personal Public Service Number (PPS) integrates your tax and social welfare records, and if other arms of the state are to deliver individualised services, there is no reason to duplicate this database.

When I call my cable TV company, my insurance company, and when I order a taxi, my record is associated with the phone number I dial from, and that record appears on the screen of the agent, increasing convenience and security on my account. (I still have to give security information to frustrate any fraudster who gets hold of my phone.)

In the first instance, the Revenue should add the ULI of every resident to their record – this would be part of having their complete address anyway. Next, for a wide range of public and private sector functions, the PPS number of the individual should be recorded. This will allow the Revenue authorities to verify tax compliance. This is already being done so that, for example, all property transactions now must bear the PPS number of the buyer and seller.

Tax and social welfare records are confidential and should not be released; however, it will be appropriate to allow some state services to access a limited amount of data such as the names, addresses and PPS numbers of individuals to ensure, for example, that people do not make multiple applications for particular benefits, or for law enforcement reasons. A PPS number should be assigned to each child at birth, and to every person who immigrates to the country, to ensure completeness of the system.

Taxpayers can already log in to the Revenue Online Service (ROS) to update their records, and this system should allow people to input and update their email and mobile phone number if they choose to do so, although their address should be a requirement. Selected state agencies should be given technology that would indicate which of these details have been input, without revealing the contact information to anyone at that agency. If appropriate, government computer systems should allow officials to send an SMS or email to the individual, without revealing that individual's details to the operator or the agency, in the same way that many websites send email updates to subscribers, without publishing their email address. This would be particularly useful for the agencies governing transfer of property (see page 163) or vehicles (see page 259).

Data Protection
Increasing the efficiency of the state's use of data also allows an increase in the efficiency in the way this data may be misused. Almost all of the data is in the hands of the state anyway, but when it is organised for better use, the system must be set up to take account of the fact that it can be easier to misuse also, and must make sure that individual privacy is respected.

This is clearly a problem already. More than 100 civil servants were found to have improperly accessed the records of a major lottery winner. Everyone from tabloid newspapers to insurance companies, private investigators and criminals appear to be able to pay civil servants for improper access to information. None have been prosecuted.[110]

The solution to this is more information, not less:

- Any state official working with personal data should have access only to the portions of data that they need to do their job, and only use it to do their job.

- The data systems should keep a record of which files are accessed by each employee.

- The revenue website which allows people to log in and manage their tax affairs should be extended to allow people to see every record of every public servant who accesses their files, including which information was viewed, and by whom.

- People should be able to make complaints directly to the data protection commissioner if they believe that their files are improperly accessed, and the commissioner should have the power to launch prosecutions where appropriate.

- In exceptional cases, Gardaí should have the facility to access files without the subject's knowledge, where that was necessary to investigate a crime.

Cartels and Congested Markets

The government doesn't work well in Ireland, but anyone advocating the free market as a solution to all our problems hits another problem: the free market doesn't work that well either. Part of the problem is geography. On a small island, fewer competitors can exist in any given business, and customers can't easily sideline local suppliers and go further to find a better deal. It also means that what few competitors exist are more likely to know each other socially and be able to quietly organise a cartel.

Lack of competitiveness rips off consumers and increases costs throughout the economy, putting us at an international disadvantage. With our inherent problems, Ireland would be justified in having extraordinary measures to promote competition, but how is competition ensured in the most competitive of economies?

The United States Department of Justice (DoJ) is charged with enforcing antitrust laws, governing what is known here as cartels and monopolies. In almost all cases, it is a criminal offence for owners of competing businesses to agree on prices which they will charge customers. These laws also regulate company takeovers, to ensure that no company can buy out competitors or use the lack of competition to disadvantage customers. But cartels are notoriously difficult to detect, because everyone taking part is highly motivated to prevent the detection of their crime. The victims – the customers – may not even be aware that they are being ripped off, as in the case of the cartels that control the price of new cars in Ireland. (See page 128)

The DoJ has developed a leniency policy to help smoke out cartels.[111] Firstly, there are very serious penalties for antitrust behaviour, with fines of up to $100m for companies and up to a million dollars and ten years in prison for individuals involved in cartel price-rigging.[112] And the penalties are enforced; every month the press release section of the DoJ website lists the businessmen who were jailed for their activities.[113]

The DoJ has an innovative way to enforce the law. Offenders can escape jail if they volunteer evidence against the other members of the cartel, as long as they are the first to get to the prosecutors with their confession.[114] This radically alters the dynamic of cartels. Previously everyone involved had a powerful motivation to keep the crime under wraps and knew that everyone else had the same motivation. With the leniency policy, everyone is aware that everyone else can send them to jail; that the only way to avoid that danger is to be the first to make it to the DoJ.

Ireland should introduce severe prison sentences for illegal cartels, and a lenience policy along the lines of the DoJ. Because the Director of Public Prosecutions is not configured to deal with such prosecutions, Ireland needs a specialist prosecutor to deal with cartels and other major financial crime. See **Tackling Financial Crime** on page 193 for proposals on how to do this.

Supermarkets

The huge disparity between the prices of products in supermarkets north and south of the border gives rise to a reasonable suspicion that price-gouging is going on, taking advantage of the more limited competition in the Irish market. The supermarkets claim that the price difference is down to different tax rates and other costs.

Their case is not supported by their refusal to reveal their profit margins for their Irish subsidiaries[115] – they are only available aggregated with the UK operations. And their case certainly is not made credible by the leaked details that Tesco's Irish profit margins are 58 per cent higher than elsewhere.[116] [117]

The arrival of the German discounters in the Irish market is a welcome development, and it seems to have put some downward pressure on prices in general. In summer 2009, major Irish supermarket chains, including Dunnes, Tesco and SuperValu, introduced what they boasted were major price cuts,[118] with Tesco even launching a dedicated website to advertise the price cuts which tellingly were first introduced only in stores adjacent to the border.[119] It might be tempting to believe that this constitutes the solution to the problem. It does not. The fact that supermarkets can boast price cuts of 30 per cent or more shows just how bloated margins are.

The solution to uncompetitive pricing is to inform and empower the consumer. Advertising on behalf of supermarkets or consumer advocates is unlikely to be effective because of the complexity of the weekly shop for most families. Therefore, all supermarkets should be required to publish prices for every product on their website, in a format easy for screen scrapers to access. The data should include the price, name, bar code and any other product details.

This would allow screen scrapers to compare the prices of brand-name products, and associate equivalent own-brand products from different supermarkets, allowing a like-for-like comparison.

Many supermarkets collect data for sale to direct marketing companies about every product that each customer who has a loyalty card buys. No doubt this data is useful to them, but it could also be very useful to the customers. The supermarkets should be required to create a feature on their websites where customers could lodge their email address, along with the numbers from their customer loyalty card, and all their credit and debit cards. When any of those cards is used to make a purchase at the supermarket, the supermarkets should be required to email, in a standard format, the receipt for that purchase to the customer – the receipt would contain all the product data that goes on the websites for the screen scrapers.

The screen scrapers would then be able to offer a service whereby consumers could upload their last week's shopping list and be told which supermarket would have been best value for that shopping trip. Such pressure on the supermarkets would increase competition and ensure the best value for the customer.

This feature is also important to give consumers useful information about the contents of their foods – see **More Information** on page 69. Wise supermarkets might allow direct access to their online ordering system from the screen scraper website, so once a customer saw what supermarket was best value, another click or two would have their shopping done.

To avoid manipulation of the system, supermarkets should be forbidden from changing their pricing more than once per week, and a specific time and day should be agreed, such as 9am on Mondays.

Pub Licences
During the boom, a pub licence was a huge asset, because it gave the right to serve a product that everyone without this licence was forbidden from serving. If you had the licence, you didn't have to compete, because the government, at taxpayer expense, eliminated the competition for you. It would be difficult to think of a more congested market. Anyone who has holidayed in southern European resorts will be familiar with the people that pubs hire to stand at their entrances. Many Irish pubs hire people to stand at their entrances as well, but the difference is that on the continent the task is to persuade passers-by to come in; they hold out menus, they tell you this is the best establishment in town, they promise the first drink free or give out some other voucher. In Ireland the people at the door are there to keep you out. During the boom, very ordinary pubs were sold for fantastic amounts.[120] [121] In November 2006, it was reported that

> In the year to date, some 28 Dublin pubs (representing 3.61 per cent of the total number of pubs in Dublin) have been sold with a total capital value of around €130.74 million, according to Morrissey's Auctioneers ... with the average sale price being around €4.67 million[122]

This means that Dublin pubs were worth a total of about €3.6bn, or more than €3,000 for every person in the city. While it is difficult to separate the capital value of the licence from that of the premises, it is certain that the pub licence became an enormous capital asset in itself, particularly because pub licences specify the physical size of the drinking area. Serving alcohol is a simple and highly profitable business. It is completely standardised, unlike running a restaurant or café, and if one sticks to the rules, the huge margins will finance the huge repayments on the mortgage. This arrangement has negative consequences, such as

- Anyone running a pub must sell as much drink as possible to meet the repayments.

- Any distraction from this will impact the bottom line.

- Any person in a pub not drinking alcohol, or not drinking enough alcohol, will cost you a lot of money, so publicans must discourage such people.

- Very loud music, to prevent conversation, and a poor selection of food and non-alcoholic drinks are the norm in most city pubs.

- Non-alcoholic drinks are sold at exorbitant prices.

- Rural pubs may not have the music so loud, but the non-alcoholic alternatives are worse.

It is not only the market congestion that causes problems. Pubs are given a fixed closing time, and exceptions can only be made by applying to a judge at the district court. This creates a culture where drinkers feel the need to drink all the alcohol they want in a short space of time, before they are ejected on to the streets to meet other people all coming out at the same time. It is difficult to think of a surer formula for disorder. The notion that judges, with no training in planning, are qualified to make judgements about when to close pubs is without basis, apart from the fact that they often end up adjudicating on the resulting disorder.

There have been attempts over the decades to tinker with the opening hours of pubs and nightclubs in an attempt to alleviate this problem, with no real impact. In a classic example of confusing cause and effect, there have even been attempts to bring fast-food outlets within their own licensing regime, limiting their opening hours too.[123]

Publicans are clever enough to keep quiet and allow groups promoting abstinence to make the case against reform; however, many of the restrictive measures don't reduce the harm caused by alcohol. They make it worse. Restricting the number of pubs, and thereby incentivising them to sell very little except alcohol in huge quantities has no health benefits. Corralling drinkers together creates a group dynamic that pressurises people to drink, and to drink more. The huge margins made on alcohol put pubs at a competitive advantage over establishments that cannot serve alcohol.

And the huge profits of the drinks industry constitutes an economic and political force that can fight off any reform designed to reduce harmful consumption. Publicans successfully fought off the proposal of licensing café-bars,[124] [125] so if a group of friends want to meet, all must go to a pub, and be exposed to pressure to drink alcohol, even if only one of them wants to have a glass of beer or wine.‡ Publicans were also quietly delighted with the exclusion of under-18's from pubs, keeping the hard-drinking culture, rather than a family-friendly atmosphere. Finally, as the Supreme Court ruled in the case that deregulated the taxi industry, it is unfair and unconstitutional to exclude someone from a trade or profession solely to benefit the current operators. The licensing laws should be scrapped in their entirety:

- There should be no limit on the number of establishments that can serve alcohol, other than one set by the market.

- The new planning authority (see **Planning Permission** on page 169) should regulate aspects of the pub trade, such as opening hours and suitable locations as they do for other businesses.

- In general, the presumption should be that there is no restriction on the opening hours or physical size of the premises.

- Where such restrictions are justified – such as close to residential areas – different closing times should be set for different pubs, with later and earlier times rotating between different establishments.

Since well before the end of the boom, much has been made about the crisis in Irish pubs. In May 2006, at the height of the Celtic Tiger, it was reported that 600 pubs had closed in the previous two years,[126] with the smoking ban and increased vigilance against drink-driving being blamed, and serious suggestions were made to undermine both these laws so as to increase the incomes of publicans. This figure appears to originate from a press release from the Licence Vintners Association (LVA). When the author queried the figure, the LVA declined to clarify whether this was the net number of closures, or included pubs moving to a new location. While it is not clear whether the cited number of pubs closing is the net figure or includes pubs being closed to use the licence for a new pub elsewhere, the vast prices paid for pubs in 2006 does not support the contention that hundreds of them were simply shutting up shop for financial reasons at that time.

But even if this is the case now that the boom is over, so what? The fact that publicans and their supporters advocate risking peoples' lives[127] [128] for their financial gain illustrates the exaggerated sense of entitlement that has flowed from the political power that they wield, and the protection from

---

‡   The café-bar proposal was unlikely to have improved the situation much, just allowing new entrants into the cartel. Unless the licensing regime is removed entirely, the licences themselves will have great value, and anyone who owns one will need to discourage customers from consuming any other product, to justify the expense.

competition that they have been given. Pubs are businesses, and businesses go out of business every day. Sometimes that is unfortunate, but often it is for the best because they are replaced with new enterprises that benefit society more. Publicans have no more right to extraordinary measures to keep them in business than did people who printed airline tickets, made VHS videos or input credit card transactions.

It is claimed that the pub is the only social venue in many parts of rural Ireland, but people who use this as special pleading on behalf of pubs rarely explain why it is the case. Publicans have used their cartel and their political and financial muscle to keep out competition, such as with café-bars. If that cartel is broken, it would allow the development of more diverse and consumer-friendly social venues.

Alcohol and Social Policy

There is one valid reason for not completely deregulating the alcohol market. Alcohol is a powerful drug, and there are valid social concerns that removing restrictions to its access could have significant negative social effects. There is evidence in other countries to back this up. Finland traditionally had high prices and strict controls on alcohol, but when the closely related Estonians joined the EU in 2005, it was recognised that there would be no possibility of restraining Finns from buying huge quantities of much cheaper alcohol. The government reduced alcohol prices by one-third, and the real price reduced even further because many people went to Estonia anyway. There were immediate and significant increases in the consumption of alcohol, and in alcohol-related hospital admissions, and long-term health damage caused by alcohol is also rising.[129]

It is obvious that this is not desirable. However, this is no reason to fail to reform the perverse and unjust licensing laws.

- Any increase in alcohol prices desirable for social policy should be in the form of taxation that goes to the state, not supernormal profits for a cartel.

A Pint is a Pint

Publicans fought hard against the metrication of their industry. Since they are so attached to their pint, it would be nice if they would actually serve that amount to customers. Pubs on the continent, almost without exception, use glasses that are larger than the measure being served and have a fill-line where the top of the liquid should reach. Irish pint drinkers, on the other hand, are often cheated out of the full measure by being served a significant portion of foam. Publicans should be required to change their entire stock of glasses to this model, and serve the complete measure that is paid for. A short phasing-in period should be allowed while the existing glasses are recycled or fall out of use through breakage.

Banking Competition

Despite the arrival of foreign retail banks (now threatened with the departure of Halifax), the cost of banking in Ireland is far higher than in other countries, and customer inertia is a big part of the problem. People don't like getting overcharged, but don't like dealing with the hassle of moving their current account either.

People don't like to have to move their direct debits and salary payments and are afraid of penalties if bills get forgotten. It is not surprising that banks who are losing a customer are not very cooperative, and don't make life easy.

It may seem counterintuitive, but it is also in the interests of the bank that is gaining a customer to make life difficult for the few people who go to the trouble of switching their accounts. Banks know that they will benefit from the lack of competition if they make life hard for activist customers, regardless if they are on their way in the door or on their way out.

The newly arrived banks are actively recruiting customers, but their market share is not big enough to have a significant impact on competitiveness. The solution is for the financial regulator to require banks to make switching much easier. Here's how:

- Create a single-page form for current account switching.

- Make the form available in all bank branches and downloadable from all retail banks' websites.

- Make bank account numbers and sort codes portable, in the way that mobile phone numbers are, so that there is no need to update direct debits, salary payments or other transactions.

- On the form, ask only for the information required to identify the account that is being transferred: name, address, sort code and account number.

- Allow the customer to present the completed form to their new bank, along with the appropriate identity documents.

- Require the new bank to present the completed form to the old bank, and the old bank to pass on all the details so that all direct debits and credits can be passed to the new account automatically.

Funeral Homes

It isn't surprising that funeral homes operate in a dysfunctional market. Without exception, their customers are at a particularly vulnerable point in their lives when they seek their services. The evidence that funeral homes may be making supernormal profits is not hard to find. New, purpose-built buildings for funeral homes are sprouting up everywhere.

They don't look cheap either; marble-clad exteriors, extensive car parks and prime locations don't indicate a cost-conscious industry. However, for all the investment in property, they don't seem to have made much of an investment in technology. A Google search of Irish websites for "Funeral Homes" reveals few links to the websites of these companies. Of the top 10 hits, only two are of funeral homes, and after that there are almost no more. The Golden Pages lists 619 of these businesses.

Of the two funeral home websites, neither contains any information on pricing or any form to request a quotation, so a grieving relative is faced with finding and telephoning each funeral home in the area and requesting pricing individually. With very much more to worry about, it's not surprising that most people simply telephone the first funeral home they came across and agreed to make arrangements without discussing pricing. The Irish Association of Funeral Directors has an amateurish website[130] that offers little useful information to clients and a watery code of practice that says of pricing only that:

> Members should have available a complete price list showing their charges for merchandise, services and facilities and also a complete list of the payments they will be required to make on the client's behalf.

There is no requirement to give the price list to the customer, or even make them aware that it exists, and there is no requirement to tell the customer that they are choosing an inappropriately expensive option. An unethical funeral home whose business was based on exploiting and bullying people at their most vulnerable would have no difficulty complying with the code. More strongly worded elements of the code are reserved for making sure there is no competition for business:

> Soliciting funerals is not permitted.

The solution is to require all funeral directors to supply their entire price list online in a standard format that can be used by screen-scraping websites. Add the ULI (see **Screen Scraping** on page 49) of each funeral home, and customers can input their ULI and see the exact price of the funeral that they desire. The funeral homes would be free to each create their own website, but their trade association could provide the service for all its members on a single page.

If funeral homes are operating in a competitive market, then this will be no disadvantage, and they will have given extra convenience to their customers. However, if it is true that they are making supernormal profits, this would make it easy for people to find the best price and put intense competitive pressure on funeral homes that overcharge.

Food and Agriculture

No, that's not the wrong way round. The Department of Agriculture, Fisheries and Food are the people who have it backwards; its very name shows the order of its priorities.[131] The entire department is oriented towards serving the producers, with the consumers being little more than an inconvenience. The department positively boasts that it barely meets the farm inspection standards required of the EU.[132]

Society has an obvious interest in making sure that all its members have access to an abundance of good quality food that allows people to live as long and happy lives as possible, and whose production is sustainable and does not harm the environment. Concern for the businesses of people who produce food, from farmers to multinational manufacturers, must come second to this.

Obesity

Changes in diet and activity levels are contributing to a sharp rise in obesity. In just ten years from 1990 to 2000, obesity rates in Irish men leapt from 8 per cent to 20 per cent. This has immediate health impacts. Rates of childhood type 2 diabetes – exclusively related to obesity – are also soaring in Ireland.[133] School uniforms are now being supplied with up to a 106cm (42-inch) waist.[134]

Dr Edna Roche, head of the child-weight management clinic at Tallaght Hospital, typically sees children between eight and 13 but has had patients as young as two years old. She listed the problems that this can cause in addition to the psychological problems:

> ...the reality is that if you have weight issues as a child you run the very real risk of gall stones, high blood pressure, cardiovascular problems, difficulties with the onset of puberty, orthopaedic problems, and sleep apnoea. Some children have serious respiratory problems, and need breathing masks at night to help them sleep because sleep apnoea means they can stop breathing at night.[135]

Part of the problem is our genes. Humans are programmed to eat – we need to do it to survive. Our ancestors never died of overeating before they got the chance to reproduce, so we never gained a mechanism to control it, and when prosperity presents the problem for the first time, we are ill-equipped to deal with it. Just watch how a child will studiously lick the cream from a biscuit, eating the highest-calorie element first, to make sure her stomach doesn't fill with lower-calorie biscuit first.

Humans are evolved to seek out the nutrients they need. There is strong evidence that even young children will subconsciously prefer foods that contain the vitamins, minerals and other elements which they need at that moment.[136] For example, when we are short on vitamin C, our brains point us towards sweet, brightly coloured fruits. Modern processed foods, however, can mimic these foods, without most of their nutrients, so our programming pushes us to eat more and more, chasing the vitamins that aren't there.

But don't just blame your genes if you can't get into your jeans. Our diets have changed radically in the recent past, coupled with a collapse in activity levels. Patterns established in childhood tend to continue for a person's lifetime.[137] [138] The solution is with the children, because very probably, the adults are lost. Also, initiatives should be designed to integrate with other activities in life. Solutions that are based on good intentions are unlikely to endure. We should:

- Design our spaces and lives so that children have the freedom to get exercise as part of other activities – see **Space for Children** on page 85

- Educate children on how to cook good food – see **Food Education** on page 124

- Reconnect children with the reality of producing food – see **Dig for Victory** on page 74

These solutions are discussed in other sections because they integrate with other objectives, but there are other interventions that the government needs to make.

Good eating habits are nurtured in childhood, but even a family which has the best habits and sits to the table for three meals a day – 1,000 times a year – cannot compete with the intensity of the message that delivers up to 4,000 junk food advertisements to children a year.[139] This is all the more serious because there is clear evidence that watching these advertisements increases the intake in junk food[140] and the risk of obesity.[141]

In recent years, food companies have been required to disclose information about food contents on the pack. Cleverly, they have always complied and often far exceeded the regulations, giving a vast amount of detail in tiny print that would leave even a nutritionist bewildered about the difference between monosodium glutamate and monounsaturated fat.

This leaves the marketing department free to make all sorts of vague claims about the "goodness" of their products. It is astonishing that, for example, a high-salt, high-sugar product such as Kellogg's Special K can be advertised as "low fat" in a context clearly designed to imply that it is a diet food likely to make you thinner. A study from the British Heart Foundation found that such claims succeeded in fooling 90 per cent of mothers when buying food for their children. Another Kellogg's product, Coco Pops Cereal and Milk Bars, which have more fat and sugar than the average chocolate cake, are labelled as "a source of calcium, iron and six vitamins". This succeeded in fooling 63 per cent of mothers in the survey into believing it is healthy food.[142]

Some have proposed a junk food tax to deter consumption.[143] This is unlikely to yield any benefits (other than tax take) because there is no evidence that price-sensitivity exists on the type of foods consumed, even if it does influence choices within the type. The huge cost of low-quality delivery pizza indicates that there are far more complex factors in food decision-making. The solution is less information and more information.

Less Information

There exists a proposed traffic light system of showing whether a food is high, medium or low in fat, sugar, salt and other key ingredients.[144] Unsurprisingly, the big food companies are resisting this ferociously, saying that they believe "customers want more information".[145] And that's fine, but let's give them the traffic lights too, and make them even simpler.

- A body should be created to commission detailed research on the intake of food by all sections of society.

- They should be entitled to detailed recipes of all foodstuffs put on the market.

- They should commission research to verify the contents of a random sample of food products.

- With this information, they should calculate a single result for each product – red, yellow or green, with all the good and bad ingredients in the food being taken into account.

- **Red** means that most people in society should eat less of this food.

- **Yellow** means that most people in society eat about the right amount of this food.

- **Green** means that most people in society should eat more of this food.

- The traffic light colour should be displayed prominently on the packet, along with the phrase explaining it.

- All advertisements for foods would be required to display the colour prominently for the duration of the advertisement, and display and read out the explanatory phrase – "Product x is a red-light food because most people in society should eat less of it to stay healthy".

- Restaurant chains or franchises with more than five outlets should be required to display the traffic light on all their menus and advertisements.

- All judgements should be based on published, falsifiable criteria, and the reasons behind the traffic light assigned to each product should be given.

- All meetings between the body and representatives should be minuted, and the minutes routinely published online.

- Employees of the regulating body should be prohibited from working for any company associated with those that they are regulating for 10 years after they leave its employment.

- The costs of the body should be met by all food companies, proportional to the amount of red-labelled food that they place on the market.

- Food companies found to supply incorrect data would be required to fund the independent testing of all their products for an extended period.

The advantage of the traffic light system is what the junk food companies hate it for – its simplicity. Not only does it communicate clearly to the customer, it gives parents battling in the supermarket an easy way to explain their choices to children demanding the latest celebrity-promoted sugar hit. Even before they learn to read, children can be taught that only a small quantity of red foods will be allowed. For adults, adding a red light to an advertisement would fatally undermine efforts to falsely promote a product as healthy or slimming.

More Information

The food companies cleverly bewilder their customers, saying that they are entitled to the information. So let's have it: every gram, every calorie, every vitamin, every mineral. This information should be published on a scrapable website, alongside other details such as the size of the package and the bar code.

This would allow the creation of third-party websites that would dynamically compare the products and give a wide range of information to the consumer. In the section on **Supermarkets** on page 59, there is a proposal to oblige supermarkets to email customers their receipts in a machine-readable format, for the purpose of price comparison.

This information could also be uploaded to websites that scrape the information about the contents of each product, giving each customer a detailed analysis of the cumulative nutritional value of their entire shopping basket. Websites could be created to assist people in planning healthy and balanced shopping trips and to offer suggestions for replacing red light products with better alternatives.

This process would place intense competitive pressure on the manufacturers of red-light foods to improve their products, so the benefit of the information would spread out from more activist consumers to all members of society.

The CAP Doesn't Fit

In 1945, Europe was starving. The war left indelible memories of hunger in the minds of those who created the Common Agricultural Policy (CAP) 13 years later. CAP's creators focused on maximising food output – it would have been astonishing if they had done anything else. But they did not foresee the effects that their policy would have on the food market and food production.

In any other market, overproduction would depress the market price of the product. The least efficient producers would go out of business, rebalancing supply and demand. The reverse happens when there is a shortage – prices go up, increasing the profits of the producer and tempting more producers into the market. At the time, the CAP seemed sensible. Food is unlike any other product – people can't wait for their breakfast for a couple of years as new producers respond to increased prices. Even a slight shortage of food has drastic consequences, and as Europe struggled to fill empty bellies, the problems of overproduction seemed distant.

Food production soon soared as the CAP removed any possibility of a market signal to farmers to produce less when there was a glut. Farmers embraced every fertiliser, every pesticide and every high-yield variety they could lay their hands on, because they were guaranteed a good price no matter how much they produced. The CAP was the least fussy customer around – it cared only for quantity, not quality, and no producer can be immune to pressures from their customer.

Thankfully, the BSE epidemic did not spread to humans, but it wrought havoc in the beef industry. It was caused by feeding cattle to cattle. Carcasses that couldn't be sold for consumption were ground up and mixed with whatever other chemicals were thought to be beneficial into sacks of "nuts" (pellets of artificial feed). This was never the way nature intended cattle to eat. With the cycle of cross-infection so short, the only surprise is that there weren't more epidemics. And that isn't the worst thing that cattle were fed.

The Irish government was one of the last to ban growth hormones in cattle (under strong pressure from the EU). In May 1991, Fine Gael Senator Tom Raftery decried this move in the Seanad, asking the government to defy Europe.[146] He commented that the banning of the hormones cost farmers £100 (€127) per animal through lower growth, but he didn't seem to appreciate the irony that he was proving just how radical the effect of these hormones was. The agricultural lobby, in every sector from beef to pork, poultry and arable has always resisted any consumer protection legislation. And who can blame them? They are only acting rationally. The CAP demands quantity, and to hell with quality, and the CAP is their customer.

On 6 December 2008, all Irish pork was withdrawn from sale because contamination from highly toxic cancer-causing dioxins was found in samples of the meat produced by pigs who had consumed feed from an unlicensed County Carlow food recycling plant.[147] Immediately an impressive operation swung into action, designed to minimise damage, not to the consumers, but to the farmers. The phrase repeated over and over in the Irish media was that eating contaminated pork was the equivalent to the risk of smoking one cigarette.[148] [149] This had absolutely no scientific basis. What was scientifically established was that feed that caused contamination had 200 times the level of dioxins considered safe,[150] although this figure was only published in the British press.

The news was of such importance that RTÉ's weekday news programme *Morning Ireland* got up early on the Sunday morning to announce the news to the country over their breakfast rashers. The incident did huge damage to the international image of all Irish food, and *The Irish Times* reported that the "World press has a field day with the pork crisis".[151] Farmers' leaders immediately began talking of the compensation package, but the compensation was to be for the industry that had used cheap unlicensed feed, not the consumer.[152]

Finally, on 11 December, the Irish Association of Pigment Processors' Cormac Healy announced that he had reached agreement with Taoiseach Brian Cowen and Agriculture Minister Brendan Smith on a €180m compensation package paid for by the taxpayer, and that his members would agree to resume production. The pork industry employs 7,000 people,[153] so this equates to €25,700 from the taxpayer for every person employed in the industry to compensate for five days of lost production.

Single Farm Payments
In recent years, intervention – using taxpayers' money to buy up farm produce that the taxpayers refused to buy themselves – has been replaced with the Single Farm Payment. Farmers are paid regardless of whether they produce anything or not. It is like social welfare in reverse – the less you need it, the more you are paid. Beef baron Larry Goodman is paid €10,000 per week.[154]

The Irish Farmers' Association (IFA) are quick to quote a very low figure – €13,000[155] in 2009 – as the average farm income, but slow to point out that this figure includes the income of part-time and hobby farmers, but excludes their off-farm income. In addition, some farmers made vast sums during the boom selling land for development and road building.

The real test of income that land yields is the price that it commands, and Irish land is, by a vast margin, the most expensive in the EU, 10 times dearer than French land and double the price of land in the second-dearest country, Luxembourg.[156]

Begin with a Brand
Despite the recklessness of the farming sector, Ireland is still seen as a clean and green country. As the consumer of the new millennium demands quality food, Ireland can build on this image and command a higher price for its produce. Organic food sales in the US are growing at 17 to 20 per cent a year, compared to two or three per cent for other foodstuffs.[157] We must build a brand. The marketing people can think up a snappy name, but for the moment we can call it Clean Food Ireland. Ideally Clean Food Ireland will be created and administered by a semi-state agency. An Bord Bia and all the other food promotion agencies will be subsumed into this agency.

Promotion

Clean Food Ireland will carry out all of Ireland's marketing of food at home and abroad. The brand will have a catchy slogan and logo, and they will licence qualifying Irish producers to use it on their products.[158] Traditional advertising will be a part of the promotion of Clean Food Ireland but mostly the marketers will have to get the brand exposed at every opportunity. The aim will be to promote knowledge among consumers worldwide of the two other roles of the agency: education and enforcement.

Education

The aim will be to get Irish farmers to meet the highest possible standards demanded by international consumers to move away from high inputs of artificial fertilisers and pesticides, and intensive industrialised food production. There will be no "big bang". The brand will begin low-key, with minimal requirements for participating.

Education and training projects will gradually raise the bar, beginning by eliminating the most harmful chemicals and objectionable practices. Part of the conversion will be achieved with natural turnover in the farming population, but mostly by trainers running on-farm demonstrations for a farmer and all his neighbours. The trainers will also explain the theory behind the practice – in particular, that prices will always be higher for the products which the consumer wants.

Enforcement

A separate but related agency will be responsible for enforcement, with spot-checks, visits to farms and analysis of produce. It will expel without warning any farmer cheating on the system, but after a cooling-off period, he or she can apply for readmission on the basis that they pay for an elevated level of testing on their products for a specified period. Unauthorised use of the brand will be a criminal offence.

Voluntary Participation
It's not compulsory, the old Irish adage goes, but you have to do it. This is the attitude that will be adopted towards participation in the scheme. It must be voluntary, partly because such detailed regulations of farming would probably be unconstitutional, but mostly because membership should be seen as a privilege. However, a clear signal will be sent that anyone serious about being a food producer will be expected to meet the standards set down. The Irish government has little power over the CAP grants and subsidies – the EU controls all these – but there is a wide range of concessions that the Irish government and its agencies give to farmers: training from An Teagasc, REP schemes and everything from international promotion to seed testing and farmer early retirement schemes. All of these concessions should be made conditional on being a member of the scheme, and where EU payments are still made to farmers outside the scheme, the Department of Agriculture will have a stated policy of prioritising the applications of scheme members.

Uneasy Reform
Ireland is already perceived as a clean, green country, but right now, that image is more than flattering. It doesn't always reflect reality. As the pigmeat scandal showed, if we don't shape up, we will be caught out. The values of the brand chime in well with the international perception of Ireland. Exploit it properly, and the benefits of the brand will be enormous. There is huge and growing demand for food that is cleanly produced, and that demand will lead to premium prices.

Initially, Clean Food Ireland will be seen as a cheaper alternative to organic, but as the brand grows and the standards are raised year-on-year, the two will become synonymous. Despite all this, there will be ferocious opposition from the farming sector. Consider the hysterical reaction to the Nitrates Directive, from the EU, reducing the use of certain types of fertiliser to prevent harmful run-off into our drinking water. Ireland has no choice about implementing it; the decision is purely an EU one. The IFA and the ICMSA have lobbied fiercely against the Nitrates Directive, claiming, according to the ICMSA:

> The Nitrates Directive, in the circumstances outlined, could prove disastrous for the most progressive dairy farmers in this country ... [farmers] must ask all politicians, how they intend remedying this insane proposal that effectively spells the end of intensive dairying in this country.[159]

This might be understandable if the directive was in some way a threat to farmers' livelihoods. Aside from poisoning their customers, such intensive use of fertilisers in most cases causes an oversupply in the market, driving down their prices. Farmers and their leaders haven't a clue what is good for them. However, what is good for farmers is good for Ireland, and much courage and leadership will be needed to implement Clean Food Ireland. But it will be worth it.

Dig for Victory

As the Nazi bombs fell and U-boats stalked supply ships, Britain faced another fearsome weapon – starvation. As an island without the capacity to feed its population, every scrap of food mattered, and an ancient tradition was revived. Every piece of waste land, particularly in urban areas, was converted to allotments. City people could grow their own food, and 1.4 million allotments fed many hungry stomachs. The tradition is still strong, with 330,000 Britons holding allotments today, and another 100,000 on waiting lists,[160] with the cost being extremely modest.[161]

There are many reasons for promoting gardening and allotments in Ireland today. Firstly, as an amenity, gardening can be a very positive and rewarding pastime. The environmental cost of transporting potatoes from Cyprus and runner beans from Kenya can be reduced by giving people the opportunity to grow their own. People, particularly city dwellers, need to increase their activity levels, and activity that is integrated into other tasks which have their own benefits is far more likely to be sustained.

But the most important benefit of allotments would be to reconnect people – especially children – with the origins of their food. Jamie Oliver, in his Channel 4 TV series, demonstrated how showing children how their food was produced made it far easier to wean them off junk food. This is vital for combating weight problems – see **Obesity** on page 66. The state should provide, at a low rent, allotments within a short distance of the home of any person who requests them. Here's how:

- Take land that has come into state ownership, through repossession of distressed loans (see **NAMA** on page 43), and unclaimed property (see **Know What We Have** on page 160), from Local Authorities (See page 177) and any other available source.

- Give it to a new state agency.

- Charge the agency with dividing it and distributing it to nearby people who apply through a dedicated website.

- Charge a small amount to fund any initial improvements needed, particularly adding topsoil.

- Require an annual online submission of a list of things grown from each allotment holder.

- Associate this information with the ULI of the allotment and make this information publicly available and searchable (see **Screen Scraping** on page 49).

- Create a forum website for allotment holders to share advice and information about all aspects of growing food.

- Allow people on the waiting list to make submissions to the effect that an allotment has fallen out of use, particularly compared to the submitted list of what is grown.

- Establish a small inspectorate, no more than ten inspectors, to adjudicate on whether a particular allotment has fallen out of use, and if it has, transfer it to the next person on the waiting list.

Barbed Wire

Barbed wire epitomises lazy farming and lazy thinking. It is grey and has poor visibility for animals as well as humans. Some farmers believe that it is an alternative to building sturdy fences, imagining that animals can reason like humans and understand to stay away from it. They can't, and many animals are injured or killed by it.[162] [163] In a soundly constructed agricultural fence, there is no need for barbed wire, so its use is mainly in sloppy or temporary fences, often to fill a gap in a hedgerow. Because animals do not understand the danger until they are injured, many then become panicked, and frantic attempts to escape from it can injure them further. The importation, sale and use of barbed wire should be banned.

Culture

Culture matters for tourism and for other things. People come because they are attracted to an image of the country that appeals to them on many levels. Culture is also important to almost every other industry in a less tangible way. Products from Bailey's Irish Cream to Ballygowan and Guinness trade heavily on their Irish image, and this clearly works for them.[164] [165] Irish pop, rock and even traditional music can be heard in countries whose names, let alone music, are unknown to most Irish people. Personalities like Bono and Bob Geldof have an international stature that chimes with what marketing people might call the brand values of Ireland. The vastly successful *Riverdance* both benefited from and contributed to the international prominence of Irish culture.

We perform well in everything from Hollywood actors to literature (four Nobel prizes). Celtic mythology is also hugely popular as an inspiration for everything from children's stories to computer games. Ireland has few enemies around the world; we probably benefit from the perceived antagonism with our nearest neighbour – everybody loves the underdog. This is ironic, given that the language which Britain gave us is one of the reasons why our culture is so accessible.

These cultural strengths benefit Ireland in immeasurable ways – we can never find the tourist who came or the entrepreneur who invested because of a cultural event, but the cumulative effect cannot be ignored. In addition, it is unlikely that the Celtic Tiger would have prospered as long as it did without attracting so many highly skilled, young foreign workers, and the cultural profile of Ireland was one of the things that made Ireland attractive to them.

Inspiration Counts

The benefits of culture are not limited to how others perceive Ireland. They are important for ourselves too, and they affect how we perform. Athens hosted the Olympic Games in 2008, an event that was uniquely important for the self-esteem of the country that inspired the games.[166] In their home games, Greek athletes won 16 medals, coming fifteenth on the medals table, far higher than ever before.[167] The inspiration didn't stop there. The month before the opening ceremony, Greece took part in the 2004 UEFA European Football Championship. They had only once before even qualified to take part in the championship (1980), but they stunned commentators by winning the entire event.

Denmark had done something similar 12 years before. The country did not even qualify, but took the place of Yugoslavia, excluded because of its internal wars,[168] and then won the entire tournament. It was the year that nationalist fervour in Denmark led to the rejection in a referendum of the Maastricht Treaty.[169] As Anglo-Danish comedian Sandi Toksvig put it, 1992 was "the year that Denmark defeated Europe twice".

People's performance seems to be measurably improved by an intangible enthusiasm which goes along with national pride. Inspiration counts. We cannot create or inspire culture on demand, and allowing the state to decide what is good art or culture is not advisable; but there are some actions that we can take to help things along.

Bring Back the Films

From *Crocodile Dundee* to the film *Australia*, that country has skilfully used the big screen to promote itself culturally. Ireland nearly got it right with the tax incentives that brought the making of *Braveheart* and *Saving Private Ryan*, but the benefits of these were lost through bad management.

The cost of these tax breaks is purely notional, since the films that were attracted would never have come to Ireland without the tax breaks. Films have a three- to five-year development cycle. Tax breaks must be guaranteed for at least that period so that they are still in place when a project moves from planning to production. Big-budget films such as *Michael Collins* are important for our own self-image, but we should not get hung up on the films made here having an Irish theme. The use of Ireland as a location, regardless of the film's theme, is sufficient payback to justify attracting the production. New Zealand benefited hugely from the display of its landscape in the *Lord of the Rings* series,[170] even though the theme was not connected with the country.

Tourism

Ireland is highly dependent on tourism, which grew significantly during the boom. Earnings from tourism went up by over 10 per cent a year – the fastest growth recorded in the EU15. Between 1990 and 2000, the number of tourists visiting Ireland from overseas and overseas tourist revenues both doubled,[171] and these figures continued to grow up to 2008, with revenues of €5bn and employment for 280,000 people.[172] But the benefits have not been spread evenly, with the growth being concentrated in Dublin.[173] [174] Part of this is to do with the increasing taste for short city-breaks, but rural areas have not been doing themselves any favours.

One-off housing has been scattered around the most scenic areas of our countryside, at the insistence of rural politicians.[175] Many other developments have been spectacularly irresponsible, such as building sprawling housing estates for holidaymakers in Courtown, which delivered sewerage directly on to the beach the holidaymakers were there to enjoy.[176] Why anyone would want to spend their holidays in such a housing estate is another question.

The success of politicians such as Éamon Ó Cuív and Jackie Healy-Rae at defeating policies against one-off housing scattered across the most scenic areas of the country is a clear example of the Tragedy of the Commons. The solution is proper enforcement of planning standards – see **Planning** on page 157.

Let's Party

The US embassy in Dublin holds a party on the night of each US presidential election, inviting hundreds of opinion formers. Some Irish embassies around the world do the same on St Patrick's Day, but this should be significantly expanded. The cost would be negligible if Irish food and drinks companies could be persuaded to supply their products as sponsorship. The guest lists are the most important feature. They should be concentrated on opinion formers, but particularly on younger up-and-coming TV personalities, newspaper columnists, politicians and others who can pass on a positive view of Ireland. The parties should involve no explicit promotion or speeches of any kind; just music, food and drink. All of it Irish.

Sport

Gaelic games inspire at home, but are relatively unknown abroad. The fact that they are absent from almost all tourism promotion shows how little ambition we have in that area. A business idea is better if, for some reason such as a patent or a scarce resource, others will find it difficult to copy the success. It means that if you succeed, others will not be able instantly to reproduce your success, diluting the benefits of your good idea.

Ireland has, in Gaelic games, a unique resource that competing countries would have almost no chance of reproducing. They are highly visual and therefore amenable to being advertised on television and promoted within chat shows and other free media. While there is already excessive demand for tickets for high-profile games, many games have attendances well below capacity. Marketing these to tourists has a clear benefit both for the GAA and Ireland.

Fáilte Ireland should be directed to make Gaelic games an integral part of marketing Ireland, not only with advertising, but also by introducing opinion makers in key tourist markets to the games, and using marketing techniques to gain features in targeted media, such as newspaper supplements, magazines and TV holiday channels. The GAA should support the venture by ensuring that buying tickets is easy for tourists.

We should not stop at encouraging tourism based on watching matches. If rock-climbing and trekking in the Andes can be promoted as activity tourism, why not promote learning and playing Gaelic games with Ireland as a destination?

Concerts

Nobody with access to the BBC could miss the blanket coverage which the Glastonbury festival gets every summer.[177] Ukraine is getting in on the act with the month-long Kazantip dance-music festival.[178] Aside from the significant revenue of these concerts, the parallel revenue from tourists incorporating them into a stay in the country is huge. By contrast, Ireland has treated concert-goers with contempt in the past, with councillors pandering to the worst local interests and exploiting the fact that planning permission must be sought for each event.

The concert promoters don't do themselves any favours either. Tickets for the Electric Picnic cost €240 in 2009,[179] and considerable ill-feeling was created in the past by adding all sorts of fees on top of the headline price. Such high prices and bad behaviour are indications of a congested market, where current operators have little fear of competitors. Part of this problem cannot be resolved, because of the limited supply of headline acts that concert-goers want to see, but the situation could be significantly improved, by creating a planning environment that encourages well-run concerts and music festivals of all sizes. See **Planning Special Projects** on page 170. Aside from the immediate benefits, this will leave many people around the world with fond memories of their youth in Ireland and well-disposed to the country for the rest of their lives.

Irish Pubs

For good or ill, Irish pubs are important to our culture, both for ourselves and for tourists. Publicans have been busy slaughtering the geese that lay their golden eggs in recent years, so modernising the laws that govern serving alcohol is important not just for justice and market efficiency, but also for our tourist trade and our internal national culture. Proposals for **Pub Licences** are on page 60.

Immigration and Culture

The chauvinistic Irish nationalist DP Moran (1869–1936)[180] had a narrow view of nationality, but his view that nothing was Irish unless it arrived after St Patrick and before Strongbow was as daft when he wrote it as now. Ireland is a mongrel nation. As with Britain, the bulk of the population is descended from Iberian settlers who arrived 6,000 years ago,[181] but cultural influences have been arriving ever since.

Ireland has been influenced or settled by the Celts, Romans, Christianity brought by Patrick and others, Vikings, Normans, Elizabethan planters and other groups of English and Scots, Huguenots, Czechs, Vietnamese boat people, German and Dutch hippies, refugees from wars in Bosnia, southern Africa and elsewhere, Nigerians, Poles and other economic migrants, and returned emigrants with their partners and children of all nationalities.

No matter how much it may have irked DP Moran, there is no line that can be drawn around our Irishness. In a globalised mobile world, every nation can expect newcomers. Any nation that tries to fossilise its culture will be quickly impoverished.

No one can know how Ireland will change, but we have a couple of good examples of how not to do it. In the 1960s, Germany encouraged Turkish *Gastarbeiter* – guest workers – to develop its booming economy, but the guests were not made very welcome. The government developed a policy of deliberately isolating the Turks from the rest of society. Dormitories were built within factory compounds, and initially workers were not permitted to bring their families and were discouraged from learning German.

When the social problems which this caused became evident, families were permitted and housing improved, but the Gastarbeiter were still discouraged from participating in German society in any way. Many German-born children and grandchildren of immigrants are not permitted to be citizens of the only country they know. With scant investment in the society they live in, and little connection to the culture and even the language, it is not surprising that they often occupy the worst positions on indices, such as education, crime, employment and income.[182]

As bad as the German experience was, the Dutch managed to do it worse. They have entirely segregated neighbourhoods where few people can speak Dutch, living in communities that could have been beamed down from north Africa. Now fanatic minorities within the Muslim community are gaining traction,[183] while the anti-immigrant Party for Freedom, whose leader was banned from entering the UK as an undesirable person,[184] won 17 per cent of the votes in the 2009 European elections.[185]

It is vital that Ireland, new to the experience of immigration, does not repeat these mistakes. The waves of early migrants to Ireland integrated and contributed to a coherent nation. One group of migrants – the Ulster Scots – did not integrate with the nation with consequences that are too well-known. We should take steps to make sure that current and future immigrants become full members of Irish society.

This does not mean that migrants must abandon their connection to their countries of origin. Earlier immigrants have brought new skills and enriched our culture, and there is no reason why this should not continue. Mostly this is an organic process that does not need any state intervention, but the state must be careful to facilitate it. Education at all levels, including workplace training (see **Training** on page 135) should be audited to make sure that it addresses the needs of immigrants. The exemption from learning the Irish language at school given to immigrants and their children should be abolished and replaced with a curriculum that is realistic and relevant and focuses on the Irish used in public life.

This is not all one-way traffic. The native Irish should also learn about the newcomers. School curriculums should include material on the countries of origin of our major immigrant groups. Teaching our citizens about the history, language, culture and current affairs of immigrants' countries of origin could be done best by members of the immigrant communities themselves. This is not just for social inclusion; it is likely that these countries will become more important trading partners in future, particularly Poland and China – see **New Alliances** on page 201.

Gay Culture

Gays are good for business. Quite apart from the human rights aspect of removing discrimination against gay and lesbian people, evidence from the United States indicates that cities with a high gay population do better economically and culturally than those without.[186] [187] The reason for this is unclear, but it may be that well-educated, mobile gay people migrate from intolerant areas to more welcoming locations, bringing their skills and creativity, and contributing disproportionately to the cities they move to.

In addition, areas that have a good record for gay rights are more likely to attract mobile, high-spending tourists, whatever their sexuality, because places that send out the signal that anyone who is different is not welcome are unlikely to be attractive.

Which do you think attracts more visitors – New York and San Francisco or Montgomery, Alabama, and Jackson, Mississippi? This is another reason, but not the best one, to vindicate the rights of all citizens– see **Gay Rights** on page 225.

The Irish Language

Vast resources have been pumped into teaching Irish in our schools. The economic value of Irish is nil, but the same is true of other subjects. In a cold, heartless world, most of what we learn at most subjects is useless knowledge – the value of knowing that Killary harbour is a fjord or when Strongbow landed is also nil. However, education is priceless. The value of a connection to your historical, physical or cultural environment is priceless. It is exactly the type of thing that, because it can't be priced in money, is often valued at zero.

The linguistic arguments against Irish are mostly rubbish. People who claim that students have a "burden" in learning Irish rarely cite evidence, because there is none. There is no evidence that learning another language consumes space in a pupil's brain that could have been used for something else. Language learning is an innate ability,[188] and learning one language does not pose any less of a challenge than learning two or three – and certainly has no impact on the ability to learn the seven-times tables. Around the world, the Euro-centric view of monolingualism is not so common. Children frequently speak one language at home and another at school.

The proponents of Irish have their fair share of daft logic too. First on the list must be the claim that learning Irish is useful because it helps the student to learn other languages later in life. Some go so far as to imagine close similarities between Irish and continental languages. This is rubbish. Irish is part of the small Q-Celtic group of languages, along with Scots Gallic and Manx. It is more distantly related to Welsh and Breton, but that's it. Irish is no more closely related to any existing language than it is to Latvian or Albanian.

A student in second-level education learning German will be helped, the theory goes, by the experience of learning Irish in primary school. Maybe. But not so much as if the student had done German at primary level. For the promoters of the Irish language, economic utility is not a wise thread to be unravelling. They should have the confidence to assert that the Irish language does not need to justify its existence economically.

The fact that so much nonsense is cooked up as logic by both sides of the Irish debate shows that it is not really a debate about the Irish language at all. It is often a proxy for a debate about our own self-worth, held between two sides that both lack the courage to state their case openly. One side is ashamed of our past of poverty and humiliation; the other is fearful of modernity and change. Both sides would do well to sort out their issues rather than project them.

Exceptions

At present the only exception to the compulsory Irish rule is that learning Irish is optional for non-nationals and their children. This policy is unfathomably stupid. Even for those who speak no Irish, the language provides a connection with the cultural and social life of Ireland. The experience of the exclusion of immigrants from mainstream society on the continent should tell us that cultural integration is important. There should be no exceptions from participation of society, and curriculums and exams suitable for pupils who begin Irish later in life should be made available, with an emphasis on cultural understanding.

Reform

The main "reform" offered is to make Irish optional in our schools. Would we make English, maths or history optional? What really needs reform is the hostile and mean-spirited Irish-language requirement for jobs from special-needs teachers to barristers.

Some of the dafter rules about Irish for getting points and grants in the Leaving Cert have been abolished, but there remains the practice of giving a 10 per cent bonus to students who take their exams through Irish. The only justification ever offered for this is because "Irish is harder". This is nonsense. No language is intrinsically harder than another for a native speaker, and the Irish language lobby is going down a dangerous road if it claims otherwise. (If Irish is harder, shouldn't we just stick to English?)

Students should sit subjects other than Irish and English in whatever language they are most comfortable with and be marked on an equal basis. Most of the jobs that require passing an Irish exam operate it as a fig-leaf. Four barristers who spoke to the author were all upfront about the fact that they could never competently present a case in Irish. They passed the test with a mix of school Irish and a few evenings cramming, based on inside knowledge of what is likely to be asked in the exam.

So what would they do if asked to represent a client through Irish? Again, all had the same answer – refer them to another barrister, just as if the case had another aspect they weren't expert in. This is just what Femi Daniyan, a student barrister originally from Nigeria, suggests. Learning Irish from scratch is a major barrier for him.[189] This and all other restrictions masked as protection for the Irish language should be swept away. There is no reason to believe that the Bar, the civil service or any other organisation won't recruit enough Irish-speakers to cope with demand in the normal course of events.

Stádas

The campaign to make the Irish language an official working language of the EU, called Stádas by its supporters, was ultimately successful. By contrast, Catalan, with millions of native speakers in the EU,[190] is not. The translation costs since 2005 run into tens of millions of euro per year, with hundreds of thousands of pages of obscure EU regulations to be translated.[191] Closer to home, the Official Languages Act requires the costly translation of the most obscure documents,[192] such as the Clare County Development Plan, which alone cost €10,000 to translate in 2005. Not a single copy has been sold.[193]

The energy put into these campaigns by Irish-language supporters is disturbing, because it was clear from the start that, when successful, it would lead to a bonanza for Irish-language translators, drawn from the same very small pool of people who ran the campaign.

No doubt many well-meaning people supported the campaign to allow Irish MEPs speak in Irish in the European Parliament, but the translation of lengthy technical government documents and EU laws and regulations into Irish, without any indication of need, is a wasteful folly. All the effort that went into the Stádas campaign, and the money that its success cost, could have had a transformative effect on the language if it had been channelled into something constructive.

Space for Children

Ireland has contempt for children. There is no other way of expressing it. Ireland has more golf courses than playgrounds.[194] We have an extraordinary rate of childhood suicide,[195] and one in 10 adolescents resorts to self-harm, with children as young as five years old presenting at hospital for this reason.[196] But the tragic extremes don't tell the full story of the casual destruction of children's quality of life for the convenience of adults.

Ireland's record for vindicating children's rights is poor. The 2009 Ryan Report documented at least 800 abusers and many thousands of victims in residential institutions run by religious orders on behalf of the state. It is clear that significant profits were made by the religious orders, who pocketed both the payments from the state and the profits from the menial work done by the children.[197]

It is simply not credible that such an avalanche of horror was a secret in the true sense. No doubt most people were unaware of the full extent of the abuse, but many had a good idea and did nothing, out of fear and indifference. When the powerful abused the powerless, adult Ireland chose to look away. But the current generation likes to imagine that all these abuses were the work of our parents' generation; that we are far too humane, too enlightened and too clever to be so indifferent to the rights of children. Bullshit.

The poverty of earlier generations led to a round-up of the most vulnerable children for unpaid work in industrial schools or a quick buck from childless Americans. The objects of our greed may have changed, but our willingness to brush aside the rights of the voiceless is equally callous. Today our greed is much more centred on control of public spaces and making sure that the messiness of childrearing and adolescence does not interfere with our selfish lifestyles.

The 1996 Control of Horses Act[198] was transparently designed to ensure that a pastime of working-class children did not offend the sensibilities of middle-class adults. Commentators expressed their concern in terms of animal welfare, but anybody listening could hear that the real concern was distaste for seeing children on horseback wearing tracksuits rather than jodhpurs. There was almost no discussion of the fact that these children were in areas most at risk from heroin abuse; nothing about the value that keeping and caring for an animal would have for the self-esteem of young people; and nothing about the fact that caring for animals deters criminal activity.[199]

The only concern, repeated like a mantra on AA Roadwatch during the 1990s, was that loose horses were "dangerous". There is no evidence of a single death or injury that resulted from this danger.

We could have used this spontaneous interest from the most deprived children in society to develop and nurture a positive pastime. The concerns about safety and animal welfare could have been addressed by providing training and stable facilities within youth clubs. The then finance minister had no problem finding €14.8m of taxpayers' money to hand over to the wealthy owners of the Agricultural and Equestrian Event Centre at Punchestown.[200] The vast bulk of the funds for the act were devoted to seizing horses, rather than providing facilities for young people.[201] The sole website of such a facility appears not to have been updated since 2006, and the phone number listed was not answered.

At the time, one 12-year-old boy in Cherry Orchard, west Dublin, saved up to buy a mare and was delighted to find she was in foal. He spent almost every waking hour caring for them, until they were seized from a piece of waste ground by South Dublin County Council. Unable to come close to the exacting standards for getting a newly required horse licence, the council refused to return them to him. They slaughtered mare and foal.

The abuse of children from privileged backgrounds may be more subtle, but it is still damaging. Relevant research in Ireland is difficult to access, but in 1971 in the UK, 80 per cent of children aged seven and eight made their journey to school unaccompanied by an adult. By 1990 that figure had crashed to just 9 per cent.[202] There is no reason to believe Ireland is any different, and there is ample reason to think it could be much worse. As traffic gets busier, more parents insist that the kids are driven to and from school, as well as any number of organised activities, mostly indoors and mostly highly structured and controlled by adults. Childhood has become an endless circuit of being ferried from one enclosed space to another.

The 2002 census of Ireland revealed for the first time that more girls drove themselves to school than cycled to school. Not university students; schoolgirls – primary and secondary schoolgirls.[203] That figure takes some digesting. They need to be at least 17 and have parents wealthy enough to supply them with a car. But the number of schoolgirls who were over 17 and had parents willing and able to supply them with a car exceeded the total number of girls of all ages who could cycle to school.

Children develop in stages, physically and emotionally, and independence is won in small steps. The degree to which our raging road traffic has curtailed so many of these steps is not just poorly understood or not realised. It is actively ignored. When adults are faced with the degree to which we are damaging children's quality of life, we turn our faces away. Just like our parents did.

A device recently came on the market called the Mosquito Teen Repellent, which the promoters claim "is the solution to the eternal problem of unwanted gatherings of youths and teenagers in shopping centres, around shops, your home and anywhere else they are causing problems".[204] It emits a high-pitched noise designed to be heard by children, even babies, but not by the narrower auditory range of adults. Legal sources indicate that this is a clear case of criminal assault.

Playstations, laptops and DVD players in the bedroom may seem idyllic to adults who grew up in the 1980s or before, but these gadgets are the bribes previously only given by absent fathers. (Two Christmas presents? You're so lucky!) It is notable that a high proportion of these gadgets have a babysitting effect. It is easy to plant the child in front of one of these devices rather than engage with them. The real reason that children need so much entertainment in their bedrooms is that they aren't allowed out to play. While some parents cite fear of child abduction as the reason for constantly monitoring them, the facts don't back this up. A child is as likely to be killed by lightning as abducted by a stranger.[205]

But the fear of road traffic is real. Ireland has the second-highest child fatality rate for road collisions in the EU. Nearly 200 children aged 14 and under were killed, and almost 8,000 were injured in the three years up to 2008. Legislation has been put in place to reduce the speed limit outside schools, but it has been implemented in just six locations.[206] This is uncomfortable for adults, because, unlike the largely imaginary stranger danger, it is not possible to blame traffic on a distant other. Adults are to blame; and the damage caused to children is real. There is solid research to indicate the damage which this lack of unstructured outdoor play does to the psychological development of children.[207]

This says nothing of the physical harm being done to children. There is a section on **Obesity** on page 66, but inactivity has other serious health effects on children, including heart disease,[208] asthma[209] and impaired mental functions.[210]

Playgrounds
It is likely that the state will acquire a lot of urban undeveloped land (see **NAMA** on page 43). There is little point in developing this for housing because of the excess that already exists in the market. One use that sites could be put to is to develop new playgrounds to make up for the current lack of facilities. The spaces should go far beyond slides and swings and have a diversity of designs, to attract children of all ages and interests. The

designs should include skate parks, nature playgrounds and water playgrounds.

There should be a range of designs to avoid having the same playground repeated across the country. A dedicated section of the Department of Education should be charged with commissioning the construction and maintenance of the playgrounds:

- An international architectural competition should be announced for the playgrounds.

- Children should play a central role in judging the competition.

- Eight to ten winners should be selected, and each winner commissioned to build variations on their model at locations distributed around the country.

- A website should be established to give information about the new and existing playgrounds, in particular the maintenance; and the web address, along with the ULI of the playground, should be prominently displayed at the playground.

- Maintenance of the playgrounds should be contracted out to different maintenance companies, to ensure competitive discipline, with each playground assigned to a specific maintenance company.

- Maintenance contracts should be paid as a fixed annual fee to keep the playgrounds in good working order, rather than a fee per repair or call-out.

- Members of the public should be able to report any maintenance concerns, and such reports should go directly to the relevant maintenance contractor.

- Maintenance contractors should confirm all repair incidences via the website.

- Performance of the maintenance companies should be monitored, with penalties for contractors who do not meet agreed service levels.

New Parks
A source in Dublin City Council said, "It's all about tea breaks." Dubliners may be surprised to learn that inside St Stephen's Green is a large building complex, including a surface car park. A lot of gardening effort has gone into hiding the development from the public, but can't hide the complex from satellite imaging.[211] According to the source, staff in the Parks Department like parks that are either large enough (like the Phoenix Park) or ornate enough (like St Stephen's Green or Merrion Square) to warrant a permanent staff and a building for them, with a tea room, a toaster, somewhere to sit and read the paper. It is a classic example of a service being organised for the convenience of the suppliers, rather than the consumers.

This means that we have a smaller number of larger parks, which in turn means that we live and work further from a park, and our lives are poorer as a result. Now that NAMA can supply the land, we can build many small parks in neighbourhoods that are distant from green spaces.

Pocket Parks are defined as a:

> ... small outdoor space, usually no more than ¼ of an acre, most often located in an urban area that is surrounded by commercial buildings or houses on small lots. A pocket park is typically located in an area with no public park nearby, in an area with no places for people to gather, relax, and enjoy the outdoors. There is no set design for a pocket park; each one is different depending on the size of the space.[212]

Many empty sites could make perfect pocket parks, and no inflexible work practices should get in the way of the opportunity. The parks departments of local authorities should be centralised, and if difficulties arise in persuading the existing staff to maintain the new parks, then that maintenance should be outsourced on the same basis as the maintenance of playgrounds.

The Streets
The motorised economy of the Celtic Tiger has made us forget that streets are supposed to be social spaces where neighbours can interact and children can play. Heavy traffic, and speeding in particular, deter people from socialising on streets, and this is probably a factor in the fact that burglaries are higher on streets where there is more traffic.[213] Legislation to allow 30km/h speed limits around schools was passed in 2005 but, under pressure from drivers, was implemented at just six schools in the following three years.[214] Steps to improve driver behaviour are set out in **Transport** (see page 256), but as well as reducing traffic accidents, these policies should be implemented with a view to making residential streets into vibrant spaces that are safe, particularly for children.

Broadcast Media

There are many competing models for media around the world:

- state newspapers, radio and TV stations and websites run as government mouthpieces or with varying degrees of regulation and independence
- media that are run to gather an audience for advertising and generate profit
- media that are run for profit by gathering subscriptions from the audience
- media run by press barons pushing their own agenda
- media that are run by interest groups to further their agenda
- media that are run by volunteers in order to provide a service

There is no one correct model; they are all correct. Truth is not something that can be decided and announced; all voices to be heard should be heard and the audience trusted to make its own decisions. Ireland, as a small country, is bound to suffer from a lack of media diversity. Because its size cannot support as many outlets as a larger country, particular care must be taken to nurture media diversity.

In Ireland, RTÉ is funded by an unhappy mix of advertising revenue and the TV licence fee. TV3 and the national and local independent radio stations must fund their entire output from the advertising that they sell. While availability of the internet is a useful counterbalance to the narrowness of the media market in Ireland, our market is so small that it is important to make sure that media diversity is maintained.

The National Broadcaster

RTÉ is criticised, sometimes unfairly, for the quality of its output. RTÉ has always suffered from the split personality of never being sure whether it is a BBC-like public-service broadcaster or an ITV-like commercial station, and at times it has not performed either role well.

Its position is not flattered by having to compete with overspill from some of the world's largest and most professional broadcasters. A quick flick through the national broadcasters of southern or eastern Europe will quickly show just how awful broadcasting can be. Also RTÉ's brightest stars can be snapped up by the huge budgets of British broadcasters, an option not open to most continental broadcasters, because of language barriers.

But that is no reason for RTÉ not to be vigilant about its standards. The licence fee is hugely lamented, mostly by newspapers owned by the same companies as own Sky TV, whose subscription charges are far higher than the TV licence. It is difficult to see this as anything other than an effort to put pressure on a competitor. The government also can use the licence fee to put pressure on RTÉ not to be too awkward in its coverage. Without even cutting the licence fee, the cabinet has the power to delay or reduce increases in the fee and allow RTÉ to be strangled by inflation. The result is obvious – anyone who has seen how Channel 4 News challenges the UK government will realise just how timid RTÉ News is.

But the licence fee is not without problems. Unlike the BBC, RTÉ mixes licence fee money with advertising revenue to pay for its programming, leading to complaints from TV3[215] and other broadcasters that they are being exposed to unfair competition. RTÉ's website says that:

> RTÉ has never used any public funding to depress advertising rates; why would it depress its own revenues?[216]

This is not the point. Mixing licence fee and advertising money is a clear case of below-cost selling. As of 2007, the licence fee accounted for 44 per cent of RTÉ's income.[217] Therefore, to fund €1m worth of programming, RTÉ need only sell €560,000 worth of advertising.

Competing broadcasters must either make their programming for less or sell the advertising in those programmes for more, clearly an unfair situation. Some propose giving some of the licence fee to commercial broadcasters or banning advertising on RTÉ.

Neither of these solutions are acceptable. Banning advertising on RTÉ might make a financial killing for TV3, but it would mean more than halving RTÉ in size and would reduce diversity in the media. Doubtless the main beneficiaries would not be Irish but British broadcasters, who beam their channels into the country. The brief experiment with 30 minutes of Irish content on Sky News Ireland was quickly terminated,[218] and a huge range of these stations already sell advertising into the Irish market[219] without employing a single Irish person.

Demands for a share of the licence fee from other broadcasters (sometimes in exchange for them making public service programmes) are equally problematic. Commercial broadcasters are profit-making companies; their product is their audience, and the customer is their advertisers. They have no motivation to serve anyone other than their customers, and any amount of regulation to try to force them to act against their own interests is likely to end in failure. This is also true of RTÉ, to the extent that it depends on advertising.

TG4

Debates about the Irish-language broadcaster generate as much heat, and as little light, as the debates about any other aspect of the Irish language. In both cases, the debates are more of a proxy for other arguments – see **The Irish Language** on page 82. Some people believe that the Irish language station deserves funding because of its status, notwithstanding the large proportion of English-language programming stations that it shows. Others argue that it is unjust that they be forced to pay through their taxes for a station that they never watch and frequently cannot understand. For an innovative and fair solution to TG4's funding, see below.

Reform

Competition is vital in broadcasting, and that should include, but not be limited to, commercial competition. It is best to have the widest mix possible, with licence-funded, public and private advertising-funded and any other models competing fairly. Here's how:

- RTÉ should be required to choose the stations that it wants to be public service, and which should be commercial.
- The licence fee should go solely to the non-commercial stations.
- The commercial stations should be permitted to sell advertising in the market to survive – perhaps RTÉ Radio 1, Lyric FM and RTÉ 1 TV would be the non-commercial stations, but this choice should be left to RTÉ.
- RTÉ's News and Sports divisions already have separate accounting systems – they should sell their programming to both the commercial and non-commercial divisions.
- The licence fee should be fixed in legislation, increased (or decreased) automatically along with growth in the economy, so that it is a fixed proportion of GDP, to maintain RTÉ's independence.

This addresses the issue of independence for RTÉ and unfair competition against commercial broadcasters. But RTÉ is still a highly insulated organisation, where many jobs are guaranteed regardless of individual or group performance. Here is the solution for that:

- Create five non-profit foundations.
- The licence-fee funded side of RTÉ is the first.
- TG4 is the second.
- Create the remaining three by allowing RTÉ staff to group together, to create proposals for producing RTÉ content.
- If there are more than three proposals, allow RTÉ staff to select three.
- Transfer the relevant RTÉ staff into each of the foundations.

- Give the three new foundations 10 per cent of RTÉ's programme-making budget each for two years, and a balanced package of peak and off-peak airtime, comprising 10 per cent of the total.

- After two years, allow licence-fee payers to choose which of the five foundations their licence fee goes to – they must pay their licence fee, but they can choose who to pay it to.

The purpose of this is to create competition which is not commercial competition. The licence fee would be guaranteed, but programmers and broadcasters would not be guaranteed cushy jobs if they did not deliver programmes that audiences valued.

Under this arrangement, TG4 would get funding that its supporters think it merits, without offending its detractors. Competition for the licence fees would create competition between the foundations, which would motivate them to keep the standard of programming high.

The foundations would develop individual characters, and motivate their supporters with inspiring programming, but would be immune to the whims of governments and advertisers, and the foundations could produce, buy or commission programming that neither governments or advertisers would fund. Any surplus made by a foundation, as a publicly-funded body, would be reinvested in programming. All the foundations would share studios and other facilities in RTÉ, to minimise their loss of efficiency through economies of scale. Because of the small audience for TG4, it would be advisable to allow them uniquely to continue to mix licence fee and advertising revenue.

Collecting the Licence Fee

The TV licence fee still needs to be collected. Although the evasion rate is declining, still more than 10 per cent of households have unlicensed TV sets.[220] An Post has had the job of collecting the TV licence since it was the Department of Posts and Telegraphs and RTÉ was 2RN, based in the GPO.

Giving the enforcement to An Post may have made sense in a previous century when the post office was the place that you went to send telegrams or buy a dog licence, but this practice is hopelessly outmoded and a waste of public funds. We must pay for hordes of inspectors, prosecuting offenders, and jailing many people who fail to pay the fines – and it doesn't even work. The *Irish Examiner* reported:

> Half of the people caught without TV licences were not prosecuted by An Post inspectors because it cost the company too much, a Government report revealed yesterday ... Those who were brought to court were fined an average of €174 each but only 4% subsequently purchased a licence in the three months after the court date.[221]

This is a textbook case of failure because the wrong person is doing the job – see point 10 on page 15.

Between cable, satellite and other systems, 75 per cent of households pay someone to deliver their TV signal,[222] mostly by monthly direct debit. By definition, all these households have a TV. A simple regulation should require all of these services to add a payment for their subscribers' TV licence to the direct debit, and then pass this payment on, along with a list of the ULIs of the homes and businesses that they have collected it for. This would eliminate a huge proportion of the evasion, along with the cost of collection and the cost of enforcement, which could then be focused on the dwindling number of households that do not subscribe to any of these services.

Competition

It is important to maintain diversity in media ownership. This is vital to make sure that a wide variety of voices are heard. The only argument raised in the UK in favour of concentration of ownership is that this allows large British media companies to compete on the world stage, but this is irrelevant in Ireland, since even the ownership of all Irish media would not be significant in a global setting.

Recently Denis O'Brien's Communicorp became the owner of Dublin's 98 FM, NewsTalk 106-108 FM, Spin 103.8, Spin SouthWest and Today FM.[223] It is clear that having a single owner for two Dublin music stations and the only two national commercial stations is not conducive to healthy competition,[224] particularly when he controls a large share of Independent News & Media, which owns many national and local newspapers in Ireland.

But the takeover that led to this situation was approved by the Broadcasting Authority of Ireland (BCI), who lack any hard criteria to make the decision, and whose decision on the matter was couched in unfalsifiable language, using words such as "satisfied", "feel" and "undue".[225] Regardless of the merits of this takeover, the process is unacceptable. It is another example of the "beauty contest" type of decision, where public officials making subjective judgements have the chance to enrich private individuals. While there is no suggestion of malpractice in this instance, it is too naive to imagine that the private profits made will never find their way back into corrupting the decision-making process. Here is the solution:

- The population covered by each broadcast station (local, regional and national) should be measured.

- The result should be counted as the points of each station.

- No takeover or new licence should be permitted that would give any owner more than 20 per cent of the total points in the system, in any area.

In a rural area, this would most likely prohibit the owner of a national station from acquiring even one local station, but it could do so in a well-served urban area. The decisions are predictable, fair and publically verifiable; and they preserve media diversity.

Community Radio
Community radio has long been a very poor relation in Ireland. Its enabling legislation and BCI regulations limit stations to very weak signals and, most unfairly, to broadcasting at times of the day when few are listening, and often for very limited date ranges.[226]

Radio listening is a process of habit, and stations build up audiences over long periods. However, they will lose them quickly if there is a break in transmission, which is why all commercial stations broadcast 24 hours a day and invest heavily in back-up transmitters and power generators.

All of the restrictions on broadcasting hours and dates should be swept aside, and the only restrictions on transmission strengths should be to ensure that they do not interfere with other stations.

Radio Licences
In February 2004, the BCI made a decision on four FM radio frequencies that they were due to advertise for the Dublin area.[227] They decided not to advertise two of them; to leave two spots on the dial blank.

The reason given was that two existing stations, NewsTalk 106 and Spin 103.8, were in a delicate financial position, and perhaps unable to withstand such an increase in competition. On other occasions, the BCI has declined to issue a licence where they felt that none of the applicants were "suitable".

Simultaneously, the BCI energetically pursued pirate radio stations, with Garda-assisted raids on hill farms where they believed transmitters were located. Press releases that followed claimed that pirate radio stations could disrupt everything from legal radio stations to emergency services, but contacts between the writer and the BCI revealed that this was just a theoretical possibility; it has not actually happened in recent years.

Technical Issues
Pending the adoption of new technology, there is a technical limit to the number of radio stations available. There's only so much space on the dial, but most of that space is blank. The website of the US Federal Communications Commission[228] lists 65 licensed radio stations in New York city on FM alone. There is no technical reason why an Irish city can't have a similar number. If the demand for licences were to approach that number,

it would be reasonable for the government to step in and ensure that one type of station did not dominate. Regardless of demand, the government has a duty to ensure that each user of the spectrum can operate without interference from the others.

Freedom of Speech

Two of the pirate broadcasters closed down by the BCI in 2003 were the Dublin stations Phantom FM and Jazz FM. They specialised in playing styles of music that were not heard on any other radio station in Ireland. Afterwards, they were not heard at all, although Phantom has since been awarded a licence. Freedom of speech is worthless if the freedom extends only to what a censor deems "worthwhile". While it is unlikely that many members of the BCI or the government even know what Urban or Alternative music is, they should recognise that a radio market based on their tastes alone would not serve the country well.

Yet this is what is happening – applying for a radio licence is by means of a beauty contest where the best presentation wins the licence. No one seems to mind that the output of the winning radio station often bears little resemblance to the original application. This has the pernicious effect that the choice of radio stations is skewed in favour of the type of radio favoured by middle-aged men.

Allocating Licences

The BCI's enabling legislation was motivated in part by a desire to favour those who paid bribes to its author, Ray Burke,[229] who has since served a prison sentence in relation to this crime. There is no good reason to exclude operators from the radio broadcasting market, and it is unconstitutional to do so. In addition, the "beauty contest" system of making highly subjective decisions about which applicant most deserves a licence is wrong.

Applicants and judges are both keenly aware that a lot of money is resting on the decision. While there is no suggestion that any member of the BCI or BAI (or any applicant since Century Radio) has acted improperly, it is bad practice to create a situation where the temptation is to offer or accept bribes in return for a favourable decision. The role of the BAI (which took over all the duties of the BCI in 2009) should be limited to the fair allocation of space on the dial and the orderly conduct of the market. It should have no role in deciding the "correct" number of radio stations or their content.

In issuing fewer licences, the BAI is clearly acting within the law, but outside the constitution, because it is barring citizens from taking up a profession solely to protect the financial interests of existing operators.

Libel

Personal injury lawsuits allow an injured party to sue the person responsible for the injury to compensate for the costs of their injury. Lawsuits for breach of contract or copyright infringement work on the same principle. The libel laws are intended to allow someone whose good name has been damaged by a falsehood in the media to recover the "cost" of the damage to their good name.

It doesn't work, although you could forgive Monica Leech for disagreeing. She was awarded €1,872,000 from the *Evening Herald* after a series of stories libelled her.[230] The *Herald* complained, unsurprisingly, that this was an amount calculated by a jury that was not permitted to get any guidance from the judge or anyone else.‡

The *Herald* has a point. In 1993, 44-year-old Angela Fortune was left blind and brain damaged when she suffered seizures before and after the birth of her daughter. When her case got to court in 2004, she was awarded €950,000. It is difficult to see that Monica Leech – still a fit and active woman, healthy enough to enjoy her millions – was injured twice as much as Angela Fortune, whatever the content of the articles.

Libel laws in the US were virtually abolished by a 1964 Supreme Court ruling which held that journalists at the *New York Times* were immune from suit unless they could be shown to have written something that they knew was false – honest mistakes did not make a libel because anything else would compromise freedom of speech.[231]

The corruption of Haughey, Burke and Lawlor in particular was widely known in media circles, but fear of legal action prevented it from becoming public for years. Absent from the discussion are an unknown number of stories about unknown scandals that are still kept under wraps by legal threats. A few pints with any Dublin journalist will leave you with the impression there are many of these.

So why do juries reward rich people who can afford to take libel trials so well? Juries are not seeking to reward the rich; they are seeking to punish the press. The €1.8m was not a measure of the damage to Monica Leech; it was a measure of how much the jury wanted to punish the *Herald*. Along with its stablemate the *Sunday Independent*, it has a long history of printing salacious stories, often seeming to encourage the reader to believe things that are not true and not said in the story.

The Defamation Act which came into force at the start of 2010 updates some of the workings of the libel law and makes other drastically retrograde steps,

---

‡ This has now been changed under the Defamation Act 2009.

such as making blasphemy a criminal offence. The libel system should not be tinkered with; it should be abolished. It remains available only to a tiny segment of the rich and powerful, so its abolition would not impact the vast majority of the population at all.

Broadband and Telecoms

If you don't already know, you'll just have to believe it. Broadband in Ireland is bad. Very, very bad; and that is a very, very bad thing. Many areas cannot get broadband at all. For those who can, the entry level package, as of March 2010, is 1Mb;[232] in Germany the entry-level package is 16Mb.[233] In South Korea, broadband reached 70 per cent penetration in 2003.[234] In 2010, Ireland are still not even close to that,[235] but the Koreans are on track to supply their population with 1 GB internet speeds[236] – more than 1,000 times faster than Eircom's standard package.

Broadband is vital to the future of our economy, even if the politicians who trot out that line so often don't even understand what it is. Irish companies are trying to trade in the information age via ass and cart, while the continentals are trading via bullet-train and the Koreans via space rocket. The core problem with broadband targets is that they are a moving target. In 2006, it was reported as progress that our broadband penetration rate had gone up from 6.7 per cent to 9.2 per cent; however, this was not progress. We were going backwards on the league tables and were overtaken by the Czech Republic. We were already well behind Portugal.[237] In December 2009, it was reported that 16 per cent of Irish businesses had no broadband connection at all.[238]

It is nonsense to regard upgrading our ass and cart to a pony and trap as progress, if our competitors on the continent are moving from bullet train to space rocket. The first thing the Department of Communications and Natural Resources must do is set targets that are expressed in terms of the prevailing technology when the target is met. In such a fast-moving race, it is pointless to take years to catch up to where our competitors were years ago.

The correct way to set the goal is to measure where Ireland stands in relation to a range of competitors and move up the league table in relation to those competitors. If technology develops and allows our competitors to move forward faster, it should allow us to do so too. Next, these goals must be imposed on Eircom. As the monopoly provider, they already have a universal service obligation for telephone service. Even in the downturn, they remain a fantastically profitable company,[239] but have a poor record of investment in infrastructure, and as mentioned on page 14, they have the potential to become far more profitable if they implement new technology.

Eircom should be allowed the freedom to contract out the obligation to provide broadband to other companies, such as using the wireless technology WiMax for inaccessible areas.

The Dial-up Cash Cow

Some people will have forgotten the digital whale-song made by a modem dialling up through a telephone line for access to the internet. For others, the screeching sound lives on, as many people can only access the internet via analogue or ISDN dial-up. In the fast-developing internet world, this technology belongs in the Stone Age. Even Eircom's pathetic 1Mb "broadband" connection is 20 times faster than a standard dial-up modem. Korea's 1 GB connections are 20,000 times faster.

Connecting to this tin-can-and-a-string internet service for just one hour per day, in 15 minute chunks, would cost €70 per month[240] – far more than most broadband packages, even at inflated Irish prices, but it costs nothing for Eircom to provide, and the more you need to use it, the higher the price gets.

While Eircom has a huge financial incentive to deny customers broadband, it is unreasonable to expect it to make any real efforts to provide the service. The solution is simple: change the incentives. On all telephone lines where Eircom has failed to provide broadband, the regulator should require Eircom to provide ISDN or analogue dial-up internet access, free of charge.

The 0818 Rip-Off

Back in the days of sky-high charges even for local calls, 1800, 1850 and 1890 numbers looked like a bargain for the consumer. While 1800 numbers are free to the caller, the others now look distinctively like a rip-off, particularly when many mobile and landline packages include either a fixed or unlimited number of calls to landlines. While codes such as 1890 advertise as "for the price of a local call", they fail to mention that this refers to the preregulation price, which is far higher than anyone would expect to pay for a local call, or any other call today. Many people believe that, since they pay a flat rate for all their local calls, these will be included, when often they are not.

The real scam is in the recently introduced 0818 "national rate" code.[241] In reality this is a premium rate number, costing as much per minute as a 1520 premium-rate number on landline.[242] Ring from a callbox or a mobile and you will pay up to 49c per minute for the privilege,[243] but because pricing is based on the now-defunct long-distance pricing, there is no obligation to mention the pricing when these numbers are advertised. Suppliers of these numbers boast of the revenue that companies can make from their unwitting customers.[244] Other companies take advantage of customer resistance to calling these numbers by making calls to their sales line free with 1800 numbers, then use 0818 to charge to connect to their customer service line when something goes wrong, doubtless hoping that many customers will run out of credit before they come to the top of the queue. A charge of 49c per minute works out at €29.40 per hour, so selling shoddy products can be quite profitable. The fact that these companies earn a fortune just keeping their customers on hold is transparently unfair.

The telephone regulator should act to make sure that all telephone customers are aware of call charges and aren't disadvantaged by sharp practice:

- Comreg should require all advertising of non-geographic numbers to include the exact price of the call and prohibit all telephone companies from charging callers more – no "calls from mobiles may cost more" get-out clause.

- The cost of the call should receive no less emphasis in an advertisement than the number itself.

- Advertisers who sell products or services over the telephone should be prohibited from using a more expensive telephone number for any follow-up service.

Fault Tracking

Getting broadband (or a telephone service) can be challenging, but keeping it can be just as difficult. To have a telephone service, all phone companies must be connected, but they are much more connected than they may appear. Regardless of what company you pay your bill to, the wire that brings it to you is owned by Eircom, and the exchange that wire leads to is also owned by Eircom, who are paid a wholesale rate by your provider for supplying the service. Independent telephone companies also pay Eircom to house their equipment in Eircom exchanges.

It would be surprising if Eircom were motivated to keep the lines of their competitors in good repair, and engineering sources from other telephone companies tell of their equipment in Eircom exchanges being unplugged, and labels removed from bundles of hundreds of wires, rendering them near useless. When a fault occurs on the line of a smaller telephone company, they must first test their equipment and then pass the fault on to Eircom, to check theirs. Fault reports can get lost in a bureaucratic maze where nobody will take ownership of a problem, with lines taking weeks to get reconnected.

No doubt, Eircom will say that their staff would never intentionally disconnect the equipment of another company or fail to deal with faults in good time. But without transparency, there will always be a temptation for someone to pass the buck rather than do their job. There is a solution that can improve the situation:

- Comreg should require all telephone companies to use a single online fault tracking system.

- All fault reports should be logged and given a unique tracking number.

- The company taking the report should be required to take the mobile number of the customer reporting the fault and send them the tracking number by SMS.

- The system should be used to make inter-company fault reports and record the time that the report is made, along with the section and individual that the report is passed to.

- An automated SMS should be sent to the phone of the customer each time the status or the ownership of the fault changes.

- The system should also be used to record the time and individuals involved when responsibility is passed within a telephone company.

- All of the information on the website should be made available for screen-scraping websites.

- Information that would identify individuals should be represented by a code number, the key to which should be available to Comreg.

This would allow customers to track their fault reports closely and put pressure on companies who do not perform. It would also allow third-party screen scrapers to monitor and report which phone companies perform best.

Screen scrapers could also quickly identify individuals and departments that have higher fault rates and slower clean-up times than average, and identify those (by code number) to the telephone companies and to Comreg if the companies do not take action.

Burglar Alarms

In theory, the sound of a burglar alarm in a neighbour's house would make you reach for your mobile, dial 999, and the Gardaí would swiftly arrive and collar the burglar. In reality, most people will ignore a burglar alarm for as long as they can bear. If the alarm persists, they may look for the source, but are very unlikely to contact the Gardaí unless they see other evidence of a break-in. They are well justified – a Garda source confirms that in only about 1 per cent of cases does a sounding alarm actually indicate a burglary.

The average burglary lasts about two minutes, so the alarm is of little value, because any help coming is unlikely to hurry to the alarm that cries wolf. The downside to burglar alarms is real: a screaming, pulsating noise, designed to be unpleasant. In theory it stops after about 20 minutes, but then rearms. So on a stormy October bank-holiday weekend when the wind rattles the neighbours' loose window, you can have your eardrums pulverised until the neighbours return on the Monday evening. So why bother fitting alarms al all?

Fitting alarms is cheap. The Irish edition of the 2009 Argos catalogue offers self-fit alarms for as little as €41.79. At the time of writing, the Golden Pages website lists 543 firms competing for the business in Ireland. There are almost no barriers to entry into the business – all you need is a kit and a screwdriver. Because there is nothing else to compete on, people who supply and fit burglar alarms compete exclusively on price. The benefits may be scant, but the cost is so low that customers are unlikely to be picky. The person who could insist on a quality system – the householder, the customer – is the person least likely to be disturbed, since the alarm is only armed when they are away. Neither the supplier nor their customer has any reason to choose a quality system.

A quality alarm would be easy to devise: remove the klaxon and keep the intruder detection system. Programme it to telephone the householder's mobile or a neighbour or a commercial monitoring service when triggered. A couple of panicked rushes home would soon have the householder insisting to the supplier that the system works effectively and eliminate false alarms. Suppliers who don't comply would quickly be out of business. Everyone (except incompetent suppliers) would benefit. So why doesn't it happen? Why don't market forces make the best system prevail? In the current situation, everyone is acting rationally:

- The supplier feels no demand from the customer to make reliable alarms, and would be at a commercial disadvantage if this cost was added to their system.

- The long-suffering neighbour does not react when the alarm sounds because there is only a 1 per cent chance that a burglary is really in progress.

- Householders do not demand a system that sounds only when there really is a burglar, because they suffer no cost from a false alarm.

But there one party is not acting rationally: society – the government. A rational government would ban burglar alarms as they are currently designed. Monitoring burglar alarms is a cost. It doesn't cost money, because the owner relies on their neighbours ringing the Gardaí when they hear it; but it is a cost nevertheless. It costs neighbours headaches and lost sleep.

The flaw is that the person who benefits from the burglar alarm is not the same person who pays for that benefit. Technology allows one person to impose that cost on another. As well as being unfair, it doesn't work. The householder could be accused of acting selfishly, but is only acting rationally. If free monitoring is available, it doesn't make sense to pay for it. And if it is free, why use it carefully?

Actually, there is already a law about this. Section 108 of the Environmental Protection Agency Act 1992 provides a series of hoops and hurdles for an aggrieved neighbour to jump. It involves taking a civil case in the District Court proving that the noise was an annoyance and, having won that case going back to court again proving that the noise continued to be an annoyance after the time of the first court case. Needless to say, it is rarely used.

A real solution would be easy: licence reputable alarm installers to issue certificates that any given alarm system has been modified to comply, and allow six months or a year for full compliance. Revoke the licence from any company that misbehaves.

After that date, give Gardaí with the paperwork to issue on-the-spot fines (say, €1,000) to the occupants of buildings with a klaxon sounding. The fine would be reduced to €200 if it was paid within seven days and accompanied by a certificate that the system has been removed or modified to comply.

Energy

Concern about climate change and pollution have been central to the Green movement for decades, and they have argued for a decisive switch to renewable energy. They are right, but for all the wrong reasons. Everything we eat, everything we use and everything we wear would be unthinkable without a huge input of energy. Our economy and society is utterly dependent on our energy supply. The oil shocks of the 1970s showed that even a small reduction of the supply of one energy source caused serious economic disruption. And there is serious disruption on the horizon.

The Saudi Mess
The unyielding bough breaks. A tree that does not bend with the wind is more likely to snap in the storm; rulers who are most successful in resisting reform are the most likely to be overthrown.

On 1 August 2005, the 82-year-old Fahd bin Abdul Aziz al-Saud, the king of Saudi Arabia, died. His half-brother Abdullah bin Abdulaziz al-Saud succeeded him.

It is difficult to describe just how corrupt and venal is their kingdom. Aside from the vanity of naming their country after their own family, he is an absolute monarch in the only country on earth that has no constitution or basic law of any kind. His word, literally, is law.

He and the 3,000 princes who are his cousins, brothers and nephews are mayor of every city, director of every company, every minister and every ambassador. They hold every single position of power and influence in their country. (One of them is hiding in a cave somewhere on the Afghan–Pakistan border.)

Their 26 million subjects are intensely religious, mostly following Wahabee Islam, rejecting the profane with such fervour that they buried Fahd in an unmarked desert grave to avoid any suggestion of idolatry. Alcohol, sexual promiscuity and even the most basic rights for women are rejected, and this morality is enforced by the Mutaween religious police. The Mutaween's activities are well described by Wikipedia:

> They have the power to arrest any unrelated males and females caught socializing. They also have the power to ban consumer products and media as "un-Islamic", such as the Barbie dolls, Pokémon games and toys, and various Western musical groups and television shows...[245]

In 2002 the Mutaween prevented schoolgirls from escaping a burning school because they were not wearing the appropriate headgear. Fifteen girls died as a result.[246] While teenage girls must burn to avoid sin, enforcement is lax in other quarters. From Dubai to Saint-Tropez, the bored princelings can be found drinking champagne and snorting cocaine with queues of prostitutes supplied by the Russian mafia.

On 4 May 2004, the *Guardian* newspapers reported that British police were investigating a €25m bribe paid by BAE, the British arms manufacturer, to Prince Turki bin Nasser, to persuade him to buy their fighter jets. Saudi Arabia has no use for fighter jets – it doesn't even have pilots qualified to fly them. The Saudi regime pays up to five times what western militaries pay for the same jets as part of a money-go-round that has no purpose other than to transfer money from the government into the pockets of the princes. BAE pays the bulk of the purchase back to Saudi Arabia as bribes to various princes to secure the deal. The prosecution of BAE was later halted on the orders of the British government, nervous of losing the business, and BAE shares soared as a result.[247]

Of all of the sins of the bloated royal family that outrage the millions of devout Arabians, one sin drove one of the princes to reject his extended family and take up arms. Osama bin Laden's stated reason for wanting to overthrow his family's rule is that they allowed infidel troops – the US army – to invade the holy land. It is not difficult to understand why an ordinary Arabian would feel that their rulers are guilty of one long continuum of sin, from using drugs and prostitutes to defiling the land of their prophet.

Almost all of the September 11 attackers came from Saudi, like their leader. There is, of course, heavy censorship in Saudi Arabia, so we do not know exactly how unstable the country really is, but it is clear that Saudi Arabia is a powder keg, with allegiance to the ruling family being one of the few things stabilising the country. The new king is now 85, and he is likely to be the first in a line of short-lived kings, because most of those in line for the crown are half-brothers in their seventies at least, meaning that Saudi Arabia will be run by elderly and dying men for years to come. Unless the prince in the cave makes a return. And all of this powder keg is sitting on top of one-third of the world's oil.

Other Oil Sources
While Saudi Arabia may be the most extreme example, from Venezuela to Iran to the Caucuses, the correlation between the location of oil under the ground and political instability above it seems to be too exact to be a coincidence. It is. The despots of Arabia and other oil-rich countries would never have survived unreformed if they did not have oil money to purchase the finest repression that money can buy and, as most of the world moved

towards democracy in the second half of the twentieth century, they could resist doing so. Now they are left with spectacularly corrupt governments such as in Nigeria and Saudi Arabia, or as in the case of Iran and Venezuela, the extremist regimes that replaced them when the bough finally broke. The world is very vulnerable to a sudden constriction in the oil supply caused by political instability.

Running Out

Oil won't run out in our lifetimes. Probably. But it might just run thin. In 2004, a sharp rise in oil prices began, and in June 2008, oil prices peaked above $140 per barrel. Adjusting for inflation, it was far higher than it had ever been before, even during the 1970s oil shocks. This created a lot of comment about the demand from China and India creating a step change in the price of oil, with escalating demand and dwindling supply leading to ever higher prices. It has since fallen back to below $65 dollars a barrel, ending this discussion. Back to business as usual. Except it is not. The new low oil prices are all above $60 per barrel, but prices between the 1980s and 2003 were generally about $25 per barrel.[248] Even the early steps in the oil price escalation in 2004 and 2005, when prices went above $60, were regarded as so high they were likely to have serious economic implications.

The real story is that prices previously regarded as highs are now seen as lows. The economic swings which the world goes through will inevitably cause swings in the price of oil, but the pattern is inevitable. Highs are higher than previous highs, and lows are higher than pervious lows, because, however ingenious we are at extracting oil from the ground, for every new barrel found, six are burnt.[249]

Winners and Losers

A higher price of energy benefits the sellers and costs the buyers. The oil producers are clearly net energy exporters. Also, many countries both produce and consume energy. The USA, by far the biggest consumer in the world, also produces large amounts of oil and coal. Although it is a net importer, a serious energy crisis and its costs would harm the interests of some Americans, but others would benefit from an increase in the price of their produce. There would be major upheaval in their economy, but not all the effects would be negative, with tax revenues and economic growth lost in shrinking areas partially offset by growth in other areas.

Other countries import almost all their energy, and they are highly vulnerable to shortages and price increases. The effect of an energy crisis would be entirely negative on them. The increased cost of energy would simply have to be handed over to producer countries. Ireland is one of those.

The Greens Are Right

Even if it is for all the wrong reasons, the Greens are correct. From an energy security viewpoint, Ireland needs to enormously increase its domestic energy output. If this came from renewable sources, it would reduce our greenhouse gas emissions, but the climatic benefit of this would be negligible.

The answer is blowing in the wind. There is huge potential for wind power in Ireland. At last we can thank our climate for something, but aside from the energy benefits, there are other issues. To gain social acceptance for a giant building programme of windmills, the trick is to make sure that the benefits are well distributed. The website of Sustainable Energy Ireland says:

> Denmark is a world leader in community ownership of wind farms. Up to 20% of Denmark's energy needs are currently met by wind, of which 80% is generated by 2,100 community-owned farms.[250]

Denmark has a higher population density and less wind than Ireland, so there is no reason why we can't do better and produce 50 or 60 per cent of our energy from wind power. Indeed Ireland can benefit from last-mover advantage – technology has moved on, and Ireland could use quiet, smaller, more efficient windmills. Also, Ireland's best sites for wind farms are the most thinly populated, in the west and north-west. But the Danish community-owned method is important for more than one reason. These are also the areas that are suffering the most from depopulation and have benefited the least from the Celtic Tiger. Community-owned wind farms could provide supplemental income that would benefit the local economy. They are far less likely to arouse local resistance.

There is another reason for promoting local ownership of wind farms. If the purpose is to promote energy security, this goal would be compromised if ownership were to be concentrated in a way that would allow it to be sold overseas, diminishing the counterbalancing effect in the event of an energy crisis. If energy prices were to rocket, the purpose of the windmills would be to make sure that as well as losers, there would be Irish winners in the resulting economic shake-up. Send ownership of the wind farms overseas, and the profits of the windfall, so to speak, would follow.

The Greens Are Wrong

Some environmentalists have campaigned against wind farms because of the visual intrusion, and also because of the damage done by the need to build a road for access vehicles up to every single windmill. These reservations are fair, but outweighed. The argument that windmills are a blight on the landscape relies on a constructed aesthetic – we like what we are familiar with. We may value our countryside, but it might not be so attractive to a sixteenth-century Irish person who was familiar with its original tree-covered state.

Even if it is true that windmills reduce the visual amenity in scenic areas, they are no more visually intrusive than electricity pylons. Campaigns against pylons are few and small. Although they have disadvantages, they also have well-recognised advantages, and both are spread around fairly evenly. The cost and benefit are closely matched.

The only problem with wind energy is that it is, well, like the wind. It won't always blow when needed. Although there is a pretty high correlation between the wind and periods of high energy demand in the winter months, electricity is difficult to store. When only a small proportion of the electricity in the system is generated by wind, this variability is absorbed by turning up or down the output of other generators, in a system called spill and fill.

If a much larger proportion of the electricity in Ireland were to be generated using wind, we would need a larger base of other power stations to absorb the fluctuations. This means an interconnector with the continental grid, so we can buy or sell electricity as needed. Sometimes we will be buying nuclear electricity, which will drive the Greens nuts, but they'll have to put up with it. Anyway, it's not like the French are going to pay any attention to us when deciding what to do with their nuclear stations – the British never do.

The government should create a planning and investment environment to favour the creation of local wind farm cooperatives, along with training and other low-cost supports to kick-start the schemes. (See **Planning Special Projects** on page 170 for more details on this.) There is no reason to involve the state in the ownership of the wind farms. Credit unions may provide a model for ownership, and also a source of capital.

There is no downside to this project. The costs are minimal, and there are only two possibilities – an energy shortage will happen or it won't. If it doesn't, Ireland will have reduced its carbon output, improved its balance of payments and made rural communities more sustainable. If it does happen, the benefits will be far greater.

Electricity Demand
The demand for electricity is very bursty – it goes up and down fast, sometimes in unpredictable ways, although UK national grid managers have long known that they should have reserve power coming online for the advertisement breaks in Coronation Street, when millions of people switch on their kettles.[251] The TV companies supply the electricity companies with detailed schedules for this reason, but if an increase in wind power were to

make the supply bursty as well, that could cause problems, because the bursts in supply would not be correlated to the bursts in demand.

There are some appliances that need power at a particular time – the kettle and the TV – and if they don't get it, it is inconvenient for the consumer. Others appliances can be much more flexible, and this flexibility should be used to keep a balance in the grid. Fridges and freezers are plugged in all the time, but they use a thermostat to control when they consume power, to keep a roughly constant temperature. When they get too warm, the power kicks in to cool them down and then switches off again.

At present the timing of this cycle is purely random, but it could be manipulated. Smart electricity meters are currently being fitted as an experiment on Irish homes,[252] but it is not clear quite how smart they are. A really smart meter would allow the price of electricity to go up and down from minute to minute, as demand shifts. Electricity would be cheapest at 4am, and at its dearest during the ad-break in Coronation Street.

Fridges and freezers could then be fitted with a special plug which was programmed to cut the power for short periods when the price was at its highest. This would not reduce their overall electricity consumption, because they would then power up as soon as the price of electricity dipped again, but this would have an important effect on the national grid.

Engines run most efficiently when they run smoothly, whether they are in cars or giant power plants. Minimising the amount that they need to hit the brakes or hit the gas to match demand makes them more efficient and makes the entire system run better. Fridges and freezers are obvious targets to manipulate demand to help balance the system, but there are others. Washing machines and dishwashers are not particularly time-sensitive, and consumers would not be inconvenienced by short pauses in their running, but the big consumer on this is only just emerging.

Electric cars are coming in a big way. General Motors sabotaged its own 1996 project, the EV1, an early electric car, repossessing and shredding every single one it made.[253] This time they are here to stay. The Chevy Volt is boasting that it can travel more than 100km on the equivalent of one litre of petrol.[254] The method of calculating this is open to manipulation because there are no established standards, but it is clear that industry is lining up on the side of the electric car this time.[255]

Electric cars run on batteries, which will need to be charged. There are several models for this, including plugging them in overnight at home and what might be former petrol stations converted to battery-exchange stations where people can switch their battery for a fully charged one. Regardless of the model that is used, it would be a wasted opportunity if the model was not adapted to accommodate using electricity when other demand was at its lowest.

Nuclear Power

Some commentators have suggested building a nuclear power plant in Ireland. They are wrong. While they are correct to say that it would reduce Ireland's CO_2 emissions, it would leave many other problems. Firstly, Ireland has no internal source of uranium, and this resource would inevitably have all the supply and price problems of oil in the event of an energy crisis. Secondly, nuclear power costs so much that nobody knows the true bill. Most countries that use it subsidise it heavily from their military budgets, because its true purpose is to provide material for nuclear weapons. (This is why "civil" nuclear power programmes in states such as Iran arouse such suspicion and hostility, although the existing nuclear states would never admit it.) Such an enormous engineering project is simply too big for a small country such as Ireland. Sellafield alone employs far more people than the entire ESB.[256] [257] And if we can't manage a Port Tunnel without leaks, a nuclear power plant is unlikely to inspire confidence.

The size of a nuclear plant is also too big for Ireland, not just because we are bad at large capital projects. One nuclear plant would be hugely expensive, but it would supply more than enough to meet Ireland's energy needs; however, it is not possible to build just one. All national grids need to have spare capacity, because all power plants (even nuclear ones) have to be taken offline once in a while for maintenance. The rule of thumb is that you need spare capacity equal to the largest single power plant in the system. So building one nuclear plant doesn't work – you must build two. This would make such a scheme impossibly expensive for a small energy market like Ireland.

The Army

Our army has nothing to do. While the Naval Service and Air Corps can pretend to be useful for rescues at sea, the army has no such fig leaf. There is no military power that might possibly threaten the Republic of Ireland, where the appropriate response would be anything other than immediate surrender.

It is true that the army has provided useful services, perhaps to alleviate soldiers' boredom, but it is in no way configured to provide interventions such as flood rescue, humanitarian aid overseas or protection for vehicles transporting money for the banks. The army has tanks and anti-aircraft weapons. It even has cannons.[258] This is utterly wasteful; such vastly expensive equipment will never be used.

There is no doubt that tasks arise from time to time where a disciplined force can be useful, particularly rescue missions in time of natural disasters or other calamities. As a wealthy nation, Ireland has a responsibility to provide assistance for other countries in such situations, but the army is not a rescue service, and none of the useful tasks that it could perform involve shooting people. It is time to decommission the weapons of the Irish army. Here's what to do:

- Merge the Naval Service with the Coast Guard, for search and rescue missions, fisheries protection and intercepting coastal threats.

- Subsume the Air Corps into the Coast Guard for the same purposes; any arms not suitable for these operations should be scrapped.

- Almost entirely disarm the army and transform it into an emergency rescue force; swap its combat training for training that is useful for humanitarian and search and rescue missions, such as emergency medical skills, water engineering and organising large scale emergency feeding and accommodation.

Aside from arms for the expanded Coast Guard to challenge illegal fishing or drug smugglers, the only armed element to remain should be the Army Rangers, which should be kept at a strength of 50 to 100 highly skilled personnel, trained under contract by overseas experts, to deal with terrorist or similar incidents.

Education and Science

The Leaving Cert

The Leaving Cert is the end of our second-level education system, but it attracts so much attention that it is difficult not to deal with it first. It also demonstrates a useful principle: people respond to incentives. Complaints have been made that our education system relies too heavily on memorising facts rather than understanding; also, that students are abandoning sciences in favour of subjects that are perceived as easier.

Telling students, teachers or parents that they should learn or teach different subjects, or approach existing subjects in a different way, is pointless if their motivation – Leaving Cert points in the Central Admissions Office (CAO) application system – pushes them in the opposite direction. If we want to change behaviour or outcomes, we must change motivations. The Leaving Cert performs two roles: it measures educational achievement at second level, and it is a university entrance exam. Any reforms must have regard for this dual purpose and not prejudice either.

There is much scope for updating what is taught in our secondary schools, and this is dealt with later, but teaching new subjects or topics will be sidelined by students and teachers if those subjects do not lead to Leaving Cert exams, and ultimately CAO points. Exams and points should be closely aligned with the direction that we want education to move in, but in doing this we must take care that the integrity of the points system is maintained.

What's wrong with the Leaving Cert? It tries to extract the sum of knowledge learnt over 14 years in 14 days of examinations. It doesn't take into account the student's character or other qualities; it doesn't cater to students who don't respond well to exam pressure, and it unfairly advantages middle class students whose parents are interested and wealthy enough to organise extra tuition.

All that is important, but here's something more important: don't make things worse. There are dozens of proposals out there, with all sorts of combinations of coursework, continual assessment and interviews of potential students. There is no point in examining any of them. Outside the exam hall, there are only two ways to assess a student. Either you judge work that the student has done or you judge the student.

Work Outside Exam Hall

Some students, the theory goes, don't respond well to exam pressure, so the work they do throughout the school year, or a series of less formal assignments at shorter intervals, will help them show their talents. Or their parents' talents. Take away the invigilator and you have no idea who is really doing the work. Add in the motivation for middle-class parents that little Johnny's place in UCD is dependent on his homework, and you can bet that they'll stay up all night doing it with him, or for him.

With the booming grinds industry, what pushy parent who didn't have the skills wouldn't hire someone to make sure that the coursework was done right? And then the work has to be marked. The Leaving Cert is marked anonymously – no favour, no connections can buy influence. If marking is done by teachers known to the students and parents, the scope for abuse in a small country with small towns is obvious.

Interviews

At present in Irish higher education, a small number of courses such as drama require students to pass an interview. This may be justified for very specialist courses, but use of interviews should certainly not be expanded. Kids know how to suck up to their parents. Middle-class culture in Ireland is radically different from working-class culture, and middle-class kids who are used to sucking up to middle-class parents will have no trouble ingratiating themselves at an interview for university admission. Working-class kids will have no such advantage.

In any case, no clear idea of what an interview for university admission would achieve, over and above an entrance exam, has ever been articulated. Probably an interviewer would just choose "people like us".

Not Perfect

The CAO points system is not perfect, but the only reason to change it would be to change it for the better, and that would mean making it fairer. The education system is already hugely biased in favour of middle-class students. Changes that would increase that bias would make it worse, not better. The points race is brutal, without doubt, but it is transparent and fair. While adding confusion to the system might be useful to some, it would not increase the number of places on any course. That would only redistribute the brutality. While there is more demand than supply, the points race is by far the fairest way of distributing course places.

That said, there are some perverse incentives for students within the points race. There are vast disparities in the number of top grades given out in some subjects compared to others. In higher maths, just 12.5 per cent of students achieve an honour grade, compared to 44 per cent in English. Even within the sciences, 23 per cent of biology students get a higher-level honour, but just 7 per cent of physics students do.[259] Do smarter students choose biology over physics, explaining the disparity? This seems unlikely, since almost all students do both English and maths, so the difference in their results cannot be explained by a different student intake.

In 2009, just 16 per cent of maths students took the higher level paper, 10 per cent took higher chemistry, and only 8 per cent took higher level physics.[260] Along with this, there is deep concern that the grades of maths and hard sciences are further decreasing, especially when compared to other subjects, particularly in the humanities.

The president of Dublin City University, Ferdinand Prondzynski, wrote of his dismay at talking to parents about the basis on which they would choose second-level schools for their children:

> What they want are the highest possible CAO points. Nothing more... It is entirely tactical, with almost no intellectual angle... they wanted Shakespeare. Was it because he developed and extended what we now call the English language and because he disseminated intellectual ideas from the classics to his own day?

> Not at all. It was because this had always been a central part of the syllabus and students know how to prepare for it to get high points. And science? No, no demand there, because it was too difficult to get high points. Yes, but didn't we need more scientists in Ireland? Maybe, maybe not. In any case, there were lots of other schools that could focus on that.[261]

Prondzynski then identifies these perverse choices as the source of serious social and economic problems in our society and calls for a debate on possible solutions. But both parents and students are being rational. They are making perverse choices because they are reacting to perverse incentives. Students are choosing rote memorisation and easy subjects over understanding, intellectual development and more challenging subjects, because the system rewards them for doing this. Prondzynski rightly wants them to change these choices. There is no point in trying to persuade them to act against their own interests. We must change the incentives.

Students get points based on their best six subjects, but they typically sit seven or eight subjects, with brighter students sitting more. It seems clear that students know that they will get more points if they ditch the "hard" subjects and concentrate on the ones which will deliver the points. Brighter students seem to be happy to scrape the minimum grade for their required subjects and get the points elsewhere.[262] There is simply no point in lamenting the fact that students are behaving rationally. There is certainly no point in exhorting them to behave irrationally.

A report by an expert group for UCAS, the UK equivalent of the CAO university admissions system, has made a detailed study comparing Leaving Cert standards to A-level ones – measuring how much work must be done to achieve a grade in each.[263] The results are quite flattering to the Leaving Cert, showing that a Leaving Cert subject is worth about two-thirds of an A-level one.

An extension of this type of a study should be undertaken to compare each of the different Leaving Cert subjects and the effort needed to merit a grade in each subject. It is likely that such a study would indicate that maths and other hard sciences require a greater effort per CAO point than some humanities subjects.

The maximum points available should be set to reflect the amount of work required to get the grade, along with an incentive for students to take up courses that were previously regarded as too hard to waste effort on, so that perhaps an A1 would earn 100 points in the English exam, 75 points in biology and 150 points in maths.

Equally, there is no point in pleading with students to choose understanding and intellectual development over rote memorisation if the marking of the exams motivates them to do the reverse, and solving that problem will require more than a mathematical readjustment. It is much easier to teach for memory tests, it is much easier to design memory tests, and it is much easier to mark them. Switching emphasis to reward more understanding and intellectual development would require lots more effort from teachers and examiners, who both tend to be the same people.

Teachers hold huge power in the system, and the fact that such a switch would require much more effort from them is unlikely to motivate them to support it very vigorously, although while teachers sometimes behave badly, they are unlikely to strongly oppose a change that would so obviously benefit the children that they teach.

Major work in curriculum reform is required, along with work on reforming the exams to reward the learning strategies that benefit students and society most. This reform should be tied closely to the development of SuperTeachers (see below), and the pay increases associated with the increased status of teachers should be dependent on staged progress moving away from rote learning.

Medicine

It is not wise to use the Leaving Cert as a basis for selecting doctors. Being a doctor takes a particular personality type, not necessarily the most intelligent. The prestige of getting a son or (more likely) daughter into medicine means that now the only criterion for selecting our future doctors is straight A1s. The result is:

- a huge dropout rate in a course that costs a fortune to run

- unsuitable people becoming doctors

- people who would make good doctors missing their vocation

The solution is to make medicine a solely post-graduate course. In recent years, this has been grudgingly added as an option,[264] but there is no justification for allowing someone who is barely 18 to make such a lifetime decision. You want to be a doctor? Go and do a degree in biology or chemistry. When you're finished, you might think differently.

After three or four years, if you still want to be a doctor, you won't have wasted any time. If you change your mind, you will have a useful degree, and you won't have wasted a place in the education system. And if you want to be a nurse you could take the same degree, because after three years some people whose self-esteem only lets them think they could be nurses might turn out to be good candidates for being doctors.

Doing Something Right

Before going any further, it should be noted that the Irish education system is good. It may not be fashionable to say it, but Catholic education is good. In the United States there is clear evidence that Catholic schools outperform others.[265] While Catholic schools in the US generally do not select students in a way which would explain their better results, it could be that more motivated and more middle-class parents select Catholic schools.

However, this is unlikely to explain their success, because there is a strong association between communities in the US that tend to choose Catholic schools (Irish, Latino and Polish) and membership of lower socio-economic groups that normally are associated with lower attainment in education. It is difficult to make a comparison in Ireland, because almost all education is Catholic education, but the Celtic Tiger would indicate that elements of our education system can match the best in Europe.

How is this achieved? Dedication. In the past, many Irish teachers were members of the clergy who had no children of their own. They saw teaching as a vocation, not a job. They invested their hopes, dreams and expectations in the children they taught. They loved them.‡ Frequently the priests, brothers and nuns lived communally, and most of their contact with the non-clerical

---

‡   In this, I do not wish to minimise the ordeal of children who suffered at the hands of the brutes and rapists who were a large minority in the clergy.

world was the children they taught, who were also the only measure of their self-worth. Of course many of the teachers were lay, but they could not fail to be influenced by the culture of dedication.

This is now, of course, the past tense. The clergy is all but gone from Irish education. How can we maintain the best parts of a system with teachers who do not have the same motivation as the teachers who taught them?

Buying Dedication

There is still a lot of dedication in the education system. The clergy did not have a monopoly on it. They might be gone from education, but the sense of vocation is not. There will always be caring and idealistic people, and many of them still go into education. We get dedication for free, and that makes it tempting to expect that dedication comes as standard issue with a diploma in education. It doesn't. There are two reasons for taking a job: because it's the job you want, or because you can't get the job you want, and this is the next best thing.

Nobody aspires to work at McDonalds, but they do fine because they don't need dedication. Google pays far above the industry rate for many of its employees, so that it can have its choice of the most talented people. So the question is: do we want our children educated by people who got to be teachers by being the best of many candidates or by people who took the job because they lost out in the competition for better jobs?

Our children individually, and Ireland as a whole, will benefit by making teaching attractive enough to create competition for the jobs, and that means money. Being a teacher used to be on the list of prestige jobs along with solicitor and doctor. To put it back there, we need to give teachers the same prestige as those professions, and that means giving them the same or similar money. It is true that the work outside the classrooms significantly increases teachers' working hours. But even that leaves teaching as a job that demands less time than almost any other full-time job. That said, teaching is a very demanding job. Facing twenty to thirty demanding pupils and keeping them orderly and attentive for even five hours a day is daunting. Educating them at the same time is even more so. But teachers can behave badly too.

Teachers Behaving Badly

The ASTI is implacably opposed to releasing information that would lead to the compilation of league tables of schools and their exam results.[266] So is the TUI.[267] The 1997 Freedom of Information Act gave citizens the right to view a wide variety of government files. When it was passed, several newspapers requested the statistics on exam results for every school in the state.[268] Teachers' unions fought the release of this information ferociously.

Why? Teachers say that league tables of exam results are crude and don't reflect much of the work done by schools. They are right. League tables only give one piece of information out of many that could be used to judge a school. But what they don't explain is, since league tables don't give the complete picture, why do they demand that we get less information, not more? The teachers' unions were so opposed to giving out information that they demanded that the law be changed to prevent the release of information on how well they are doing their job. And they got their way in the 1998 Education Act.

They also demanded that the Department of Education break the law and refuse to release the information, and they got their way on this too. The department fought the law from the Information Commissioner all the way up to the Supreme Court, and lost at every point. The results for 1998, the only exam year between the FoI Act and the clampdown, were released. The teachers' unions claim that they were protecting the privacy of the students, even though the information did not contain any personal data and excluded schools where fewer than 10 students sat the exam in any particular subject. There are three things to say about this.

Firstly, the teachers are treating parents and students like fools. They are saying that clever teachers can understand that league tables don't tell the whole story, but stupid parents and stupid pupils can't. And being so stupid, parents will make decisions on where to send their kids based on this incomplete information. Secondly, keeping this information secret does nothing to stop parents from trying to find out which school is most likely to get their kids better results. They will seek it from every source. Keeping league tables secret will only make parents act on less accurate information. Thirdly, anyone so anxious to cover up must think they have something bad to hide.

The Department of Education has much detailed information on the academic output and intake of every school. Comparing the two indices would give a very accurate idea of how a school is doing. Two schools may both produce C students on average, but if one had an average intake of D students and the other B students, then clearly one is doing better than the other. Keeping this information secret means that there is no pressure to improve schools that are doing badly or to recognise, reward and replicate the methods of good schools.

SuperTeachers

Teachers should be paid more. Much more. Double the current rate would be a good starting point. This may seem out of step with the situation where workers in the public and private sector are taking pay cuts, but the key point is that the relative position of teachers should be dramatically improved. Before euro symbols start appearing in the eyes of the teachers' unions, the pay increases should not be given for nothing; they should not be *given* at all. Teachers should be paid the higher pay in return for losing their tenure and working in a system with radically different work practices and close scrutiny of their outcomes.

Teachers' relatively low pay is matched by fringe benefits unheard of in other professions. The first three things they might have to sacrifice would be June, July and August. Teachers currently have a precise contract with specific terms of employment, and they can't be expected to just give this up. And if they want to keep them, fine.

But teachers should be offered the opportunity to apply for a new job – call it SuperTeacher. There is nothing automatic here. Teachers would be expected to meet high academic and professional standards to get the job, and they would be expected to submit to frequent and regular evaluation of their work and to have those evaluations made publicly available. SuperTeachers would be evaluated – by pupils, parents, head teachers, their colleagues, and by professional inspectors. This is called 360-degree evaluation, and it is commonplace in multinationals in Ireland. Schools and head teachers should be evaluated in the same way.

And if teacher or head teacher evaluations don't meet an agreed standard, teachers would be withdrawn from teaching for (unpaid) retraining, at the end of which they would be evaluated. If the retraining did not improve their standards, teachers would lose their jobs. It is not difficult to predict the reaction from the teachers' unions. Their hysterical reaction to even the most modest form of accountability shows that they are deeply paranoid about any examination of their performance. They are wrong.

Technology has already trumped some of the objections to this freedom of information. The RateMyTeacher[269] website contains thousands of reviews of teachers in every school in the country. Some of the comments are puerile, some are clearly false, but it is clear that the great majority are sincerely held views. The comments and ratings (mostly positive) give a remarkable insight into teachers and schools. Teachers' unions objected so vociferously to this website that it is difficult not to but smile at their impotent fury. Callers to radio shows seriously suggested disconnecting Ireland from the internet or prosecuting RateMyTeacher's American-based operators in Ireland. The teachers had some success. Many schools have used software intended for blocking pornographic websites to jam their pupils from accessing RateMyTeacher.ie. Of course, teachers cannot prevent pupils from accessing RateMyTeacher.ie on home computers and in internet cafés. The website is thriving, and despite the chicken-lickens, the sky has not fallen.

Evaluation of teachers and schools should include:

- Exam results

- Value-added academic assessments, measuring the progress of children, taking their starting point into account

- Detailed questionnaires from parents and pupils on all academic and non-academic aspects of the schools, including the physical environment, the level of commitment of the teachers, prevalence of bullying, quality of school trips and the levels and methods of discipline in the school

All of the data should be published on a website, in a format accessible to screen scrapers, although not one which would identify or tend to identify individual teachers or pupils.

Before the Leaving Cert

The Leaving Cert comes at the end of our school system – a fortnight at the end of 14 years in education. It is extraordinary that such a short period gets so much attention, compared to everything that comes before it.

It should be obvious that good education is good for the country – but are we doing as well as we could? Not by a mile. This, by the way, is good news. It's good news because Ireland is already doing well (*quite* well) in education. If there is room to improve, that means Ireland can look forward to the benefits of an improving education system. If it improves.

What is the evidence that there is room for improvement? Inequality. There is a dramatic difference between the performance of pupils from different social classes in Ireland.[270] By far the most reliable way to get a good Leaving Cert is to choose rich parents. The contrast in college admissions between Dublin postcode areas is striking. A student in Dublin 14 has an 87 per cent chance of going to college. A few kilometres away in Dublin 10, the chance is 11 per cent.[271]

This isn't surprising. Some children start school knowing how to read and write; others have never seen a book and don't know how to hold a crayon.

It is inevitable that better-off, better-educated parents will be able to teach and motivate their children better. These children will have the role models, seeing their parents reading, and seeing the social and economic benefits of education. They are likely to know relatives who are going through the education system ahead of them. All of this is good. The Dublin 14 kids in Rathfarnham are performing to their full potential. The challenge is to give this encouragement to all pupils. Think of the benefits to Irish society if the Dublin 10 students in Ballyfermot had the same opportunities and encouragement.

Challenging Education

The Bronx is one of the poorest places in the United States. About 30 per cent of the population, including 41 per cent of those under age 18, live below the poverty line.[272] Educational achievement is far below the US average.[273] In his book *Outliers*, Malcolm Gladwell writes that only 16 per cent of all middle-school students in the Bronx meet their expected level in maths, but there is one school that has dramatically better results. In the KIPP Academy the equivalent figure is 84 per cent.[274] Students also excel at other subjects, but the Academy doesn't do it by skimming off the most promising students from other schools. Students at the massively oversubscribed school are chosen at random.

Equally, it is not parental commitment. Few parents have ever set foot in the school. Ninety per cent of them are so poor that their children qualify for subsidised school lunches, which makes you pretty poor in the US. So how is it done? Hard work, and lots of it. The school day in the KIPP Academy begins at 7.25am and lasts until 5pm, which is when other activities begin, such as homework clubs and sports activities, lasting until 7pm. On Saturdays, the school day is from 9am until 1pm, except in summer, when it is from 8am until 2pm, and they take three weeks fewer summer holidays. Two to three hours' homework is standard for 12-year-olds.

There are innovative teaching methods: all students must follow the SSLANT protocol (smile, sit up, listen, ask questions, nod when spoken to and track with your eyes), but the most common difference is that children are given more challenging learning. In his book, Gladwell explains why this leads to such levels of success, particularly for pupils from a background that would normally predict very low educational achievement. Middle-class children are surrounded by books, learning and literacy at home as well as at school, so they progress both in term time and in the holidays. For working-class students, the problem is not that they fail to progress in school; it is that they go back so far when they are out of school. This is backed up with hard data. Gladwell refers to tests of reading scores from the end of each of the five years of US high school, which appears to show that middle-class kids progress more than working-class ones in each academic year, creating a large cumulative deficit. Testing the children at both the start and end of the academic year tells a different tale.

During the school year, working-class kids advance their reading scores more than middle-class ones, but crucially, during the long summer holidays, middle-class children's reading scores improve significantly, but working-class children go backwards.

> When it comes to reading skills, poor kids learn nothing when school is not in session. The reading scores of the rich kids, by contrast, go up

by a whopping 52.49 points. Virtually all of the advantage that wealthy students have over poor students is the result of differences in the way privileged kids learn while they are *not* in school.[275]

In Ireland, the school year is 179 days, one day shorter than in the US, and our summer holidays are up to two weeks longer. Australia, Italy, Netherlands and Germany all have school years that are 200 days or longer. Korea has 220, which means that Korean children benefit from two months' more education than Irish children every year.[276]

New School Year
The school year should be significantly lengthened. This could cause severe disruption to the tourist industry and others if all families with children were to try to take their holidays in a single short few weeks, but it doesn't have to:

- All teachers should be assigned to one of three groups when they begin their profession: A, B or C.

- Teachers and their children should be assigned the same groups, by moving one of the teachers if necessary.

- The first child from every other family should be randomly assigned to a group when they start school.

- All children from that family should be assigned to the same group as their older brother or sister, regardless of what school they attended, so that the family can holiday together.

- Schools should give children six weeks' summer holidays, but the whole school should close for only weeks 26 and 27 (early July).

- In the first year, group A should have holidays in weeks 22 to 25.

- Group B have holidays in weeks 28 to 31.

- Group C have holidays in weeks 32 to 35.

- In subsequent years, the position of the holidays for each group should be rotated, so that families get their holidays at a different time each year.

- Christmas and Easter holidays would be difficult to rotate, but the same system should be used to stagger half-term breaks.

As well as lengthening the school year and keeping children from sliding backwards in their holidays, the periods of school time when one group or other is on holidays would be used, in part, for more creative elements in the school curriculum.

Social Engineering
Schemes designed to intervene in the lives of working-class children and engender in them what are, in effect, middle-class values have often been

criticised as social engineering. What right does society have to interfere with the values that working-class parents instil in their children? This is a good question. But it's the wrong question. Education is about opportunities, and if showing working-class children opportunities that they would not otherwise have is social engineering, then hurray for social engineering.

But it's not. The real social engineering is poverty and lack of opportunities. Teachers in schools catering for deprived areas have reported pupils being listless, irritable and having a poor attention span. It transpired that a high proportion of them went to school without a breakfast. If you hadn't eaten for 15 hours at the start of your working day, you probably wouldn't achieve much either. And when they do eat, it's not much better.

Food Education
The very least that an education system can do is prepare a student for life, and the ability to feed yourself and your family in a healthy and economical way is a most basic skill. Home Economics has long been a poor relation of other subjects, and only a small proportion of that was devoted to cooking skills. Knowing these skills has become more urgent with the onset of serious dietary problems – see **Obesity** on page 66.

Teaching nutrition and cooking to children is now a priority, and the subject should be a core part of primary and secondary education for all students. Apart from the importance of the skills, this is to reconnect children with the source of their food.

- Schools should be linked to local allotments, if there is no other suitable ground for growing crops – see **Dig for Victory** on page 74.

- Children should be given integrated age-appropriate nature, biology, nutrition and cooking lessons.

- Lessons should vary from planting seedlings for young children, up to planning and producing nutritious meals.

- Depending on logistics, all pupils should be given a regular opportunity to produce food for schoolmates or parents, to provide feedback and gratification for the pupils.

Typing
Before computers became popular, typing had a feminised image and an association with low-status jobs that turned off many people. There is some voice-activated software available, but there is no prospect of computers without keyboards in the near future. Inability to type can deter many people, particularly men, from pursuing valuable career enhancement.

Some spend time staring at a keyboard, their panic blinding them to the letter they are looking for. Others don't get that far. Touch-typing – the ability to type without seeing the letters that you are typing – is a liberating skill that is simple to learn. Typing will remain a crucial skill for the knowledge economy for some time to come.

- All second-level students should be taught to touch-type.

Fee-Paying Schools
Outside of the main education system, a minority of Irish children go to schools that charge their parents fees. Fees for "day pupils" – those who are not boarders – range from €2,900 to €11,430. Boarders' parents are charged from €11,130 to €20,895.[277] If wealthy parents want to pay for their children's education, then there is little reason to stop them, but the parents are not paying these fees.

Many fee-paying schools in the state have managed to secure charitable status, meaning that "donations" to them are tax-deductible.[278] Although it is unclear how much of these donations would otherwise be fees paid by parents, the option is open to them to effectively land the taxpayer with a large chunk of the bill.

In addition, the salaries of teachers in fee-paying schools are paid by the state, leaving the schools free to spend parents' fees on enhanced facilities for the pupils, reducing the pupil-teacher ratio and topping up salaries to attract the best teachers from the mainstream system. Sr Eileen Randles said if parents were required to pay the full cost of this advantage, the fee for her Loreto schools would jump from €3,600 a year to between €20,000 and €30,000.[279]

So, while you must be rich to get in the door to privilege, once you are in, the bulk of the cost of that privilege is paid by the taxpayer. Private schools suck teaching talent out of the mainstream system, but they also suck out the support of the richest, best-educated and most articulate parents who might be more politically effective at campaigning for improving all schools, if they were motivated to do so by having their children there.

- All forms of public subsidy for private schools should be ended.

Public Schools
Private schools can be readily identified by their demands for fees, but what of the status of the rest of the schools? Protestant private schools protested loudly when one of their state subsidies, worth around €100,000 per school, was removed. This particular subsidy was paid exclusively to Protestant schools for being Protestant schools.[280] While it is difficult to see how this payment was constitutional, let alone justified, it is far less clear to see what the alternatives for members of minority religions are.

Most public schools are also technically private schools. While they don't charge fees, and receive almost all their funding from the taxpayer, they are technically owned by the Catholic church. The taxpayer pays the salaries of the teachers, but, extraordinarily, the employer is the Catholic church, which can and has fired teachers for not being sufficiently Catholic.[281] This, and the fact that Catholic teaching permeates the school day with English and Irish readers focusing on religious instruction, makes it easy to see how minority religions feel entitled to special provision for their own.

But just how big is the majority? Surveys among the 87 per cent of Irish people who are Catholics[282] indicate that between 1974 and 2003, weekly mass attendance declined from 91 per cent to 44 per cent,[283] so just 38 per cent of Irish people are observant Catholics. The second-largest religious group found in the census is people of no religion, significantly larger than the Church of Ireland. There is no justification in requiring Protestants, atheists or lapsed Catholics to pay taxes to fund the indoctrination of their children in a faith that they don't, or don't fully, subscribe to. The state should have no role in pressuring or encouraging anyone to follow, or not to follow, a particular religion.

- Schools that the state pays for should be open to children of all religions and of none, on an equal basis.

- Employment in such schools should be on the basis of skills as a teacher alone.

- The curriculum should be suitable for all, and focus on teaching the subject at hand, without embedded religious indoctrination.

- School buildings should be available to any denomination that wishes to use them for religious instruction that they organise.

Bullying in Schools
Bullying in schools can be troubling for some, devastating for others. In the past, teachers' methods of dealing with these problems was, at best, to ignore them. In some cases, as detailed in the Ryan Report, teachers enabled, participated and led bullying.[284]

An intervention that has proven successful is the creation of Bully Courts, supervised by teachers, in which children hear complaints against peers accused of bullying and can impose minor punishments.[285] Bullies often attempt to normalise their behaviour and claim the tacit support of silent classmates for their victimisation. Involving the majority of children in tackling bullying counters this behaviour, refuting the impression that the bully enjoys majority support.

The success of this initiative is dependent on the support of teachers, so the success may be due as much to that support as the method itself. Thus Bully Courts should not be seen as an alternative to the teachers doing their jobs.

- All schools should have a detailed policy defining bullying and how it is dealt with.

- Bullying should be measured in teacher and school assessments.

- The level of bullying should be included in the assessment of SuperTeachers, with unacceptable levels leading to a negative assessment.

Vehicle Registration Tax

Nothing arouses the ire of Irish motorists as much as VRT, the extra tax allowed on cars, as an exception to the EU single market rules. A normally clear-thinking commentator, David McWilliams, even argued for a "No" vote on the Lisbon Treaty as a protest against it.[286] He was wrong.

Clear thinking begins with facts, such as the fact that in May 2008, James Durrigan and his company pleaded guilty before Ardee District Court to fixing Citroën cars prices from 1997 until 2002. He was fined €12,000,[287] a pathetic amount given the vast sums scammed from customers by this type of crime. Car dealer Denis Manning was convicted of a similar crime in Cork in 2007.[288] While car dealers have been hit hard by the economic crisis, there can be no doubt that there is almost no competitive pressure between suppliers, and the price cuts that have appeared will disappear just as soon as demand returns to the market.

Before the crash, Eddie Hobbs on his TV show demonstrated that there was less than €100 variation in the price of a €28,000 car throughout the country. It's not surprising. RTÉ's *Prime Time* exposed a raft of documents that showed determined, organised and highly disciplined price-fixing in car sales around the country, adding €2,000 to €3,000 to the price of every car sold in the country.[289] David McWilliams said that the existence of VRT in Ireland is an outrage against the Treaty of Rome, and he may have a point, but there are bigger outrages. Under EU law, motor dealers have a derogation which exempts them from competition laws that apply to almost all other industries.

There are 83 Toyota dealers in Ireland. For years up until the current depression, the dealerships were worth millions, because of an EU block exemption which says that, unlike any other industry, the car dealers can get together and agree the right number of dealerships in the country.[290] In any other industry, this would be a criminal offence, but not with cars. And unsurprisingly they have decided that the right number is no more competition thank you. Perhaps while they are deciding (legally) that they don't want any competition thank you, they might also be tempted to decide to all sell at the same price. That would be against the law, so it was a pure coincidence that there was less than one-third of 1 per cent of a difference in the price of a particular car between all of those 83 dealers.

A few years ago, DVD players cost €800. In the current Argos catalogue, there is one for sale at €24.95.[291] In common with the cost of all manufactured products, their price has collapsed in recent years, but not cars. If VRT didn't exist we couldn't invent it, but it does exist. The price of cars has little to do with market forces, and certainly nothing to do with the cost of manufacture. Car dealers and the multinational manufacturers charge what the market will bear – whatever they can get away with.

What the market will bear will not change with or without VRT. If VRT was abolished now, car dealers and multinational manufacturers would simply inflate their profits, continuing to charge what the market will bear. VRT totalled €1.4bn in 2007,[292]and if that money doesn't come from VRT then it will come from VAT, or income tax, or an increase in that national debt. The only thing that abolishing VRT would do is transfer huge sums out of the taxpayer's pocket, directly into the profits of multinational companies.

Bankruptcy and Debt

Sadly, the need for bankruptcy and debt collectors in Ireland is increasing. The need for running the services to deal with this is also increasing.

Bankruptcy[‡]

There are thousands of individuals in Ireland with debts which far exceed their assets and whose available income is limited or non-existent. Our dated and limited bankruptcy legislation means that individuals must cope with mountains of debt with no mechanism to make an arrangement with their creditors.

This causes considerable personal hardship for many people. More importantly, from an economic point of view, there is no effective remedy available to creditors where a debt is held or guaranteed personally. This is a particular problem for the banking system, which is facing a logjam of creditors, including a number of very large property developers, with no cost-effective mechanism to agree a binding scheme of arrangement.

The Irish Bankruptcy System

The legislative regime in Ireland is specifically designed to discourage bankruptcy. There are three possible routes, two of which involve bankruptcy:

- An individual can file for bankruptcy with the Official Assignee of the High Court.
- A creditor may petition the High Court to make a person bankrupt.
- If 60 per cent of creditors approve, a Scheme of Arrangement can be established, which will be binding on all parties.

The current arrangements do not work and are not used in Ireland. The stigma involved means very few people choose to petition for personal bankruptcy; creditors petitioning for a person to be made bankrupt must provide a full indemnity against the cost of the proceedings, which is usually seen as throwing good money after bad; and Schemes of Arrangement are costly and so not used.

Between 2000 and 2006, there were three applications for a Scheme of Arrangement brought before the High Court. In 2005, the United Kingdom had 47,291 bankruptcies. Ireland had nine. In 2008, there were 150,000

[‡] This section is based on work by journalist and consultant Tom McEnaney.

personal insolvencies in the UK, including 67,000 bankruptcies. In Ireland there were fewer than 15 personal bankruptcies.

An option in the UK is an attachment of earnings, where a creditor can apply to the debtor's employer and request instalments to be deducted from the debtor's salary and paid to the creditor. This is not available in Ireland.

Individual Voluntary Arrangements

People facing bankruptcy in the UK can avail of an Individual Voluntary Arrangement (IVA), where a third party negotiates with creditors; if those holding more than 75 per cent of a debt agree, a binding Scheme of Arrangement is made. Most IVAs deal with personal loans and other forms of unsecured debt. Last year the average person with an IVA owed £47,000 and proposed to pay back 38 per cent of this. An estimated 2,500 people with debts exceeding GBP£100,000 entered into IVAs in the UK in 2008 out of a total of 37,000 people who took out IVAs.

Unlike bankruptcy, IVAs are not made public and so avoid the stigma which attaches to bankruptcy, and do not need to involve solicitors, although a professional is required to oversee the IVA. Ireland should introduce the Individual Voluntary Arrangements laws from the UK into Irish law immediately.

Debt Collectors

There is tight regulation of debt collectors in the UK,[293] but despite this there is considerable evidence of malpractice within the industry.[294] By contrast, there is no regulation of debt collectors whatsoever in Ireland.[295] Some unscrupulous individuals are quick to exploit the lack of regulation in an area that frequently deals with individuals who are vulnerable or have poor access to legal or financial advice. One is Martin Foley, the violent Dublin criminal with a dozens of convictions[296] and other associations with organised crime. He was dubbed "the Viper" by tabloid newspapers.

It is flabbergasting that he can, perfectly legally, establish a debt-collection company called Viper Debt Recovery and Repossession Services Limited,[297] exploiting his violent reputation to intimidate people who may or may not have a dept payable to one of his clients. What it says about clients who select him to collect their debts is another thing. There have already been allegations of intimidation against the company,[298][299][300] although it is hard to see how even the simple use of Foley's company could be construed as anything else. The company is operated in a highly suspect manner.[301]

- Ireland needs licensing and regulation of debt collectors immediately.

- For the most part, the UK regulation can be copied into Irish law.

- The Private Security Authority[302] should be responsible for regulating debt collection agencies.

- All directors, owners and staff of debt collection agencies should require Garda clearance.

- The Garda clearance should be in the format of a certificate that the person is of good character and a fit person to be involved in debt collection.

- Companies in breach of the regulations or found to be employing or associated with people without Garda clearance should lose their licence.

- Companies currently operating as debt collection agencies should have no right to continue in the business if they do not meet the criteria.

The Workless Class

Unemployment has skyrocketed since 2008, but even in the peak of the boom years, unemployment never fell below 4 per cent of a greatly expanded workforce[303] – about 80,000 people. That is not to say that we failed to find work for them. During the boom, hundreds of thousands of people returned or came for the first time to Ireland and found employment,[304] and employers searched the world for workers willing to come to Ireland.[305] [306]

What happened was this: we failed to find a way to incorporate a small section of society into the economy. Regardless of how small that section, people who live in relative poverty because they cannot or will not find work during a period of such intense demand for labour represent a challenge to our social welfare system and our whole society.

The dole, now called Jobseeker's Benefit, was designed as just that – something to prevent absolute poverty while looking for a job in a lean period. The long-term unemployed are one of the most marginalised groups in society, and political rhetoric that scapegoats them for society's ills is unpalatable and inaccurate. The dole is only a small proportion of the social welfare budget (the bulk goes on pensions), and the long-term unemployed are only a small proportion of this.[307]

The real cost of long-term unemployment – people who will not or cannot get a job under any economic circumstances – is social. It is not acceptable to throw any members of society on the scrapheap. Some left-wing commentators instinctively jump to the defence of people with the least economic and cultural capital, but nobody can defend a system that permits and funds the wasted lives that result from unemployment that lasts for years, decades or lifetimes and passes from generation to generation.

There is a contradiction in the solution to this problem: reforms that appear to be motivated by a mean-spirited desire to punish the unemployed are unlikely to gain acceptance, and a programme of reform cannot serve contradictory purposes. Either its focus is to help the long-term unemployed, or it is to persecute them. Nevertheless, the cohort of people in question have not responded to intense economic incentives to enter employment, and there is no prospect of any success without an element of compulsion.

Skills Deficit
With a great number of long-term unemployed, the issue is skills, or lack of skills. There may have been many unskilled jobs available during the boom,

but even unskilled jobs require at least the skill to show up on time, in a fit state to work for the day, presented in a way that inspires confidence from employers and customers. It is not surprising that many long-term unemployed people lack the social skills required for employment. People lacking such skills are the most vulnerable to becoming unemployed to start with, and long absences from the workforce are likely to make people lose contact with those skills.

Workfare

Workfare, the name given to American schemes which revolve around requiring social welfare recipients to work for their benefits, is in operation in around half of US states.[308] It evolved from right-wing American politics and has a distinct tinge of a desire to punish and stigmatise the poor. While it does have some benefits – giving its recipients the purpose and social contact of going to work and preventing them from losing the social skills that employment requires – it has serious systemic disadvantages.

Working imposes costs that are very significant for low-paid people, such as childcare, buying work-appropriate dress and losing the opportunity to spend time bargain-hunting and buying goods at their cheapest. Forcing people to accept these costs, without the extra income that even a minimum-wage job would give over social welfare payments, is unfair.

Workfare also damages the economy. Typically, it consists of work that would otherwise be done by minimum-wage employees, the very people who are most likely to be long-term unemployed. The availability of cheaper Workfare workers is likely to displace people who would otherwise have been in regular employment and who thereby end up on Workfare themselves.

This can have a serious depressing effect on the market for low-wage jobs, particularly because Workfare workers are often contracted out to employers seeking to lower their labour costs. The result is a race to the bottom, whereby unscrupulous employers gain a competitive advantage over ones willing to pay decent wages; who are in turn forced to adopt their competitors' tactics or go out of business. For these reasons, Workfare on the US model is not acceptable.

The Solution

Five things must be done:

- Close off the route into the lifestyle funded by social welfare.

- Deliver employment training where it is beneficial.

- Break the generational transmission of social welfare dependence.

- Establish state programmes as an employer of last resort.

- Invest in detailed, structured, intensive training and personal development programmes to enable the long-term unemployed to return to being productive members of society.

Reform Unemployment Benefits

A person who does not find work at any point in the economic cycle is not suffering from deprivation that is a result of external economic conditions. The concept of unemployment benefits that can be paid for the whole of a person's life is damaging and hypocritical, and must be replaced to avoid snaring more people in the trap of lifetime unemployment.

- Unemployment benefits should be paid for a limited period.

- Base the period on the amount of time each person has spent working in their lifetime, for example six months plus one month for each year spent in employment that has not been counted towards a previous period of unemployment.

- End all unearned benefits after this time.

This does not mean leaving people destitute; however, if someone has declined paid retraining (see below) and also declined a job offer from a commercial employer or the state (see page 138), it is bad social policy, and bad for the individual to fund their lifestyle indefinitely with social welfare.

Training

Training for the unemployed does not have the best of records. Because of its expense, it has often been reserved for the long-term unemployed, the group who are least interested. Almost all training is dependent on motivation – both of the trainee and the trainer; if either doesn't really want to be there, then the outcome of the training is unlikely to be productive. Whether it is for the unemployed or anyone else, compulsory training isn't valuable enough to be called worthless. It is a total waste of the time of the trainee and the trainer, not to mention a waste of money.

In theory, Fás is the agency that looks after retraining unemployed people. Their annual budget ballooned to over €1bn during the boom, when their workload almost entirely disappeared, and breathtakingly arrogant behaviour was uncovered with the executives displaying little interest in anything other than treating expense accounts like billionaires' bank accounts.[309] [310] [311] Controls seem to have been equally lax down the line, with invoices being approved in extraordinary circumstances, including producing TV ads that were never broadcast, a car that was never delivered,[312] and investigations were launched into large invoices for nothing at all being paid,[313] as well as an employee on a full-time salary invoicing for services rendered.[314]

While the individuals involved should bear the full penalty for their behaviour, the systemic reasons for the malpractice need to be addressed. The culture of non-accountability in the public service, when met with often poorly motivated trainees is a toxic mix. When the trainees don't really want to be there, and there is little or no quality control for the trainer, the temptation is to take it easy until something close to quitting time and then wind up the day. When an entire organisation is operating on these lines, groupthink sets in, and poorer and poorer work practices reinforce each other, creating a culture where ever lower levels of performance are accepted and the original purpose of the exercise is lost.

The contradiction in Fás's roles as both a provider and purchaser of training cannot be overcome, as was evident when, in 2007, Fás caught a training supplier fiddling the results of the courses that they were running. Fás paid for the courses and continued to give business to the supplier, who continued to falsify the results.[315] Fás were hardly in a position to tackle the supplier since that would bring scrutiny on the quality of their own services.

The grandiose offices, world trips, expense accounts and self-regarding advertising budgets indicate that the culture of the organisation couldn't be further removed from serving the most economically disadvantaged people in the country. Fás is beyond salvation. It should be closed down and its entire staff made redundant. A new agency should be set up with three tightly-focused objectives:

- Assess the training needs and employment potential of unemployed people.
- Provide them with vouchers to purchase training that improves their employment prospects to be spent with approved providers on the open market.
- Vigorously validate the quality of the training supplied.

It is important to create market incentives to keep up the quality of the training delivered; here's how:

- People who have been approved for training will be given vouchers to purchase that training from approved suppliers.
- Approved suppliers would be any private-sector training companies that offer the courses in question, but these companies would lose their approval if they had an adverse audit of their training.
- All approved suppliers would be required to use a detailed online evaluation process where trainees would give regular feedback during and after the training course.
- The subsequent employment record of all trainees would be tracked (without identifying individuals) via their PPS numbers, giving details of their employment status and earnings.

- The new training agency would be responsible for detailed audits of the training providers, with random checks in addition to audits based on trainee feedback.

- All the information from this system would be available to clients before they choose their training provider, in a format that would allow them to compare all the data from different providers, including the employment outcomes and comments of previous trainees.

- This information would also be available for screen scraping to allow third party websites to compare and present the data in innovative ways.

At any time while unemployed, whether receiving benefits or not, each person should be entitled to a detailed personal assessment of their career, including a realistic assessment of their skills and skills gaps, as well as their employment prospects in careers that appeal to them and how training and education would enhance those prospects.

- Training vouchers for specific course types should be issued on this basis, at no cost to the unemployed person.

- While attending the course, the person should be paid the equivalent of unemployment benefits, plus an allowance to cover the extra cost of attending the course, including childcare.

- The online auditing system should also be used to ensure that the trainee maintains an acceptable attendance record.

- The period spent in training should not count as unemployment for the purpose of calculating the time limit on that person's length of unemployment benefit.

- Training should be entirely voluntary.

- Training should only be denied where it does not have a realistic prospect of moving the trainee closer to employment, or have some other beneficial effect.

Break the Cycle
Intergenerational unemployment is a particularly tragic problem. Children – particularly boys – can grow up without knowing any role model in their extended family who holds a job. To break this cycle, it will be necessary to pay particular attention to the needs of children in deprived areas. Education is the key to this, in its widest sense. A model for bringing up the education levels of children in deprived areas is discussed in **Challenging Education** on page 122.

In addition to these, particular programmes should be targeted at areas and schools where these problems affect a significant number of children. The Big Brothers Big Sisters organisation in the US specialises in allowing children to make friends with young adults whom they can identify with in a recreational setting.[316] The unspoken aim of this is for the big brothers and sisters to be role models for the children and give them an insight into the opportunities and lifestyle that education and employment can offer them, in a way that their parents may not be able to. Such a programme should be vigorously encouraged here.

Also, the lengthened school year (see **New School Year** on page 123) should give schools time to organise regular trips to workplaces, universities and other third-level institutions, government offices and the courts to allow children to see the physical manifestation of the different institutions of society, prompting them to visualise how they would like their lives to turn out.

State Employment

There will be people, particularly in difficult economic times, whose unemployment has run out and for whom no training is required, but who cannot find work. The state should create employment for them.

These jobs are frequently likely to be low-skilled in nature, but they should be paid at the going rate. This is a job, not social welfare. Care must be taken to make sure that such employment does not displace or depress the wage levels of other jobs. Tasks that they could work on would include:‡

- a major housing insulation programme (see **Insulate and Build** on page 175)

- a network of community crèches, particularly targeted at supplying childcare for parents on training courses

- major recycling programmes

- building new parks and playgrounds (see **Space for Children** on page 85)

- being teachers' aides and supervisors for newly expanded school activities (see **Food Education** on page 124)

- insulating, renovating, upgrading and redecorating public buildings, particularly schools and hospitals

As the employer of last resort, the state would be obliged to find employment for all applicants who have exhausted their other unemployment options. However, this is a relationship of employment and should be treated as such. Employment should be found that is within the skill level of the applicant, but in the event that they behave in a way that would not be acceptable in any other employment – through absenteeism,

---

‡ Some ideas for this type of work owe inspiration to *Ireland's Economic Crash* by Kieran Allen, published by the Liffey Press in 2009, although his vision of the nature of the employment is different.

unacceptable work rates or other disruptive behaviour – they should lose the job, just like with any other employer.

Recovering Lives
While training and changing incentives can prevent people from falling into the trap of lifetime unemployment, transforming the lives of people who have spent years on the dole through the boom will be far more challenging.

Training is the key, but the training is likely to fail if it does not address the real blocks to employment. While job skills will be important for many people, life skills will be more necessary for some. People may have left school before their teens, have serious literacy problems, have never held regular employment and may have addiction, emotional or other problems.

Each person should be entitled to a realistic assessment of goals that they can achieve in their lives and agree to a timetable attached to those goals, which are likely to require significant support. Such goals may be as simple as learning to read. The Blair government in the UK made a significant investment in courses such as adult literacy,[317] parenting[318] and the Surestart programme to coordinate services for young children[319] and many others, in an effort to end long-term social problems. In addition, teaching people to cook and eat healthy food should be included, because there is strong evidence of an association between poverty and poor nutrition.[320]

Once realistic goals are set, and the training and support provided, there is no excuse to continue paying social welfare to people who do not avail of them. One of the skills needed may be the self-discipline to come to work on time every day. In extreme cases, the motivation to do this could be achieved by making social welfare payments daily, at the start of the training course. It is entirely possible that such programmes may never return some of their clients to employment, and the goal may be to make sure that they have the skills to make sure that their children have better lives.

Tackling Isolation
Geographical and social isolation can be significant problems for unemployed people and an obstacle to returning to employment. Two easy ways to tackle this is with subsidised public transport tickets and subsidised internet access. The latter could be organised in conjunction with computer skills training courses aimed at the unemployed. Even recreational use of computers and the internet tend to improve IT skills that are useful for employment.

Valuing Children
One of the reasons for long-term unemployment among women is single motherhood. Remaining on social welfare can often be a financially more

attractive than minimum wage employment, particularly when the benefits for several children and childcare costs are taken into account. This makes single mothers the target for unrestrained contempt among some commentators both in Ireland[321] and abroad,[322] [323] particularly in the United States, where the notion of Welfare Queens[324] (code for African-American single mothers) is more prominent in urban myth than in reality.[325] Anyone anxious to crack down on single mothers living on social welfare should contemplate the fact that the main victims of such harshness are likely to be children who have done nothing to deserve their fate.

While it is unacceptable that people should opt out of society, the definition of participation cannot be so tightly defined as just having a job. Raising children is probably the biggest contribution that could be made to society. If single parents are doing this job well, disrupting their lifestyle is likely to be counterproductive. Even doing this job badly is probably an important contribution, but that is no reason not to do everything possible to support and improve parenting.

Parents, particularly single parents, should be supported, and special provisions should be made to make sure that training programmes accommodate and address the needs of parents. Couples with children should be treated as a unit, and if they wish to be a single-earner family, the training that they are offered should be tailored to that need, in particular with offering non-employment training to the partner that does not wish to return to the workforce.

In the Training Needs Assessment mentioned under **Training** above, an assessment should be made of any support that is needed for parents, in terms of everything from parenting classes to cooking and nutrition to literacy and numeracy for themselves, and supporting their children in school work. The last point is particularly important because of the role that parents' literacy plays in the success of children in school.[326] Very innovative programmes to improve the literacy of parents and children together should be replicated in Ireland.[327]

Travellers

Relations between the Travelling community and the rest of society form one of the most uniquely troubled aspects of Irish society. It is a problem that has few analogies in any other country, and therefore there is little international guidance on how to improve relations. There is not even a clear understanding of the origins of the Travelling community,[328] although there is no evidence that they are anything other than Irish.

There can be no doubt that the condition of many of Ireland's 22,400[329] Travellers is miserable. They have higher infant mortality rates, lower life expectancy, much higher rates of births to teenagers, and in almost every other health index they fare much worse than the general population, with settled Travellers doing worse than the general population and unhoused Travellers faring worst of all.[330] Half of Travellers never see their fortieth birthday.[331]

There is a public perception that crimes committed by the Travelling community are out of proportion with their numbers, but the statistics that might prove or disprove the link appear not to be collected. Pavee Point, the Travellers' advocacy group, don't appear to be anxious to clear up the issue. In their submission on the Garda Diversity Strategy,[332] they repeatedly emphasise the "care" and "caution" that needs to be taken with publishing such statistics. Nowhere in the submission is there any suggestion to improve the collection or publication of the statistics, so all we are left with is the anecdotal evidence, and the anecdotal evidence is not good.

Prominent stories range from havoc in Finnish campsites[333] to intense long-running feuds in Kilkenny[334] and Mullingar.[335] There is no question that other sections of society are also responsible for dreadful crimes, but the common theme in reports of crime committed by members of the Travelling community is the failure of the rest of the Travelling community to condemn the crimes. Travellers make up less than one half of 1 per cent of Irish society, but the numbers of people involved in some incidents seem to be extraordinary. The feuds in Kilkenny and Mullingar brought scores of people on to the streets in pitched battles with a frightening array of improvised weapons.

The wife of the rapist Simon McGinley interrupted the rape of a 13-year-old girl that led to his first conviction, knocking on the door of his van, and he drove off to continue the assault in peace. Yet she attended court with her children to hear the gruesome details of his being convicted a second time, on the strength of DNA evidence and a deposition from the victim, who was in her eighties at the time of her ordeal. The wife's bizarre behaviour outside the court suggested that she believed that some sort of injustice had been visited on her husband. No doubt many members of the Travelling community were horrified at these crimes, but the numbers willing to say so publically are dwarfed by the numbers of Travellers willing to take to the streets of rural towns armed with clubs, axes and slash-hooks intent on doing battle with rival members of their community.

The Travelling community is deeply dysfunctional, and it is difficult to see how it could be any other way. The patterns of movement, it is believed, are based on seasonal agricultural work, but the nomadic way of life is totally incompatible with either employment or education in modern society. It is hardly surprising that less than 14 per cent of Travellers are in regular employment.[336] The transitory behaviour may also be connected with the appalling visual state of halting sites around the country. In a preindustrial age, the method of waste disposal by nomadic people was to simply move on. By the time that anyone else came to the site, any organic matter would have long decayed; but this is simply not compatible with the products of an industrial economy, and there can be no doubt that the disfiguring fires and litter that mark out so many halting sites contribute towards ill-feeling on the part of the rest of society.

Behaviour that gets rewarded gets repeated, and the reaction of the authorities towards Travellers has sometimes been extraordinarily indulgent. Martin Joyce ran an illegal diesel laundering operation in Finglas, cheating taxpayers and polluting the area. He ran the scam on lands belonging to Fingal County Council, which his family have been squatting on for years. In 2007, his brother David was paid €1.1m by the County Council to leave, as under the law known as squatters' rights, someone who occupies for 12 years or more without being asked to leave gains possession of the property, unless they sign an agreement otherwise. It was reported that many other members of his family were in negotiations for similar payouts. Through the years, there have been significant finds of firearms, stolen property and other contraband at the site.[337] The notion that a county council could for 20 years fail to even ask people who were illegally occupying their land to leave, let alone allow one of them to carry on a major criminal enterprise there, gives an idea of the way in which some authorities deal with misbehaviour on the part of Travellers. In the light of this, it would be irrational of Travellers not to exploit this.

Another factor is time and energy. Given the almost non-existent participation of young Traveller men in either education or employment, they are bound to find something else to do. Without any other route to find peer esteem, it is not surprising that they become involved in crime as a means to wealth and establishing dominance. The use of alcohol, combined with and caused by boredom, is likely to make this situation even worse.

Discrimination

Travellers are not to blame for all of their own problems. There can be no doubt that prejudice in wider society, even if provoked by the actions of some Travellers, affects all unfairly. Regardless of its origins, discrimination has the potential to inhibit any improvement in the situation.

The Traveller John Ward entered 62-year-old Padraig Nally's farm, presumably to rob him – he had numerous convictions for burglary. Nally shot and wounded him, and Ward fled. If the incident had stopped there, it would have hardly attracted much comment, but it didn't. Nally returned to his house to reload, and then pursued Ward down the rural road before shooting him again, this time fatally. His actions seemed to go far beyond the reasonable force that the law allows for self-defence. Nally was tried twice, and two juries acquitted him,[338] finally pronouncing him innocent of any crime. Supporters of Nally launched a fund to assist him[339] and even planned a rally to protest at his sentence for manslaughter in his first trial, although this was called off.[340] The fact that two juries gave such verdicts says a lot about the view of average Irish people towards Travellers.

The Equal Status Act has caused significant protests, particularly from publicans who were aggrieved at the way it could be used to challenge the refusal to serve or admit people who they said were a threat to the orderly running of their premises. The act was later amended in an apparent attempt to inhibit discrimination cases.[341]

Solutions

The only solution available to fractious relations between Travellers and the rest of society is for government to treat all without fear or favour. The laws requiring school attendance should be imposed on Travellers in exactly the same way as the rest of society. The proposal to remove the lifetime social welfare payments for people not seeking work on page 135 and the proposals to restrain career criminals from reoffending in **Serving a Sentence** on page 245 are likely to have a profound impact on Traveller society. These should be implemented in a way that achieves the same goal as with the rest of society; however, the training programmes associated with each should be adapted to make sure that they address the needs of Travellers and are most likely to achieve success.

- School programmes should be carefully tailored to meet the particular needs of Traveller children, including offering literacy and numeracy lessons to their parents.

- All statistics, including those surrounding health and crime, should include data on members of the Travelling community and be publically available.

- Rather than a reason, door staff who refuse entry to anyone should be required to give a receipt, which would allow an aggrieved person to follow up the reason for a refusal later.

Travellers' advocates say that the nomadic lifestyle is part of their culture, and this is correct. However, discrimination and prejudice are deeply ingrained in the culture of much of the rest of the population. It is time for both to move on.

If Travellers wish to continue a nomadic lifestyle, that is their right, so long as they do not infringe on the rights of others. However, they have no right to deny their children proper access to education, and if Travellers or anyone else choose a lifestyle that is incompatible with employment, they have no right to expect the rest of society to fund that lifestyle.

Benefits

Child Benefits
In 2001, child benefit was increased to €85.70 per month for the first child, and higher for families with more children.[342] By 2009, it had reached €166, but was cut to €150 for 2010.[343] Families with eight children now receive €1,422 per month, €17,064 per year.[344] Though child benefit is an important and effective way of reducing child poverty, much of the payment goes to families that are wealthy enough not to need it.

In a period when the public finances are under great strain, it is difficult to justify paying €17,064 per year to a millionaire TV star. Means-testing child-benefit, however, would also cause problems. Firstly, some people who need the benefit may not take the step necessary to complete the means-testing forms, because of problems with literacy or lack of information. Means testing is expensive, and the bar needs to be set high to justify the cost of doing this.

The biggest negative effect of means-testing child support would be the undermining of the social and political support that child benefit enjoys. It has this because it benefits so many people, and a perception that receiving child benefit is a mark of poverty is likely to undermine this support, making it politically difficult to continue paying it at a useful level, or at all. As well as expensive, means tests are bureaucratic and often humiliating for the applicants.

Instead of means-testing, child benefit should be taxed, with the tax-free allowance of the parents adjusted accordingly. This would leave the payment intact, but reduce the bill in a way that would affect people proportionally to their income.

Pensions
If you save for your retirement, it will be more comfortable. So, the thinking goes, if the whole of society saves for retirement, then everybody will have a more comfortable retirement. This is a line pushed by governments looking at the ticking demographic time-bomb coming, where pensions will consume an increasing amount of national wealth. This is lazy thinking and is incorrect.

Currently, a wealthy pensioner has the money which allows her to buy things that others cannot. If everyone has more money, all they get is inflation, caused by an increasing retirement fund chasing a fixed amount of goods and services.

A wealthier pensioner uses her money to outbid others competing to buy world cruises or nursing home care. But having wealthier pensioners in general is not likely to increase the supply of these things in the economy enough to give all pensioners the lifestyle of the currently wealthy ones. It may increase supply somewhat, but only by increasing the price to tempt more suppliers into the market. Big pensions work for the people who do have them precisely because most people don't have them.

There are complex economic reasons why the level of savings in an economy is an important factor influencing economic growth. Germany and Japan have had slow growth in the past decades, partly because of very high savings rates, and Ireland, the UK and USA have had very low saving rates and over-accelerated economic expansion. For this reason, it is worthwhile for the government to encourage a sustainable level of savings, but the huge tax breaks that very wealthy people can get by having part of their salaries paid directly into pension funds are not justified.

Local Services

Unpriced goods and services are used wastefully, although the motivation for the service charges imposed by Irish local authorities was revenue collection, not conservation. Both water and waste charges faced intense opposition, mostly organised by left wing groups.[345] [346] Water charges were levied as a flat rate, regardless of use, but this was abolished in 1997[347] and replaced with waste charges.[348] This was the worst possible decision.

Rubbish Charges

In theory, pricing a resource alerts its consumers to the cost of using it and disciplines them to use it wisely, rewarding the thrifty and punishing the wasteful. This doesn't work with waste charges, because disposal of the waste is an imperative once the consumer has bought a product. In theory, waste charges would motivate customers to switch to products that generate less waste, but the waste charge is so remote from the purchasing decision that it is unlikely to have any impact on the choice of product.

In any event, volume-related waste charges have only recently been introduced; previously households were charged a flat rate regardless of the amount of waste they produced and regardless of their diligence in recycling it. Also, waste charges are difficult and expensive to enforce. If correct disposal costs money, and fly tipping and backyard burning are free, they motivate people to behave in the least responsible way. There is evidence that organised crime is involved in illegal dumping,[349] and frustrated authorities have even resorted to satellite imaging to try to tackle the problem.[350]

Waste creates an eyesore, as well as being a hazard attracting vermin and containing unsorted toxins. It must be dealt with correctly, and the environmental movement neatly summarised the order of priorities; reduce, reuse, recycle. It is not clear why the third option on the list has gained so much more prominence than the other two.

There has been one successful policy shift in waste handling in recent years.‡ The Waste Electrical and Electronic Equipment (WEEE) directive[351] places a charge on every electronic item sold, which is shown at the point of purchase, from 50c for a small item up to €30 for large fridge freezers.[352] This fund pays for the recycling and disposal of electronic items. When you buy a new fridge or TV, the retailer is obliged to accept your old one back

---

‡   At the instigation of the EU, not the Irish government

and dispose of it responsibly free of charge.[353] Other items can be deposited at bring centres at no charge.[354]

This has effectively ended all incentive to fly-tipping. It works because it imposes the charge in a way that is inescapable and proportional to the cost of disposing of the item. It also makes the cost of disposal visible at the point of purchase, although it is unlikely that the €8 charge for TVs over 28" would persuade many people to buy a TV under 28" and pay only €5, so the behaviour-modification element of the charge is slight. Nevertheless, the principles behind the success of the WEEE directive should be extended to all consumer waste. Here's how:

- A small agency should be established to assess every consumer product on the market.

- The waste element – usually the packaging – should be measured, noting the amount of each material used.

- A price per gram for disposing of each material should be calculated, adding it up to the total disposal cost of the materials used in each product.

- Recycled elements of the packaging which are sourced from post-consumer waste should not attract any charge.

- Packaging that makes recycling difficult, such as those using mixed materials, would attract an extra charge: Pringles packets, which mix cardboard, plastic and metal, could expect a hefty premium.

- A flat fee of, say €500 would be charged for the assessment of each new product placed on the market.

- Packaging companies who sell to small manufacturers would be required to have the charge calculated for, and collected from, their clients.

- Retailers would display the waste charge for each item on their shelves, and list it on their till receipts and the receipts that they email to customers – see **Supermarkets** on page 59.

- The funds generated would pay for all domestic waste disposal and recycling.

- All charges for domestic waste collection would be removed.

Environmental Police
Violent organised criminals becoming involved in large-scale dumping show that enforcement of environmental laws is a serious issue. The Gardaí, as currently constituted, are ill-equipped to enforce environmental laws such as pollution controls, because they lack the in-house skills to understand the issues, and it is difficult for them prioritise such issues over murders, rapes and other more immediate crimes.

In theory, the Environmental Protection Agency (EPA) are the specialist prosecutors in major pollution incidents, but they don't appear to be an effective deterrent against major corporate polluters. At present there is a split between the EPA and the local authorities who have responsibility for the clean-up. More closely aligning these two responsibilities in the same organisation would motivate them to vigorously prosecute major offenders, and giving them the power to take prosecutions from start to finish would allow them to respond to this incentive.

The figures currently indicate that the level of prosecutions, and the fines for those prosecutions, are so low as to provide no deterrent. They brought just 19 successful prosecutions in 2008 and just 13 in 2007, with a total of about €160,000 in fines levied each year. The total fines levied look slightly more impressive in 2009, at €600,000, but this figure is flattered by a single case that accounts for 60 per cent of this figure, the only case in recent years which was referred to the Director of Public Prosecutions, necessary to impose higher fines.[355]

Delving deeper into these figures, it is clear that pathetic levels of fines are no deterrent to companies that can make huge extra profits by draining waste into rivers or by illegal landfilling. Firstly, the EPA website seriously overstates the level of fines by including the court costs imposed on offenders, which in 2008 constitute more than 70 per cent of the figures, meaning that the total in actual fines levied against all offenders combined in that year was less than €50,000.

Secondly, the same offenders have a tendency to show up year after year. South East Recycling Company Limited, whose fine was more than 60 per cent of the 2009 total, had been successfully prosecuted for similar offences in 2008, 2006 and 2004.

An environmental police force should be established, as outlined on page 148. Litter wardens (currently employed by local authorities) should be transferred to this force, and the EPA should be subsumed into it. It should be tasked with enforcing all the laws on waste disposal and pollution, and prosecuting offenders, and dealing with the clean-up of illegal dumping sites.

In particular offenders, and directors of offending companies, should be sentenced to work on clean-up operations, such as restoring illegal landfill sites, and corporate offenders should have their fines expressed as a percentage of the company turnover. The Environmental Police should have the discretion to refer complex cases to specialist courts – see **Technical Juries** on page 247.

Water

Arguing in favour of metering water supplies and charging householders accordingly, Michael McDowell said, "If electricity was free, we'd leave the lights on all night." His opponents argued that denying water to people who can't pay the bill is unacceptable. It is difficult to imagine a more elemental need, with the sole exception of air, and there is good reason why, in a country like Ireland, people believe that water is so abundant that there is no reason to charge for it. They are wrong.

Nothing is free. Water has to be paid for via taxes or by some other method, and the process of purifying water to a high standard and delivering it to householders is not free. The volume of water use increases sharply the higher you go up the socio-economic scale,[356] so any charge that is not volume-related, particularly a flat charge, is particularly regressive.

There are major problems with water supplies in Ireland. Residents in many rural parts of Ireland suffer a dreadful quality of drinking water, which causes serious illnesses,[357] and there are severe water supply problems in the greater Dublin area, which are predicted to get worse. Plans to draw water from the Shannon to supply the east coast have drawn firm opposition.[358] Waste of water is not just expensive, it is also environmentally damaging, as water often has to be drawn from rivers at just the time that they are lowest in the summer, and the process of purifying the water itself has an environmental cost.

Investment in water supply has been lamentable in Ireland, largely because when a resource is free, it is difficult to justify spending any money on it. In addition, because domestic water in Ireland is completely unpriced, there is no incentive to use it in any way wisely. At present, almost all businesses pay water rates that bear little or no relation to their water use and certainly are not metered to discourage waste. Opponents of water charges retorted to McDowell that the cost of reading proposed water meters would be prohibitive. It is a very simple task to produce meters which would automatically report their usage. When was the last time that somebody came to read your telephone meter?

A more reasoned objection to metering is that there would be a significant cost to installing the meters; and that this investment could be better be put to fixing leaks in the water system, which is responsible for the loss of up to 50 per cent of all water supplies.[359] This is a false dichotomy; indeed the metering of water supplies is likely to improve the ability to track down leaks in the system.

- Automated water meters should be fitted to every premises, which would report their water usage live to a computerised system.

- Domestic addresses should be credited with a free daily supply of water to cover their basic needs for each resident, based on PPS address records – see **Remember Everybody** on page 56.

- Water used in excess of this allowance, and all water used by businesses, should be billed at a commercial rate.

- The funds raised should be ring-fenced for investment in the water supply system.

- Bills should be delivered electronically wherever possible, in a standard format that can be uploaded to screen-scraping websites, and include daily water usage.

- All data on individual daily water usage by businesses and households should be made available to screen-scraping websites – the household usage data should be anonymised, but the commercial use should not.

- Water conservation tips should be made available alongside tools for householders and businesses to compare their water usage to other users.

- Prizes, raffles and other non-cash recognition should be organised for commercial and domestic users who have lower-than-average use and who succeed in reducing their use the most.

- Meters should also be installed at all major junctions in the water supply system.

- The volume of water passing these junctions, along with the data on the volume of water passing all the branches from each junction would quickly give an indication of where the most serious leaks are in the system and allow the prioritisation of pipe replacement.

- Customer meters that have a constant flow of water that never goes to zero would indicate a leak somewhere on a private premises, and this could be detected and the customer alerted automatically.

- Meters should contain a feature that they can be remotely set to stop water flow in an emergency, such as when the water supply has been contaminated, and allow the householder to reset the flow for normal or non-consumptive use when they have been informed of the nature of the problem.

Waste Problems

Some waste items cause particular problems, but there are solutions.

ATM Receipts
Bank-machine receipts are a significant proportion of street litter,[360] [361] but there is a simple solution. Require the banks to give the customer the option of not having the machine print one if they don't want it and charge a small levy – say 10c – if they do. People choosing to pay for the receipts would be unlikely to throw them away.

Batteries
Batteries are a small volume of waste, but are very problematic because of the highly toxic materials contained in them. Separate recycling facilities are being developed for batteries to counter this problem. It is not possible to ascertain what proportion of batteries placed on the market are currently being recycled, but it can be assumed that there is very great scope for improvement, given that the EU target is only to achieve a 25 per cent recycling rate by September 2012.[362]

Battery technology, particularly that of rechargeable batteries, has advanced rapidly in recent years. This has been particularly driven by demand from mobile phones and laptops. Anyone who remembers the briefcase phones that boasted they could go for an entire business day before needing to be recharged overnight will appreciate the advance that made possible the slimline mobiles that we now charge for one or two hours a week. Switching to rechargeable batteries for as many appliances as possible would have a clear environmental benefit, vastly reducing the amount of batteries that need to be disposed of.

Ireland is tied into the globalised manufacture of both the batteries and the electronic products that they power, and a small country like Ireland is unlikely to have a major impact on the consumer electronics market. The aborted attempt to compulsorily replace incandescent with CFL light bulbs[363] should show the dangers of government-mandated technology. A wiser move is to mandate the outcome and allow technology companies to use their ingenuity to achieve that outcome in the best way they can.

There is considerable integration between companies that manufacture batteries and that manufacture the electronics that use them. Not all electronics are suitable for the current generation of rechargeable batteries – smoke alarms are one example – but newer versions of many products have moved away from disposable batteries to integrated rechargeable batteries.

Pressure on electronics companies would encourage them to accelerate this development of both batteries and electronics to increase the use of rechargeable batteries. If such pressure in Ireland was seen to work, it would be replicated elsewhere, further accelerating the process. Here's how:

- Establish the exact proportion of conventional and rechargeable batteries currently being placed on the Irish market, including those sold as components of other products such as mobile phones or MP3 players.

- Mandate that any company placing batteries on the market supply a proportion of rechargeables, with a fixed target, escalating each year.

- Allow companies to trade their proportions, so a company exceeding their target could sell the excess to one failing to meet it, at a market rate.

Chewing Gum

The success of the plastic bag levy brought forward an imitator, a tax on chewing gum[364] to deter the filth that sticks to almost every visible street surface in our towns and cities. Unlike the manufacturers of plastic bags, the chewing gum companies had access to powerful lobbying. The US-based companies brought in the American ambassador to Ireland to put pressure on then minister Dick Roche not to proceed with the measure. Roche caved in and instead settled for a weak-kneed contribution to the clean-up and research from the manufacturers.[365]

For all the wrong reasons, Roche was right not to proceed. A levy on chewing gum would not have worked as well as the plastic bag levy. Firstly, there does not exist the problem of consumers viewing gum as free and therefore consuming it wastefully. The product is already priced, even if that price does not reflect the full cost to society.

Secondly, not all gum-chewers spit their gum on to the streets, and the tax would levy them all equally, failing to create any incentive to improve behaviour.

Predictably, the solutions promoted by the gum companies have had little success. There is some clean-up work done, but nothing like enough to create an impact. It is a classic example of an initiative failing because the wrong person is doing the job.

In this instance the government is trying to micromanage a problem created by the chewing gum companies and their customers (against principle 10 on page 15). Government is not much good at managing, let alone micromanaging, and they lack the ability or motivation to succeed. In this instance they are:

- mandating a particular mix of research, cleaning and public education to be carried out, and

- mandating the price that should be paid for this by the gum manufacturers

There is no evidence that the government even has the skills to succeed at such a complex task, which is far outside its core competencies. A far better solution would be to leave the entire business up to the gum companies:

- Independently monitor the amount of gum stuck to the streets.

- Set exacting standards for improving the situation over a defined period.

- Require the gum companies to pay into a fund in proportion to the volume of gum that each places on the Irish market annually, agreeing between them the level of payment.

- Allow the gum companies to set their own mix of education, research and clean-up, and to manage the entire process as they see fit.

- Fine each of them a set percentage of their annual turnover if they fail to meet the required standards for improvement – the fines should be set in advance and known to all.

In this scenario, the gum companies have it in their power to succeed, and they suffer the consequences if they fail. It is a good example of the right person doing the right job.

Littering

Littering is a pervasive problem, and failure to punish it not only undermines the incentive to behave in a sociable way, it also undermines the law in the eyes of society. There is a great diversity in littering, from flicking a cigarette butt to dumping household waste by the street to organised criminal gangs dumping hundreds of tons of hazardous waste in the Wicklow Mountains. Dumping on private property is a particular problem, as it causes problems in prosecuting the offenders. Once dumping at a location begins, it can attract people dumping more rubbish, making the problem very difficult to solve.

At levels of dumping below organised crime, appropriate punishments are difficult to gauge because of the inadvisability of sending otherwise law-abiding people to prison and the difficulty of pitching fines high enough to be a deterrent, but low enough that they would not unfairly hit people on low incomes who may be trying to evade waste charges. Part of this problem will be solved by shifting the payment for waste charges on to the point of purchase, rather than the point of disposal – see **Rubbish Charges** on page 147 – but it is inevitable that there will still be a problem with littering. The solution is restitution:

- People who have been the victim of dumping on their private property should report the dumping and request a clean-up to the national authority proposed under **Rubbish Charges** above.

- The authority should also take note of public locations where there is a litter problem.

- People guilty of simple street littering should be issued with a fixed-notice penalty by litter wardens, in the way that on-the-spot penalties are issued at the moment.

- On-the-spot penalties should range from a half-day to five days' clean-up.

- Penalties in court should range from one day to 400 days clean-up (40 Saturdays a year for ten years) for organised criminals, implemented after they complete any prison sentence.

- Cleaners would be ordered to show up at an appointed hour, mostly on Saturday mornings, with photo ID.

- Litter wardens should give each cleaner a pair of gloves and a high-visibility jacket with a number prominently displayed and rubbish sacks to fill, and supervise the operation.

- Rubbish sacks should also bear the number of the cleaner.

- Any person who was disruptive or was not working at an acceptable work rate during the day would be given a warning, and if they failed to comply, would be sent home.

- Any person who, at the end of the day, was judged to not have made an adequate effort would be given the option of completing a fixed extra amount of cleaning.

- Cleaners who did not do this, or did not show up, or were sent home during the day would be referred back to court and sentenced as appropriate.

Sorting out Recycling

Visibility can change people's behaviour for the better, and when that visibility is to one's neighbours, the pressure to do the right thing is all the stronger. Colour-coded wheelie bins are now installed all over the country, each for a different type of waste, but there remains the problem of people not bothering to put the right thing in the right bin, causing difficulty for the recyclers.

The colour-coding should be retained, but only for bin lids. All new stocks of bins ordered should be transparent, to make it plainly obvious to anyone who sees it – the rubbish collector and the passing neighbour – if the wrong kind of rubbish is inside. In theory, bin collectors are meant not to collect bins that have the wrong thing in them, but in practice this is difficult to enforce. Transparent rubbish wheelie bins would make this easier, but it would also exploit the fact that most people don't want to be seen by their neighbours as people who do the wrong thing.

Planning

The Flood/Mahon tribunal demonstrated that there is an avalanche of corruption in the Irish planning system.[366] The tribunal necessarily dealt with past problems, but there is evidence that the problems are continuing. In 2001, Kerry County Council discovered that many of its planning officials were involved in serious irregularities. Killarney town engineer and senior Kerry planning officer Donal Mangan had submitted planning applications in the names of people who had no knowledge that their names were being used. He was also involved in unauthorised site clearance on lands which he owned and was involved in other planning applications without declaring his involvement. Mangan was suspended from work for seven days. Twenty-four other staff were sent a warning notice, with no penalty.[367]

The interim report of the Flood tribunal made clear that planning corruption can be hugely rewarding, with lands increasing in value by millions and sometimes hundreds of millions. But the problem is not, or not exclusively, the lack of penalties for corruption. The penalties are a dam trying to keep back a tide of money. A stronger dam might hold back the tide a little longer, but the amount of money to be made through corruption is so enormous that there is no hope of building a dam that can withstand such pressure.

While the planning system is staffed by humans, the only solution is to remove the huge incentives to corruption and to put distance between the decision-makers and the applicants, so that planners can have a measure of independence from the people applying to them. With more than one planning authority for every 50,000 people in Ireland, even if there was no corruption, there would still exist the problem that planners and applicants are frequently known to each other, and planners can come under undue pressure to make favourable decisions to their neighbours.

The proposal in the upcoming planning act to impose an 80 per cent windfall tax value uplift from rezoning[368] is welcome but inadequate. Lobbying from farmers has excluded its application on compulsory purchase orders and one-off housing,[369] seriously diluting its benefit, but the key problem is that there is no way of enforcing this tax properly unless we have a systematic way of knowing who owns, buys and sells what property. See **Who Owns Your House?** below for proposals on this.

Dogs in Mangers
In Dublin's South William Street, about 100 metres from Grafton Street – the most expensive street in one of the most expensive cities in the world –

most of the buildings have four or five stories. At 4pm on a dark winter evening, most of the ground floors are occupied, but 70 per cent of the windows in the upper floors have no lights on. The author is aware that most of these floors are either unoccupied or very sparsely used. This might be unsurprising in the recession, but this has been the case right through the boom years. How could there be so much unoccupied space during an intense property boom when companies were paying more than €600,000 key money for tiny shops near by?[370] The answer is money – too much of it.

Each building is worth millions; but these buildings were bought in the 1980s or earlier, at very low prices, and because many of them are in a state of disrepair, the rates are low. Throughout the boom, there was spectacular growth in the value of these buildings, up to 25 per cent per year – a great return on the owners' investments. The return was so great that renting out the building would only marginally have increased their return – renting would give a return of 5 per cent or less, and out of that they would have to pay for refurbishments, create a street access, meet fire regulations and possibly pay more rates for the period that the building is unlet. So the property owner has two choices:

- Do nothing and see their asset produce a return of 25 per cent.
- Organise and pay for refurbishing the building, go to the trouble of seeking and keeping tenants, risk paying increased rates and get a return of 30 per cent.

It is easy to see why someone who is already a millionaire would not bother with all that work when it would only slightly improve their financial position. And landlords aren't people who are used to doing a lot of work. Now that the boom is over, landlords who are emotionally attached to the prices and rents of the good years are likely to sit on empty buildings rather than crystallise their losses. The landlords, for the most part, are behaving rationally but society is not. In particular, it is crazy that there should be no incentive to make full use of city-centre properties.

South William Street is certainly not the only street to suffer from this slow dereliction, and it is easy to see how such a narrow, centuries-old street would be difficult to develop, but despite our property boom, there are hundreds of vacant buildings and sites all over Dublin and other towns in Ireland. Dublin 1, Dublin 3 and Dublin 8 are particularly badly hit. When property prices skyrocketed, how was it that the owners didn't sell up and cash in? Were they being totally irrational?

Business & Finance magazine reported in 2000 that the bulk of the development land in Dublin was owned by just eight speculators – Gerry Gannon, Michael Cotter, Mickey Whelan, Tom and Mick Bailey, Joe O'Reilly and Brian Wallace, David Daly, Joe Moran and Liam Carroll.[371] Between them they sat on almost all the land that could be developed, with Gannon alone holding more than 320 hectares. If the land was held by a larger number of speculators, there is no doubt that some would break ranks and sell up, having hit the jackpot. However, with each so wealthy that they controlled an average of 10 per cent of the available land, what would happen? If one of them put even one tenth of their holding on the market, that would be 1 per cent of all the building land in the city, a market-moving amount. Each hectare was valued at the time at between €3m and €4m.

There is no evidence that they colluded together to constrict the supply of land – that would have been a serious criminal offence – but they didn't need to. It is likely that they each correctly concluded that putting even one-tenth of their holding on to the market would increase supply to such an extent that it would devalue the rest of their holdings by more than the payment they would receive for the portion they were selling, so it was a rational strategy for them to drip-feed the market. In the process, they hugely increased the demand for building in totally inappropriate sites in the counties around Dublin, while leaving suitable sites undeveloped. With the boom over, many of these sites may not now be developed for many years.

This is not just a waste of the sites themselves. Derelict and underused sites drag down the value (social and financial) of all the property around them. The most spectacular example is the Guinness brewery in the south-west inner city. This sprawling site is 70 per cent derelict, because technological changes allow a brewery to work in a much smaller area, and the vastly profitable Diageo[372] just haven't bothered to do anything much with the leftover land.

This has caused a whole zone of dereliction and under-use of land in Dublin 8. To see just how grim it is, try to find Victoria Quay. You probably don't know the name – it is the south Liffey quay leading up to Heuston station as you leave the city centre. It is one long, filthy, featureless wall, one of the most inhospitable places in Dublin city. If you go there, the closest you will get to human contact is to be drenched by an articulated lorry speeding through the puddles of rainwater. Other European cities celebrate their riverbanks with sidewalk cafes, buildings with river views and all sorts of culture. You'd get more culture in your pint of Guinness than on Victoria Quay, and it's all because of the dereliction.

Dereliction sucks the life out of a neighbourhood. Not only do derelict buildings and sites become an eyesore, they discourage investment in adjacent sites and drag down their value. Desolate places make many people afraid even to be there, and they are probably right. Rudolph Giuliani, explaining his extraordinary success at fighting crime in New York, wrote about what he called the Broken Windows Theory.

> The theory holds that a seemingly minor matter like broken windows in abandoned buildings leads directly to a more serious deterioration of neighbourhoods. Someone who wouldn't normally throw a rock at an intact building is less reluctant to break a second window in a building that already has one broken. And someone emboldened by all the second broken windows may do even worse damage if he senses that no one is around do prevent lawlessness.

Property gains its value from the value of the property around it. Rather than punishing people for improving their properties, it would make more sense to punish those people who allow or encourage dereliction, and thereby encourage them to behave differently.

Know What We Have

A key problem for property taxes in Ireland is knowing who should actually pay them. At the moment, there is no single definitive record of property ownership in Ireland or its use. The first step is to record and codify this. Recent developments in technology have made this a much easier task. Computer databases that used to contain lists such as names and addresses can now also hold location information in a way that is easy to enter and retrieve. This technology is used in the GPS satellite navigation systems that show a map on a screen and guide cars street by street to their destination. Also, the Department of the Environment maintains a database to record where every one of our tens of thousands of national monuments is. A larger version of this database could record all property in the country and refer to it reliably by its ULI – see page 52. This system should contain the PPS number of the owner of every property in the country.

In 2002, the owners of a 43-hectare site called Jackson Way claimed €47m in compensation from the state for disruption that they claimed was caused by the building of the M50 motorway.[373] The ownership of Jackson Way was disguised by a complex structure of companies, and it remains unclear who the true owners were.[374] However, there is strong suspicion that money would ultimately go to people who were able to influence the course of the motorway, and knew its route before it was publicly announced. This leaves the possibility that corrupt politicians and businessmen could arrange state building projects to massively enrich themselves and hide behind an impenetrable veil of secrecy. The Planning Tribunal expended a lot of time and great expense trying to discover its true owners.

When a residential property is sold, the vendor is asked to sign a declaration saying whether it was their principle private residence (exempt from capital gains tax). There is no way to verify whether the person has made the same claim on various properties without an exhaustive search of property transactions. Anyone brazen enough to lie is likely to get away with it. It is unacceptable in a democracy that the state cannot routinely determine the ownership of property to verify tax compliance. The owner (or owners) of any property should be required to have their PPS number listed. Here's how to do it:

- Launch a five-year project to log every property in the country in a database.
- Every property transacted in that period should be added to the database at the time of transaction.
- Owners of properties not transacted would be requested to claim ownership during that period.
- Properties that are not claimed would be the subject of a search at the Land Registry, and any other sources that could determine its ownership.
- A fee of €1,000 would be charged against owners who did not register their properties.
- Occupants of property that is unclaimed would be given a 25-year bond to represent its ownership, which would make them liable to the property taxes and any other liabilities of owners.
- The bond could be bought and sold on the open market.
- If the owners presented themselves within the 25 years of the bond, they could reclaim the properties (subject to any existing legal limitations) by paying all the back taxes, plus interest, to the bond holder.
- After 25 years, the bond would become full ownership of the property.
- Unoccupied and unclaimed property is dealt with under **Value Deficit Tax** on page 162.

The database would allow routine checks to confirm compliance with capital gains taxes, other property taxes and money laundering legislation.

Preventative Measures

It's not often, but once in a while Comreg, the telephone regulator, does something right. When criminals used phone numbers acquired from South Pacific islands for internet scams, Comreg ordered Irish phone companies to block phone numbers of Norfolk Island, Solomon Islands, Tuvalu and Comoros, unless an Irish customer requested the connection.[375] This had the effect of immediately ending the incentive for criminals to use these numbers for scams and also of punishing the offending telephone companies by denying them incoming international calls. This principle should also be used against renegade states that accommodate money-laundering and other activities that help criminals to hide their assets or protect them from seizure.

The British Virgin Islands in particular are a haven for the proceeds of crime, because they allow companies registered there to hide the identity of their owners and directors, frustrating attempts to track down criminals' assets. The lands at Jackson Way were owned through a British Virgin Islands company.[376] Ireland should prohibit the ownership of property by, or payment of any state benefit to, any entity where the ultimate ownership is disguised using an offshore structure.

Value Deficit Tax

The Commission on Taxation was established in February 2008 to review the structure, efficiency and appropriateness of the Irish taxation system,[377] and it reported in September 2009.

There are basically two types of taxes – taxes on running and taxes on standing still. Income and corporation taxes raise revenue from economic activity – the more you work, the more you pay. Taxes on wealth and property do not discourage economic activity, but there is almost none of this type of tax in Ireland. The only property taxes are commercial rates, and as these are mostly paid by commercial tenants, they operate more like a tax on the size of a business. Our only domestic property tax (stamp duty) is levied on the transaction when the property is sold. Wealth can stay, entirely unproductive, in families for generations without any tax liability. The disproportionate use of taxes on activity has a distorting effect on our economy, penalising people who create wealth to favour those who inherit it.

The Commission recommended a Site Value Tax which, excluding agricultural land, was included in the 2009 Programme for Government, although it is not clear how much determination there is to implement it.[378] It would tax the value of a site, regardless of whether it was being used, or used to its full value. So a hotel occupying a city-centre site would pay no more tax than the derelict site next door. The theory is that this would remove the effect of property taxes that encourage dereliction by taxing the value of the developed property.

This does not go far enough. A derelict site drags down the value of the sites around it, as well as itself. Well-developed sites improve the value of the surrounding sites, so the Land Value Tax, while it doesn't reward dereliction, doesn't punish it either. The zoning map on mentioned on page 166 can be used to determine zoned value of any property.

All taxes should reward behaviour that benefits society and focus the cost of anti-social behaviour on those responsible. In the case of property tax, good development should be rewarded, and dereliction and inappropriate property use should be taxed. All properties should pay a Land Value Tax based on the values from the zoning map; however, in addition:

- The actual use of each property should be established.

- The occupation of residential properties would be determined by the Revenue taxpayer database – see **Remember Everybody** on page 56.

- Commercial properties would be determined by the employment records of the businesses that use them.

- All properties that do not appear on either list would be considered vacant unless evidence was presented to the contrary.

- Such a decision could be appealed by property owners.

- Evidence of occupation, such as electricity bills and water charges (see page 150), would be considered in the event of a dispute.

- Properties that are not, or not fully, occupied would attract a **Value Deficit Tax** (VDT).

- The VDT would be 20 per cent of the fully used value of the site – so someone leaving a property vacant for five years would pay its entire value in tax.

- In the first instance, the Land Value Tax and the VDT for residential properties would be collected by adjusting the tax-free allowance of the owners of the properties.

- Unoccupied properties where the owner cannot be traced and the VDT is unpaid for five years would revert to the state in payment of unpaid tax.

Who Owns Your House?

Do you own your home? The Irish lead the world ranking of home ownership; 83 per cent of homes are owner-occupied, far ahead of the next two countries on the list, the UK and Australia, who both have rates of 69 per cent,[379] so the chances are that you do, but how do you know that you own it? Almost certainly because you (or your mortgage provider) have a document in a file from the previous owner saying that they sold it to you. But how do you know that they owned it? Because they had a document from the owner before that, and so on.

Every time a property is sold, solicitors for the purchaser must trawl through this ever-expanding bundle of yellowing papers, sometimes going back centuries, with many documents written longhand in the obscure legal language of a bygone age. In addition, this system is very expensive and time-consuming, and it is often difficult to predict how long it will take. This is an extra burden of cost on the economy and adds to the transaction cost of moving house, which imposes illiquidity on the housing and labour markets – see **Stamp Duty** on page 47. Despite the money and time it costs, there are frequent disputes over property ownership, which only hit the headlines when celebrities are involved.[380] This is a system that belongs, literally, in the Dark Ages. It should be modernised immediately. Here's how:

- The database proposed under **Know What We Have** on page 160 should replace the Land Registry, the Registry of Deeds and all other forms of recording property ownership.

- The state would issue licences to any reputable business applying to act as property transaction agents – banks, firms of solicitors or others – and give them secure access to the database in a manner that recorded the institution and the individual within that institution who accessed or altered the database.

- People wishing to buy and sell property would both present themselves to such a business, with identification that proved their identity and PPS number.

- The property transfer agent would record the transaction and enter it in the database, including the purchase price.

- They would also record whether the property was to be the primary residence of the buyer and what the new address of the seller was to be.

- The purchase price of the property would be placed in escrow by the property transaction agency.

- The fee paid for the service would include an insurance policy to indemnify the property transaction agency in the event that any party suffered a loss as a result of an error.

- The licence to act as a property transaction agency would include a requirement that the agency has adequate control systems and insurance in place.

- The section in the Revenue responsible for maintaining the database would contact both parties using details from their tax records (not supplied for the purchase) to confirm that they both agreed to the transaction.

- The revenue would inform the property transaction agency of the amount, if any, due in capital gains tax or other charges over the property.

- If no objections were received within one month, the property transaction would be finalised and the appropriate amounts released from escrow to the seller and the revenue, including other taxes due on the property and any mortgages on the property would be settled.

- The law would be changed to say that ownership is determined by the record of the owner held in the database.

Options to Buy

Much of the land held by speculators during the boom was not owned by them at all. They had not bought the land; they just bought a contract with the owner that said that they had the right to buy that land for a specified price when they chose to in the future. These are called options. In Ireland these options were usually a contract between a developer and a farmer whereby the farmer was paid an upfront amount to agree to sell to the developer for a fixed price if the developer exercised the options at any point in the future.

This is problematic because it allows people to effectively own land without their names ever appearing on any documents connected with it. The options are private contracts which never need be disclosed unless a dispute arises over them. This prevents conflicts of interest from being evident, and it also allows developers to block developments by anyone else, at relatively low cost.

- Legislation should be passed to require all options contracts on property to be registered with the property transaction agency, and to make all other options contracts invalid in law.

Appropriate Land Use

In January 2008, the auctioneers group, the IAVI, reported that there were about 40,000 empty apartments in Dublin, [381] and it is likely that this number has increased since. These dwellings could be put to good use – see **New Housing Agency** on page 173 – but perverse incentives during the boom led to the most bizarre and inappropriate developments. While there were many apartment developments, large areas of our inner cities still remain derelict, but there were huge, unnecessary and now empty housing developments in other areas.

These new ghost towns are concentrated far from services and city centres – they seem to have been built specifically to ensure that anyone who did live in them would be entirely car-dependent, condemned to long commutes to work or any services. They are concentrated in the border areas, the midlands and the west of the country. One estate in Longford was described in *The Irish Times*:

> Wires dangle from the sides of most of the houses, plastic sheeting is still attached to the windows, and water pipes from the empty buildings lead nowhere. Mildew is growing on some of the walls, while weeds are beginning to sprout through some of the fresh tarmac.[382]

Rural villages, such as Rathcormac in County Cork, are swamped with unsold properties.[383] Some developments seem to be unusable because of lack of infrastructure.[384] In December 2009, an exhibition was held by a firm of architects suggesting uses for these ghost estates, with ideas ranging from the practical – knocking them down and returning the land to farmland – to the bizarre – creating a "City of the Dead" to house corpses.[385]

Of course, much of what was built in the boom is now occupied, and the build quality is mostly acceptable. Many of the properties that are now unoccupied can be put to use; but there was a distinct trend, particularly in the latter part of the boom, to build completely pointless housing estates at very low quality in locations where it was always difficult to imagine anyone would want to move to. How did all of this rubbish get built?

People usually act rationally, even if their personal rationale is detrimental to the rest of society. Bubbles are irrational, but somebody participating in a bubble is acting rationally from their point of view. If you see that many people before you made a lot of money developing shoddy property, then it is not so irrational to follow the same path. Once on that path, the incentives in the economy will decide where the development goes.

Frequently, developments on green-field sites throughout Leinster were aimed at the commuter market, for people driving every day to Dublin, often with spectacular round-trip distances. The Advertising Standards Authority held that an advertisement by Hook and McDonald estate agents claiming that a Gorey, Co. Wexford, housing development they were selling was within "easy commuting distance of Dublin by rail" was false; the first morning train from Gorey did not arrive in Dublin until 10.23am.[386]

How can it be that so much housing was built for Dublin workers in such far-flung places, when there is so much space for development within walking distance of major centres of employment? The fact that there was so much irrational development is proof that there were irrational incentives. If development in the future is to be more rational, these must be removed.

- Property in city centres can have hideously complex title problems, making it unmarketable – this can be solved by a single central record of property ownership, described in **Who Owns Your House?** above.

- Many properties in city centres are being hoarded by people who have no intention of using them – this can be solved with the **Value Deficit Tax** described above.

- Corrupt and incompetent zoning and planning in local authorities has permitted the most inappropriate developments, and this is addressed in **Zoning** below.

Zoning

The map is an incredible tapestry of colour. The curve of the canals makes it recognisably Dublin city, but it has an intricate matrix of colours, which make it unlike any other map. This is the zoning map produced by Dublin City Council, and the key to the colours explains its purpose: they say things like **Residential Retain** or **Industrial Rebuild**. With years of work, the planners decide on the most appropriate development for an area, a street or even a single building. This is the document that is used to guide planning decisions.

While some people may argue with the details, it is clear that we can make a decision as to what should go in a particular space. In some cases, this is very specific (Stephen's Green should stay a park); in other cases, it is quite general.

Rockall is worthless. The 21-metre high Atlantic outcrop 430 km from Donegal may have valuable mineral reserves in the surrounding seas, but the 700 square metre rock is no good to anybody. Put it on Grafton Street, or in the centre of London, New York or Tokyo, and 700 square metres of property would be worth a huge amount. The difference is not quite location, location, location; it is what that location provides. Land in city centres is worth more because of what surrounds it. Services are important, but so are the surrounding properties. A shop on Grafton Street is valuable because all the other shops on Grafton Street are valuable. The value in property cannot be seen in isolation; for the most part it is a function of the value of the surrounding properties and services. No property is an island, at least no valuable property is.

It is reasonable for society to impose restrictions and requirements on what citizens do with their privately owned property, because if it does not, then the Tragedy of the Commons effect (see page 18) would leave individuals and society worse off. Zoning property is a way to make the planning process simpler and more predictable. Changes to zonings can make a vast difference to the value of property, and this increase in value has a long record of corrupting the planning process. Firstly, it is unjust that such value should go to the property owner. It is society that provides the surrounding properties, the services and the infrastructure that make the property more valuable, and the fact that other property owners do not get the same permission increases the rarity and therefore the value of the zoning or planning permission for those who receive it.

Secondly, it has proven disastrous for public administration to gift the huge increases in value that can come from rezoning and planning permissions to property owners. It is completely unrealistic to expect that these millions will not find their way back into the decision-making process. The long-ignored Kenny Report recommended in 1974 that all of the increase in the value of land as a result of rezoning over and above 25 per cent would go to the state,[387] a very modest proposal which would still leave lucky landowners with a considerable and completely unearned profit. Zoning is a function of the state that confers a right on some property owners and denies it to others. It is wrong to randomly reward already wealthy land speculators at all, and the huge wealth that this has artificially created has utterly corrupted the zoning process, with enough land now zoned to house three million more people in the country.[388]

Property zoning needs to be completely reformed. Here's how:

- A single national agency, based in the Department of the Environment, should take responsibility for all zoning.

- As far as possible, zoning decisions should be based on publicly stated, measurable, falsifiable criteria.

- **Publicly stated** – all the criteria that the zoning authority uses to make its judgements should be available on their website.

- **Measurable** – the criteria should be measurable, in terms of populations of towns, distance from amenities, population growth rates; the criteria should be mostly numeric.

- **Falsifiable** – in the great majority of cases, the criteria should allow ordinary members of the public to determine the result of a rezoning before it happens and be able to clearly see if the decision does not meet the published criteria.

- Zoning plans should be published on a fixed cycle, such as every five years, following the release of census data.

- The agency should run a website where any person could enter their ULI and be informed of its exact zoning status.

- Landowners could also use the website to find out about any proposed change in zoning during the revision of the plan.

- Landowners whose property was proposed for rezoning would have the right to be notified, particularly if the rezoning would increase its zoned value and expose them to VDT.

- Landowners could request their land not to be rezoned, and this request would normally be granted, providing that it did not conflict with the stated criteria.

- The zoning record of all land would be stored and be available to the Revenue authorities, searchable by its ULI.

- When any property is sold, the process of transferring ownership would include a check of this database to see if it had been rezoned since it was last transacted – see **Who Owns Your House?** on page 163.

- When a rezoned property was sold, a determination would be made as to the proportion of the value which was attributable to the rezoning, and this proportion of the sale price would be payable to the Revenue, not the seller.

This calculation could be made largely automatically by benchmarking the property against other properties in the area of the current and previous zoning, and it would make rezoning financially irrelevant for property owners. It would eliminate corruption in the rezoning system, because nobody would be motivated to try to influence decisions.

Planning Permission

Planning permission is essentially the implementation of zoning, in the way that the courts implement the law made by the Oireachtas. The current situation is problematic because both these functions are held by very closely related departments in small local authorities. It is fundamentally bad practice to fail to have a clear division between these two interrelated functions, and such a division is probably not possible at all in such small organisations.

The defensiveness of planning departments around the country, and their resistance to accountability, indicates that they are aware that they are not behaving in an appropriate way. Councils have a record of frustrating public participation in the planning process. The €20 fee for lodging a planning objection, although created through legislation, is clearly designed as an anti-consumer measure. However, even getting to the objecting stage may be a feat. In July 2009, the Ombudsman Emily O'Reilly submitted a report to the Dáil detailing how local authorities were charging people up to €5 for photocopying each A4 page that members of the public were entitled to see, 100 times the market rate.[389]

Between county, town and city councils and others, we have more than 90 local planning authorities in our tiny country.[390] Even if this was not daftly inefficient, it inevitably means that planners are more likely to come under improper pressure from applicants that they know personally and be unable to deal with large planning applications competently because of their small scale. Planning is easily the single most corrupt area of Irish life. It should be reformed so that all applications are dealt with by a single national authority:

- The authority should be funded exclusively by application fees.

- It should be independent of any ministry, and in particular of the zoning body.

- Applications should be accepted online, in electronic format only, capturing the PPS number (or company registration number) of the applicant, as well as the ULI of the property concerned.

- The authority should have access to the database of property ownership and automatically reject applications from parties that do not have ownership of the property.

- All applications should be available online, and comments and objections should be submitted online, at no charge.

- The website should accept the email address of any person and offer an email alert to that person when an application is submitted for properties with a specific ULI or ULI range.

- Members of the public should also be able to create an alert for any application made by a particular person or company.

- Planning officers should be available to prospective developers for meetings to clarify what types of buildings would and would not be acceptable, at a fixed hourly fee.

- Such meetings should all be minuted.

- All planning decisions should be published on their website in a scrapable format with all data points, including a code number to represent each planning officer who dealt with the case.

- Minutes of pre-application meetings should be placed on the website.

- When an application is made, the minutes of the pre-application meetings should be linked to the application on the website.

- The authority should have no power to grant planning permission in contravention of zoning principles.

- Where the authority believes that an application in contravention of zoning guidelines has merit, at its sole discretion, it may refer it to a small independent board, for stated reasons.

- This board should have the power to give the planning authority permission to consider the development against stated revised zoning guidelines.

- All the dealings with this board should be published on the planning website.

- An Bord Pleanála should continue to operate as an appeals board.

Inappropriate Developments

Some developments are inappropriate in any circumstances, and for the maximum clarity, the zoning agency should issue blanket guidelines for types of applications that will always be rejected, such as once-off housing developments.

Planning Special Projects

As mentioned under **Concerts** on page 79, large-scale music festivals can benefit Ireland on many levels, but they have experienced significant problems gaining planning permission in the past. Other major projects, including major infrastructure and manufacturing plants, incinerators, sewage plants and power stations have generated a lot of opposition. Debate has often been of a poor quality, with the merits of the development and the merits of the location being confused.

The problem is that these planning applications are frequently site- and developer-led, and this is compounded by the fact that county councils are too small to have the necessary skills to make educated decisions on these matters, which are essentially national in character. The order of decision-making must be changed, and it must begin with debate. As these are national projects, the onus is on national government to come to a decision about how many, if any, of a given project should be sited in the country. When this decision is made, the zoning authority should draw up guidelines as to the features of a site for the project, including the size, type of location and required infrastructure.

Within these guidelines, the planning authority could then invite applications from developers who had a site that met the criteria. In some projects, it would be appropriate for the state to acquire the optimum site by compulsory purchase.

Retention Permission

At present, a system exists whereby the owner of an unplanned development can apply for planning permission retrospectively, with an extra cost usually less than €100,[391] a tiny amount in comparison to the cost of building. This is the worst of all worlds. The lower the extra fee, the more the developer is tempted to build first and apply later, knowing that they will put the developers in a difficult position where they are very reluctant to order someone to knock down their house, even if it would not have secured planning permission in the first place. If the fees are increased to become a real deterrent, this would create an institutional incentive to encourage a greater proportion of retention applications, because of the greater income that they would generate. The solution is this:

- The new planning authority should consider all applications without reference to whether the property has already been built or not.

- The fee for a retention application should be equal to the fee for a standard application.

- Where permission for retention is granted, a note should be put on the file of the property in the Revenue property database to this effect.

- When a property that was the subject of a retention planning permission is sold, 20 per cent of the sale price should be retained by the Revenue as a penalty fee for the retention permission.

- Where the retention permission relates only to part of a property, the value of that part should be calculated, and 20 per cent of that portion should be retained by the Revenue.

Rental Properties

The law requires that all rented residential properties in Ireland are registered with the Private Residential Tenancies Board.[392] As of August 2009, the board's amateurish website listed a total of 205,889 properties that between them had 527,621 bedrooms.[393] Ireland has the highest rate of home-ownership in the world, with 83 per cent owner-occupancy,[394] but that still leaves 17 per cent of our 4,422,100 people[395] living in rental accommodation, which is 751,757 people, or 1.42 people per bedroom. Given that renters are far more likely to be single, that means that either renting is very cosy indeed or that there are many properties that are rented but not registered.

This illustrates the problems with disconnected databases. The PRTB's register is disjointed and poorly stored in a slew of Microsoft Excel files – it's not actually in a database at all. If this was done properly, all properties would be recorded as either being the owner's residence or a holiday home or a rented property. Any property that didn't show up on one of those lists should trigger the owner being billed as vacant for Value Deficit Tax (see page 162), which would give the owner a powerful incentive to register it correctly.

Better Signposting
Navigation-by-pub may be a humorous Irish way to give directions, but signposting, street names and building numbers are disastrously bad in Ireland. This is a problem that is recognised less the better a person knows the country. For delivery services and particularly tourists, it is a major drawback. We need a single national agency, with no more than five staff, to set standards that make navigation through our streets and rural areas easy. Put simply, every road and street should be named, and that name should be displayed, facing every direction at every junction.

Property owners should be required to display their street number, where it exists, so that it is visible from outside the property. The agency should contract out the installation and maintenance of street names and the enforcement of street numbering to a suitable bidder. They should also publish their standards for signage on their website and include a section where people can report instances of inadequate signs in their area, meaning that any work the agency would need to do to check up on compliance by their suppliers would be largely done for them, for free.

New Housing Agency

There are tens of thousands, perhaps hundreds of thousands of vacant homes around the country. In Dublin alone there are 40,000,[396] and a great many of these will come into the possession of NAMA (see page 43). There are also almost 60,000 people on the local authority housing list.[397] The more than 90,000 people on rent allowance are paid €500m per year, which they hand over to their private-sector landlords.[398]

This is not two problems – it is one solution. The state, if it acts wisely, will come into the possession of a huge amount of housing. At a stroke, it can end the housing list. Even if much of the housing is in inappropriate areas, it is inconceivable that the rest cannot be used to meet the requirements of people in need of housing. If it isn't, what else is to be done with it? There is a need for good planning to make sure that housing is allocated in as beneficial a way as possible.

Building Neighbourhoods
Many areas with a high proportion of local-authority housing also have a high level of anti-social behaviour, low levels of educational achievement and other social problems. No doubt many of these problems are simply a feature of the profile of people who avail of social housing, but it is likely that these problems are magnified by groupthink and the reinforcing effect that happens when everyone around takes part in behaviour that would not otherwise be seen as normal. This is particularly the case for children. It is important that we do not create ghettos and that any population shifts that the state can influence have the tendency to encourage all areas to have a good social mix.

In the past, local authority housing has not only tended to be concentrated in particular areas, but was stratified, so that different types of tenants were bunched together. Often it appears that there was no reason for this other than a desire to build highly uniform developments.

It is important to make sure that people have as much of a stake in their own home, and their own neighbourhood, as possible. This may result in a loss to the state – giving away housing at below market values – but since this financial value would be impossible to realise anyway, it makes sense to accrue the most social benefit. All local authority tenants should be put on a path towards owning their own home.

- A single national office should take possession of all vacant housing that comes into state possession, whether through NAMA, vacant local authority houses or otherwise.

- The local authorities currently managing the housing lists should be asked whether any currently has a database suitable for managing the entire country – if they do it should be taken over, and if not it should be created.

- The office should also take control of all applications for public housing and manage the system in a single database.

- The ULI of each vacant property should be recorded in the database.

- Other features, such as size, number of bedrooms, wheelchair accessibility and any other items of relevance should also be recorded.

- Each applicant should be asked to pinpoint the area or areas where they want to live and the housing requirements they have, and this information should be entered in the database.

- A detailed socio-economic profile of the applicants should also be recorded, as well as a profile of the existing occupants of the properties in the surrounding areas.

- Properties should be allocated on a basis of matching people with the property that best meets their needs and of creating or keeping as close to a balanced social mix in each area as is possible.

The right to buy a home can be a powerful incentive towards social improvement, and even if the tenants have not yet exercised that right, its existence is likely to encourage them to maintain their home in better order. In this, there are two competing values. The purchase prices must not be so high that they are unattainable for the tenants, but they must be high enough to maintain some element of realism. Tenants who buy their home must have the right to sell it on – otherwise they don't really own it – but if they do, they should not be entitled to another social housing property in their lifetime, and if they sell it on at a profit within a short time, the state should claw back a declining portion of the profit.

- A market price for each property should be established and this recorded at the time that the person is given possession of the property.

- Rents should be set based on the ability to pay and reviewed on this basis annually.

- Rent paid should go towards the capital value of the property set at the time of allocation, and the tenant should be given regular statements.

- Tenants should receive a statement of the total rent paid and the remaining capital value unpaid once per year.

- Tenants should be given the opportunity to buy out the remaining capital value of their home at any time.

- If that property is sold on by the tenant, the difference between the purchase price and the sale price should be payable to the housing agency, less ten per cent for each year that the tenant owned the property outright.

- Tenants who are evicted for anti-social behaviour or misdeeds should lose the right to have the rent they have paid treated as capital payments.

Flood Insurance

The price of all new homes should be required to include 25 years' flood insurance, paid by the developer, and of course then internalised in the price the developer charges the homeowner. This will slightly reduce insurance costs for the homeowner and slightly increase their mortgages, probably cancelling each other out, although the bulk-buying of the insurance could lead to a small net discount. However, it would internalise the cost of the flooding risk into the highly visible price of the house.

Without a doubt, insurance companies would carefully examine the flood risk in the areas that they are insuring and price their insurance accordingly. This would give house-buyers a strong incentive not to buy houses in areas at high flood-risk and, therefore, give developers a strong incentive not to develop in flood-prone areas.

Insulate and Build

Ireland's energy requirements expose us to a significant threat of a global constriction in the oil supply, which would lead to a rocketing in the price of all energy. This risk alone is enough justification to make large investments in reducing our energy consumption, without ever considering the reduction in pollution and greenhouse gas emissions that would result. Heating accounts for 44 per cent of our total energy needs, by far the largest single consumer, double that used by transport.[399] Insulation is a very easy and effective way to reduce our energy consumption. A €20 lagging jacket can save €90 per year on the heating bills of a typical house.[400]

Because of the collapse of the building industry, there is very little building work going on in 2010, leaving many thousands of builders unemployed. On page 138 there is a proposal for the state to become the employer of last resort for people who can't find work. An obvious task for the unemployed builders is to put them to work insulating every home, business and office in the country, so that they meet the highest possible thermal standards.

- Builders should be trained to assess the insulation needs and potential of all types of buildings.

- They should also be trained to examine historic energy bills and assess the potential energy and financial savings possible from the insulation.

- A major insulation programme, for every home in the nation, should be begun.

- The cost of the labour should be shared equally by the state and the householder.

- The cost of the materials should be met by the householder.

- Energy supply companies should be required to cooperate with a scheme whereby the portion payable by the householder is added to the energy bills of the house and paid off at a rate that equals the financial benefit of the energy saving, so that the householder experiences no increase in outgoings.

- Once the cost of the insulation is paid off, the householder would benefit from a significant reduction in energy bills.

The skills of many builders who came to the industry during the boom would need to be updated to match this work, and this training should be a high priority for the training scheme mentioned on page 135 for state-provided training of people who can't find work. Training builders to insulate existing properties is a valuable goal, but why stop there?

Passive Buildings

A passive house is a building which requires little or no energy input for heating or cooling to keep it comfortable.[401] Typically, the energy consumption for heating and cooling is about 5 per cent of that of a conventional house.[402] This design is achieved by making thicker walls, using innovative windows and taking care with the materials in each aspect of the house. Examples built in Ireland include a house in Galway[403] and an office building in central Dublin.[404]

About 20,000 passive buildings have been built around Europe since the standard was developed in 1990.[405] Some of these features add to the construction costs of the building, but others – such as the absence of need for installing a heating system – reduce it. As with all new technologies, the cost is likely to reduce quickly as it becomes ubiquitous. Passive buildings in Germany have already been constructed with no extra construction costs above that of standard buildings.[406] Of course, once the building is built, it is dramatically cheaper to run, saving the occupants thousands of euro every year for its entire life.

- With immediate effect, all planning permissions issued should mandate the passive standard – since there is little building happening at the moment, this will not create a burden on builders or developers.

- The programme of state-provided training mentioned on page 135 should include training all builders who want to remain in the industry to convert their skills to building passive houses, schools, offices and other buildings, and all new buildings in the state should be built to this standard.

Duration of Permission

At present, planning permission in Ireland has a life span of seven years. It is not wise to allow developments that are approved with out-of-date technology. Permissions should last two years, at a maximum.

Local Authorities

A common refrain in recent decades in Irish politics has been that local government does not have enough power or enough funding. This statement is made as an unsupported truism without any need to justify why local government should get more power. Local government is responsible for 20 per cent of all state expenditure,[407] and there is no evidence to indicate that they achieve better value for money than central government, so precisely why they should be rewarded with an increase in either power or funding is not clear.

The Department of the Environment lists the functions of local government as:

- Housing
- Planning
- Roads
- Water supply and sewerage
- Development incentives and controls
- Environmental protection including rivers, lakes, air and noise
- Recreation facilities and amenities
- Agriculture, education, health[408]

but this is a vast overstatement of their functions. Agriculture, education, health, most environmental protection and almost all roads are controlled and funded by ministries or other national agencies. Their provision of recreation facilities is paltry in a country that has more private golf courses than public playgrounds. The building of local authority houses has ground to an almost complete halt. The little that remains – planning and waterworks – varies from utterly corrupt to merely incompetent. How this can justify one-fifth of all state expenditure is bewildering. So what do they spend the money on?

The salary for each of the 883 part-time members of the 29 county councils and five city councils in Ireland is about €17,000,[409] but with a wide variety of allowances and expenses, the average amount they take home is over €33,000.[410] There are also the town and borough councils to pay for.

The distribution of town and borough councils is bizarre, to say the least. Excluding the special arrangements in Dublin, there are just five cities deemed to deserve a borough council. Kilkenny, with a population of

8,591,[‡] is one of them, but Drogheda, population 35,090,[411] is not. There are 75 town councils, including Granard, Co. Longford (population 933), Lismore, Co. Waterford (790), and the town council that serves the 401 souls of Ballybay, Co. Monaghan. That county, with a population of just 56,000, has a wealth of local government. It has five towns that are deemed to justify a town council (Monaghan Town, Carrickmacross, Castleblayney, Clones and Ballybay), but Fingal, with almost half a million people, has only one, Balbriggan. Dún Laoghaire-Rathdown, with 200,000 people, has none.

Mark O'Keeffe, the Fianna Fáil candidate in Macroom, may not be best pleased with the levels of representation in local government. He secured 2,397 first preferences in the 2009 local elections but failed to win a seat.[412] His party colleague, Gary Wyse, got just 315 first preferences in Waterford East and took a seat on Waterford County Council.[413] If Wyse only claims the average expenses of a councillor, he will earn €165,000 over the five years before he needs to seek re-election, €523.80 for each vote he got.

The origin of this vast imbalance lies with a failure to reform local government to reflect the huge population shifts in recent years. This could cause an imbalance in representation, unfairly biased against Dublin and its satellite towns, but it doesn't. Local government is so ineffective that it does not provide any worthwhile service. What does the abundance in local government do for Monaghan? It is not easy to tell, but a good way to work it out would be to look out for the services that are performed with gross incompetence. Local government, toothless enough to start with, has had many of its remaining powers stripped away in recent years, and it is difficult to spot any ill-effects. The disorganised incompetence of the Health Boards has been replaced by the micromanaged incompetence of the HSE, but health is too big a topic to be a good example here.

The unrealistically high level of political representation in local government leads to an exaggerated sense of entitlement, whereby people come to believe that counties and towns with tiny populations "have a right" to a host of services paid for by central government that are simply not viable for such small areas. These unrealistic demands are given credence by the huge number of local politicians who, with nothing better to do, seek visibility by supporting or creating local campaigns. In August 2009, the two Fianna Fáil TDs for Sligo resigned the party whip in protest at the

---

‡   22,179 people live in the conurbation that is Kilkenny, but only 8,591 people live inside the boundaries of the Kilkenny borough council, another failure to redraw boundaries to match population shifts. There are also intense turf wars around the cities of Cork and Limerick, with the counties unwilling to cede powers over areas of urban growth.

withdrawal of totally medically inappropriate cancer services from Sligo Hospital.[414] (See **Centres of Excellence** on page 213.)

The Taxi Fiasco

Local authorities lost their power to regulate taxis to the Taxi Regulator in 2004.[415] The utter fiasco that local authorities made of this simple service is difficult to believe, and it is notable that the situation was not resolved until the courts ruled that a corrupt attempt to give the taxi monopoly even more power was an unconstitutional restriction on the rights of other citizens to enter the profession. Before that, Dublin City Council, and most other local authorities, had restricted the number of taxi licences it issued, creating an artificial market where licences changed hands for up to €100,000 and organised crime flourished.

Most licences were owned by people who had never driven a taxi, but rented the licence out for hundreds of euro per week to those who did. It seems clear that this was a method of laundering the proceeds of crime, with the licences being held in the name of people who were not the beneficial owners. The involvement of the criminal Frank Dunlop, renowned for bribing politicians, in lobbying for the taxi drivers makes it seem likely that money from drug-dealing, prostitution and bank robberies ended up in the pockets of corrupt councillors and officials. Now all has changed. With a staff of just 23[416] (less than one for each local authority that previously administered the service), the taxi regulator has vastly improved the service.

The lesson is simple: local authorities are too small. They cannot deliver services that are in any way complex, because the level of knowledge needed to manage that complexity simply cannot be contained in a town council that covers 401 people. Local authorities are too small because Ireland is too small. If we start dividing up our little country, there just isn't enough expertise to manage a separate taxi service for each little bit. Ballybay may be different from Dublin, but it isn't so different that the two can't be covered by the same taxi regulator. It is very difficult to think of any service where Ireland is too large a unit to deliver that service nationally.

Scrap Them

The areas that local authorities are responsible for show up in this book with remarkable regularity. There is not a single redeeming feature of local authorities. If they were just expensive baubles to flatter the egos of third-rate politicians, they might be tolerable, but it is worse than that. There is almost no area of their responsibility that does not need major reform, such is the incompetence of the management. Almost everything that they touch turns to ashes, from maintaining the electoral roll (see page 184) to planning permission and zoning (page 166) and organising the water supply (page 150). Once the functions of local government that need major reform are reorganised on a rational basis, there is nothing left. Ireland is a tiny country, smaller than many units of local government in other countries. We don't need local authorities. They should be scrapped.

Unused land held by local authorities should be given to NAMA for distribution and use for the public good (see page 44), and the functions of local authorities that have not already been assigned to other bodies should be assigned to a single national body.

Electoral Reform

Many critiques of electoral systems focus on arranging the system to ensure that more or less of a particular type of candidate is elected. This is nonsense. The proper function of democracy is to ensure that pressure is put on leaders to do the will of the people and to remove those who don't. Once in office, the system should pressure them to behave as good legislators, as judged by the voters.

Some people make the point that the electoral system should be designed to achieve a particular result, such as avoiding or encouraging coalitions, or small political parties, or extremist political parties. Almost all of these demands can be traced to the desire to achieve an unfair electoral advantage, such as the two failed referendums in which Fianna Fáil tried to introduce the British electoral system to Ireland.

Ireland's multi-seat STV system is far superior, because it ensures that the votes of a far larger proportion of the electorate go to electing our parliament, but it is not perfect. The best electoral system should make sure that:

- every voter's vote weighs equally
- every party gets, so far as practical, a share of seats in the parliament that matches their share of the vote
- the winning candidates from each party are the candidates with the most support within that party

Our STV system achieves these goals pretty well, although the system is not perfect. In 2007, Fianna Fáil won one seat for every 11,150 first-preference votes, while Sinn Féin got one seat for every 35,852[417] first-preference votes.‡ So the best system would also:

- elect representatives that represent the broad range of interests in the country, in terms of region, gender, social and economic class
- encourage politicians, once elected, to act in the interests of the whole country

Our electoral system fails these tests miserably. Representatives are 86 per cent male, with an average age at election of 53.[418] § While Irish

---

‡ First-preference votes are not the only votes important for winning seats, and this disparity must be seen in conjunction with the fact that Sinn Féin performs poorly at winning transfer votes.

§ The average age of the founding fathers of the United States was 42, and four of the most influential delegates – Alexander Hamilton, Edmund Randolph, Gouverneur Morris and James Madison – were in their thirties, although they were hardly an advertisement for gender or ethnic balance.

constituencies give a good regional spread, it is clear that some professions have far more clout than others in the Dáil.[419] Doctors, farmers, publicans, teachers and lawyers take the lion's share of the seats. Engineers, manufacturers, entrepreneurs and manual workers hardly get a look in. While it could be argued that voters choose smart professional people, this does not explain why teachers and publicans should hold such an advantage over engineers and entrepreneurs.

What is notable is that the protected sectors – people employed in the public sector, or in areas that are protected by subsidies and regulation – have a vast advantage over those who work in competitive and internationally traded areas. It is difficult to tell which is the chicken and which is the egg here. People who work in the protected sector don't have to worry too much about their jobs and can afford to spend their energy on things that make it likely they can get elected, such as going to meetings in the middle of the day.

It is also possible that the reason these professions are so protected is precisely because they have such a grip on political power. Either way, what is important is that a system with such a disparity in representation is not healthy.

Over-representation can also harm the national interest. The last seat in each constituency is typically decided by a couple of hundred (sometimes a couple of dozen) votes, so very small, well-organised groups can swing the vote and put a candidate over the top in return for extraordinary concessions from the candidate's party. This can give some groups power vastly disproportionate to their numbers, such as the Aer Lingus workers who were given "letters of comfort", apparently guarantees of jobs for life, on the instructions of then Minister for Tourism and Transport Seamus Brennan, who was keenly aware of their power to deliver votes to marginal Fianna Fáil candidates in north Dublin constituencies.[420]

This is not to be confused with a small political group getting a foothold in the Dáil in proportion to their vote; merely ensuring that the political power of a group does not exceed what they deserve, given their vote.

Too Many TDs

Ireland has been hit by crises, but it seems that our politicians don't have much to say about it. In June 2009 (and not for the first time), the Dáil stopped operating because nobody had anything to say about anything.[421] Our TDs are well enough paid, so if there is nothing for them to do, this is a clear case of overstaffing. New Zealand has 122 parliamentarians[422] for a country with the same population as Ireland, compared to our 226, and New Zealand is not a member of any organisation such as the EU, which is responsible for a high proportion of Ireland's lawmaking. There is no justification for the number of TDs to exceed 100.

Changes to Make

Electoral reform is a delicate subject. It is important that any reform preserves the advantages that we have. The goals of electoral reform are to:

- ensure that, as far as is practical, the parliament reflects the will of the voters
- prevent small groups having disproportionate interest, without disenfranchising them
- encourage politicians to legislate for the national good, not sectional interests

A list system would achieve these advantages, but they have problems of their own.

List System – Best Loser

The best-loser lists in Germany are where parties' top losing candidates are awarded seats to bring their party up to its deserved number of seats. With this, some constituencies have two MPs, where others of equal size get one, and some voters' votes have twice the value of others. This is not ideal for a democracy. This system also is capricious in that a party that gains less than 5 per cent of the vote, or three constituency seats, is not awarded any top-up seats in parliament, meaning that for smaller parties, getting votes in the right places is more important. A single vote can lift a party from having no seats to thirty or more.

List System – Party Set

It is common in Europe for parties to set a national or regional list, with the party leader at the top. Depending on their success in the election, the candidates further down the list win seats. In Ireland, this system would be totally unacceptable, because dissent within parties is essential for our democracy. Given the nature of our larger parties, we could be certain that the party leadership would ensure that awkward members would find themselves at the bottom of the list.

Currently, the party leadership must contend with the possibility that if they try to thwart a popular rebel, she may run as an independent and take the seat from them. This system would result in parties of yes-men and women. Regional lists are preferable, to ensure that the parliament is not dominated by people close to the centres of political and media power, but the regions need to be large enough to make sure that we are not electing glorified parish councillors.

New Electoral System

The solution is to have primary elections to choose the lists:

- The country is split into no more than four constituencies – the current European Parliament constituencies would be fine.

- Each constituency is allocated a share of a total of 100 TDs based on its population.[‡]

- Two months before the general election, every voter – not just party members – goes to the polls and takes the ballot paper of one party of their choice.

- They rank the candidates from that party in order of their preference.

- The votes are counted and the candidates of that party are ranked according to the rules of a preferendum.[423]

- The general election proceeds, and two months later, voters are given the option of voting with an X for a single party.

- The general election votes are counted in each of the four constituencies, and parties are awarded a number of seats that best matches the share of their vote.

The Electoral Register

The electoral register in Ireland is a disaster. It contains an unbelievable 700,000 errors,[424] 30 per cent of the total entries. A roomful of monkeys with typewriters could do better, and that could well be the chosen data-entry method of the local authorities responsible for compiling the register, given the spelling errors on the multiple entries for the author on various electoral registers, including at addresses up to 20 years out of date.

The electoral register should be abolished. The PPS database that is maintained by the Revenue is far more accurate. In addition, many people, including employers, the subject of the records and the Revenue themselves, are highly motivated to keep it accurate. It contains all the data that is required – name, address and date of birth of the person. The only possible extra requirement is to record the citizenship status of the people on the database, to determine what elections they are entitled to vote in.

This information should be added, and the Department of Justice, Equality and Law Reform's naturalisation process should include an update of this record, to keep it accurate. In the run-up to each election, the Revenue should supply an extract from their database to send out polling cards.

---

‡   There would never be a need for boundary changes, just adjustments to the number of TDs to match population shifts. On this basis, the 2006 census would give 28 TDs to Dublin, 26 to the rest of Leinster, 25 to Munster without Clare and 21 to Connaught, Cavan, Clare, Donegal and Monaghan combined.

Electronic Voting

I bought a new computer to write this book, and I splashed out. Flat screen, powerful processor, snazzy optical mouse, DVD burner, the works, costing €599. A budget machine, priced €309, would have done, but the latest technology was too appealing. That price was for a single computer, but you might expect that someone buying 5,000 computers would have more negotiating power. The Department of the Environment didn't.

Unbelievably, the Department of the Environment paid €5,000 for each of the computers that were intended to be used for the electronic voting system, and the electronic voting computers were nothing like as powerful as the €599 one used for this book. In fact, the electronic voting computers were less powerful – *far* less powerful – than the €309 budget computer. These were not in any way special machines; they were old, out of date Microsoft Windows computers with the outdated and unstable Microsoft Access '97 database software on them. Somebody made a killing.

The disaster that was the attempt to introduce electronic voting was largely down to the incompetent handling of the process, but also about our complex electoral system. For one thing, it proved that there was little chance of electronic voting being cheaper than our current pencil-and-paper system, and that is enough to justify leaving well enough alone.

Polling Stations

Some computerisation, however, could benefit democracy. The requirement to vote at a particular polling station is an anachronistic hangover from the days before information technology and modern communications. It inconveniences voters, because the polling station that they are assigned to may be in the opposite direction to their journey to work or school runs, and the voter might pass several other polling stations on their journey. At present, each of these polling stations keeps a printed list of the people entitled to vote there and draws a line through the name of each person who votes. A very simple modernisation of this system would put a single online computer at each polling station, linked directly with limited access to the PPS database that is the electoral roll.

The polling officers would then record on the computer system, rather than on a piece of paper, that the person has voted. This would allow voters to vote in any polling station in their constituency, increasing convenience and voter turnout.

Marked Register

The marked register – the register of electors that was used in the polling station, with a single line drawn through the name of each person who has voted – has been made available to politicians.[425] There is a story, perhaps apocryphal, of a constituent telephoning the late Tony Gregory TD for help with a problem. Gregory asked the caller whether he had voted for him, and the caller assured him that he had, not aware that the TD had reached for his copy of the marked register and seen that the person had not voted at all. Gregory gave the shocked constituent terse advice on exactly what to do with his problem and terminated the call.

Whether the story is true or not, the right to secrecy of the ballot should extend to whether someone has voted, as well as who they have voted for. The element of the PPS database recording who has voted should be reset at the close of polls, with any data indicating who has or has not voted being deleted.

Party Funding
At present, politicians and their parties can accept donations from individuals and companies. Limits have been reduced to €4,000, with all donations over €2,500 requiring disclosure, and they apply to campaigning organisations as well as parties.[426] Once elected, the parties are then entitled to state funds which are intended for running the party and may not be used for electoral purposes, although it seems clear that if the state pays for the administration of a party, the party is then free to spend on elections those donations that it would otherwise have had to spend on administration. These measures are sensible, because it is unjust to allow political parties which are supported by the rich to have an unfair advantage over others in elections, but even €4,000 would be an enormous amount for most people to donate to a political party in a year. The spending limits that operate in elections seem to be ineffective, since a large proportion of candidates cannot afford to even approach the limit.

There is also scope for abuse. Declan Ganley, the founder of Libertas, gave €200,000 of his €300m fortune[427] to that organisation, but in the form of a loan.[428] It is unclear when, if ever, the loan will be repaid, and this raises the issue that wealthy people, including people with no right to vote in Irish elections, could influence the outcome of elections by giving loans, along with a nod and a wink to indicate that if it is never repaid, and there will be no enforcement. This is on record as happening in the UK.[429] Another possibility for abuse is that a wealthy organisation could direct their businesses to provide goods or services to parties at far below the market value for them to use in elections. This has already happened in the past, although the motivation at the time was not to avoid spending or donation limits, but to defraud the Revenue of VAT.[430]

The objection to state funding of political parties is that this forces the taxpayer to pay for politicians. It is not valid. Firstly, as we have seen in the recent past, the damage that politicians can do is many orders of magnitude greater than the cost of running a political party. Secondly, elections must be paid for, even if they are kept modest. If the taxpayer does not pay, then democracy is devalued because somebody hugely wealthy will, and will also call the tune.

- All political parties should receive funding to fight general elections from the state, in proportion to the people who choose their ballot paper in primary elections.

- Political parties should be required to hold a single set of bank accounts for all their elections expenses and pay all expenses from that account.

- All funding from the state should be paid into those accounts, and all transactions on those accounts should be published in their entirety, as they happen.

- Elected deputies who wish to devote a portion of their salary to party ends should be permitted to do so by having the money paid directly to the party account.

- All other political donations should be prohibited.

- Parties should be prohibited from taking loans from entities other than financial institutions regulated within the state.

- The full details of all such loans should be published as they happen.

- No person should be permitted to act as guarantor for any such loan.

Fixed Term Elections

At present, the Taoiseach decides the date of an election, unless the government loses a confidence vote in the Dáil. Neither of these are satisfactory ways of deciding the date of an election. The Taoiseach calling an election on a date of his or her choosing is a clear invitation for the government to try to manipulate the date of an election to its own advantage. An election triggered by the government loss of a confidence vote in the Dáil is more rational, in that a government cannot govern without a majority.

In recent years, Dála have generally run for almost their full terms, but in the early 1980s, there was a spate of elections, with three in 18 months alone.[431] It is important that elections do not become devalued by frequency to the point that democracy is undermined. Italy is often cited as a country where this has happened, although it is not clear if the frequency of elections is caused by the debasement of politics or vice versa. Opposition parties in Ireland or any other democracy are, by definition, below what they regard as their optimum performance, so are tempted to have an election at any point to return to what they may see as their rightful strength, regardless of the benefits of the election for society.

Also, in recent years the traditional day for an election has been tinkered with. All elections since 1938 had been held on a Tuesday, Wednesday or Thursday; in 1997 the day was switched to a Friday amid discussion of allowing the maximum number of people to vote, in particular allowing students to return to their parents' house to cast their vote. The 1995 divorce referendum was held on a Saturday, transparently aimed at ensuring a high turnout among the urban voters and students, moving Ireland closer to the continental model of weekend voting.

Weekend voting proposals can be problematic because of the reluctance of some Christians and Orthodox Jews to vote on their Sabbaths. Also, the practice of closing national schools to facilitate elections is disruptive to education.

- A constitutional change should be made to require fixed terms for the Dáil, with five years between each election.

- Elections should be held on the Saturday between week 20 and week 21 (late May) before any school holidays begin, so that fewest people will be away (see page 123).

- Polls should open from 6am to midnight, longer than any shift that somebody might be working that day and so that Orthodox Jews can travel and vote after sunset, when the Sabbath ends at about 9.30pm.[432]

- Referendums should be required to be held on a Saturday with the same voting times, on a date set in the enabling legislation.

In the event that the government loses the confidence of the Dáil, the Dáil should be given the opportunity to elect a new Taoiseach. If the Dáil fails to agree a Taoiseach, the president should call an unscheduled election to elect a Dáil to serve the remainder of the Dáil term. The date of the next scheduled election would not be changed, so politicians seeking advantage by manipulating the date of the election would have to balance this with the fact that the Dáil term would be shorter and that they might suffer a negative public reaction from such antics.

Major Financial Crime

Taxes, the billionaire Leona Helmsley said, are for the little people.[433] One could be forgiven for thinking that she was responsible for enforcement policy in Ireland.

Ireland has been the site of recurring tax evasion, major corporate fraud, insider trading, bribery, price fixing and other major financial crime through the years. Some cases have been revealed in the media, who are sometimes brave enough to even name the perpetrators, but there are almost never prosecutions, let alone jail sentences for the perpetrators. The loss to taxpayers, customers and shareholders runs into many billions.

By contrast, 334 people were convicted of social welfare fraud in the first 11 months of 2009, with 45 people given the Probation Act, 208 given fines, nine given community service orders, 19 given suspended sentences and two imprisoned.[434]

Italian food giant Parmalat collapsed in 2004 when a gigantic fraud that left a €14bn hole in Parmalat's finances was uncovered. The four-year investigation that followed was massively complex and ended with the jailing of the company's founder for 10 years. It involved many interlocking companies across Italy, the US and the Cayman Islands; and a tiny subsidiary, Eurofood IFSC Ltd, based in Ireland, was at the centre of the fraudulent operation.[435] [436]

Irish Gardaí are all trained at the Templemore College in County Tipperary, which "has been designated an Institute of Higher Education ... The 2-year Student/Probationer Education Programme is accredited by the NCEA with an award of Degree in Police Studies. The college also offers a Bachelor of Arts (Police Management) Degree for senior Garda Officers."[437] It has been observed that the huge disparity between the prosecution of fraudsters at the top and the bottom of the social scale is evidence of a class bias in law enforcement, and this may be true.

However, at least an equal problem is that, even with the best of intentions, the Gardaí are hopelessly outgunned in education and resources by major financial criminals. The Gardaí simply cannot be asked to juggle resources between burglaries and billion-euro fraud. There is nothing in the make-up of An Garda Síochána that suggests they are the right organisation to pursue crimes which are sometimes so complex that only a handful of people in the country can understand them.

What is required is an effective method of detecting and prosecuting major financial crime, and this should be done by a single dedicated organisation which has the skills, resources and motivation to succeed, and which is not distracted by any other tasks.

Money Laundering

The tribunals, along with many law enforcement authorities around the world, have made an important discovery: major crime is a means to an end – money. Attempting to restrain amoral criminals from their activities is almost impossible. It is far more effective to change their motivation by making their activities unprofitable, hence the focus on money laundering. At present, if you want to open an account of any type with a financial institution, you are required to provide various types of proof of identity, in an attempt to prevent people from opening accounts in false names. In the event of a tax or criminal investigation, the bank or the account holder may be required to divulge details of their accounts. This is not enough.

Firstly, a determined effort can overcome the requirements for proof of identity. Secondly, this of no use to the authorities unless they know by some other means that there is criminal activity going on. Such an enquiry can only ever confirm what they already know. The state should require that every type of account – credit or debit – should have the holder's PPS number attached to it.

- When a customer opens an account, they should be required to supply proof of their PPS number, and this number should be attached to all the accounts that they have with that institution.

- Banks should be required to contact all their account holders where the information is missing and advise them that they must supply proof of their PPS number within one year.

- Withdrawals should be tightly restricted until the PPS number is supplied.

- Funds in accounts that are not claimed within one year should revert to the state, with a record taken so that the account holder can make a claim later, to cater for people who were unable to come forward at the time.

- Accounts where the PPS number does not match the personal details on the account should be frozen, pending an investigation by the Revenue.

- The movement of funds between accounts should then be made available to the state for data-mining.

This is, in effect, a diminution of banking privacy, but it is limited, and justified. Data-mining would allow automated queries to find suspicious patterns without revealing any identifiable details from an individual's bank accounts. Where data-mining gives reason to believe that a crime is being committed, the state is justified in using the information to investigate and prosecute the crime.

Once the state has visibility on the money coming in and out of accounts, the prosecution of tax-evasion, particularly on a large scale, becomes much easier. Elsewhere in this work there are proposals to attach PPS numbers to all property transactions (see **Who Owns Your House?** on page 163) and cars, boats and aircraft (see **Vehicle Records** on page 257). With this information, it is possible to run a database query to find individuals who have deposited and spent more money in any given year than they have earned or borrowed. While they may have an innocent explanation, it would be at least worth asking someone with no apparent income other than social welfare how they are able to buy expensive properties and cars, as drug-dealers and other criminals have done in the past. This information should be used by Revenue to target their tax audits.

Tribunals

The tribunals that have been a feature of Irish political life do not have a good reputation for value for money. In some cases they have got to the truth about corruption in Irish public life, but at gigantic expense. That expense has been used by those who don't like the findings as an argument that political corruption should not be investigated at all. A key flaw of the tribunals is their inability to convert evidence of wrongdoing into prosecutions and convictions. Despite this, the subjects of investigations are entitled to full legal representation as though they were on trial, as a result of a 1970s legal precedent,[438] meaning that each of sometimes dozens of people can have large legal teams of barristers and solicitors, all being paid huge amounts. It may be possible to attribute some of the length of proceedings to legal egos, but we must also consider how they are motivated. Lawyers are paid for by the day, so it is impossible to imagine that, given a huge incentive to drag proceedings out as long as possible, they would not respond to such an incentive.

To an extent this is not avoidable. People accused of serious crimes cannot be justly denied the right to mount a defence, but it is clear that other countries can have much more effective ways of prosecuting major white-collar crime. The prohibition on tribunal investigations leading directly to prosecution originated before the court ruling that all participants were entitled to full legal representation.

The system of Tribunals of Enquiry should be entirely abolished and replaced with special prosecutors, along the lines of those that operate with Grand Juries in the United States. A special prosecutor is an external lawyer who can be appointed by the US Attorney General or Congress to investigate government officials for misconduct while in office; they have proven successful at rooting out wrongdoing there.

The Director of Public Prosecutions in Ireland is simply not configured in a way that would allow it to prosecute this type of crime, and there is no evidence that there is any reason to complicate the DPP any further.

All pretence of political impartiality should be dropped. Groupings with more than 10 members in Dáil Éireann should be given a fixed budget, proportional to their numbers, to hire a special prosecutor of their choice. The prosecutors would have powers to compel witnesses and offer immunity deals to those who would otherwise refuse to comment on the grounds of non-self-incrimination. Hearings would be held entirely in private, and once the prosecutor felt she had enough evidence, she could launch a prosecution in the courts.

Tax Amnesties
Tax amnesties in the past have rightly attracted much criticism. A system whereby wealthy tax cheats could gain immunity from prosecution, penalties or even paying their taxes by simply paying a fraction of the taxes that were originally due was exceptionally unfair and motivated people to continue their cheating. People who availed of the 1993 amnesty were required only to pay 15 per cent of the tax originally due, with no interest, no penalties and immunity from prosecution. Because penalties in such cases are twice the unpaid tax, this means the cheats got a minimum of a 95 per cent reduction in their liability. In addition, the fact that tax cheats could make payments without specifying what tax was evaded allowed them to make small payments, safe in the knowledge that if they were ever the subject of a Revenue investigation for the rest of their lives, they could halt it immediately and claim that the amnesty payment was in relation to that particular incidence of tax evasion. Despite all of this, we need a new amnesty.

It is not possible to prosecute offences that have already been prosecuted or ones for which amnesties have been given, but we can create a new offence regarding future behaviour. We should create a new criminal offence: retaining the proceeds of crime. Regardless of whether the original crime has been (or can be) prosecuted, it is plainly immoral and not in the common interest to allow someone to retain ill-gotten gains. In addition to any criminal penalty, courts should be empowered to order criminals to return funds and other property to their rightful owners, and they should have the power to order them to be detained indefinitely until they comply. The provision should apply equally to bank robbers and tax evaders.

As a parallel measure, a crime should be created of assisting someone to evade this law. This would be aimed particularly, but not exclusively, at professionals who may be tempted to advise or assist their clients in disguising proceeds of crime, or moving them out of the country, and it should carry a long prison sentence.

Tackling Financial Crime

Insider trading is a stock market term that refers to insiders – people who have knowledge not generally known – trading in shares at the expense of the rest of the market. In the United States, this crime is taken very seriously, and Ivan Boesky, Charles Keating (an associate of presidential candidate John McCain), Andy Fastow and Jeff Skilling of Enron, Bernie Ebbers of WorldCom, Dennis Kozlowski and Mark Swartz of Tyco, Eugene Plotkin of Goldman Sachs and Jennifer Wang of Morgan Stanley have all served long prison sentences for this crime.[439] To comply with legislation on insider trading, shop-floor workers at Irish branches of US multinationals who have received shares as part of their annual bonus are regularly told that they are not permitted to trade in those shares, usually in periods running up to product launches.

In 2007, the Irish Supreme Court ruled that Jim Flavin, head of DCC, had held price-sensitive information about Fyffes' share price at a time that he ordered the sale of €106m worth of Fyffes shares.[440] DCC is a large procurement, sales, marketing, distribution and business support company that has little public profile because it has no retail function.[441] Jim Flavin was also a director of Fyffes, so he was about as inside as a trader could get. DCC netted a profit of about €85m from the deal.[442] Jim Flavin has never been arrested or prosecuted in relation to this deal. Regardless of whether Jim Flavin has committed a crime, it is clear that the prosecuting authorities in Ireland are simply not equipped to deal with offences such as insider trading or cartels. There is a model for a separate prosecuting authority – the British Serious Fraud Office.[443] The fact that it is regularly called the Serious Farce Office and the Seriously Flawed Office in the British media does not indicate that it is well respected, and with good reason. Its record on prosecutions is poor, to say the least.[444] Ireland should learn from these mistakes, but there is no doubt that a single, dedicated service for prosecuting major financial crime is needed.

- An investigating and prosecuting body organised around 20 or so small autonomous teams of three to five investigators, each team with a mix of specialist skills, should be created.

- This body should be designated as Gardaí, within the meaning of the Constitution of Ireland, and members should have ranks accordingly – see **More Gardaí** on page 227.

- The body should take over the functions of the Fraud Squad and the Criminal Assets Bureau.

- High-calibre graduates from financial courses should be recruited internationally and trained as investigators.

- Administrative support and specialist skills such as data recovery and legal research should be available to the investigative teams.

- They should be empowered to begin investigations on their own initiative, as well as on foot of a complaint.

- The organisation should be required to submit an annual report which would include the average cost per investigation for the organisation and also would be broken down by investigative team.

- The annual report should also quantify the average benefit of each investigation to consumers and to the taxpayer, also broken down by team.

- The organisation should have the power to prosecute crimes in the courts and to offer immunity from prosecution in exchange for evidence supplied.

- An internationally recruited director should manage the day-to-day running of the organisation.

- An Irish-recruited chief executive should have the power to award bonuses to investigators, based on the annual report, but without day-to-day control of the organisation.

- Staff in the organisation should be forbidden from taking up any position with a company within their powers of investigation for ten years after they leave the employment of the service.

The object is, of course, to create a competitive atmosphere among people who have no allegiances to established power structures in Ireland.

Quangos

Ireland has a lot of quangos, including (take a breath) Advisory Board for Irish Aid; Advisory Committee on Cultural Relations; Advisory Council to the Commission for Taxi Regulation; Advisory Science Council; Aer Rianta; Affordable Homes Partnership; Agency for Personal Service Overseas; Appeal Commissioners for purposes of Tax Acts; Aquaculture Licences Appeals Board; Area Development Management; Army Pensions Board; Arramara Teoranta; Arts Council; Attorney General; Ballyfermot Partnership; Ballymun Partnership; Bioresearch Ireland; Blanchardstown Area Partnership; Blood Transfusion Service Board; Bord Altranais; Bord Bia; Bord Fáilte Éireann; Bord Glas; Bord Iascaigh Mhara; Bord na gCon; Bord na Leabhar Gaeilge; Bord na Móna; Bord na Radharcmhastóirí; Bord o Ulstér-Scotch; Bord Pleanála; Bord Scannán na hÉireann; Bord Uchtála; Bray Partnership; Broadcasting Commission of Ireland; C.E.R.T.; Campus and Stadium Ireland Development; Canal Communities Partnership; Censorship of Films Appeals Board; Censorship of Publications Appeals Board; Censorship of Publications Board; Central and Regional Fisheries Boards; Central Bank and Financial Services Authority of Ireland; Central Fisheries Board; Central Statistics Office; Chester Beatty Library; Chief State Solicitor's Office; Children Acts Advisory Board; Chomhairle Leabharlanna; Chomhairle um Oideachas Gaeltachta agus Gael-scolaíochta; Citizens Information Board; Civil Defence Board; Civil Service Commissioners; Clondalkin Partnership; Cloverhill Prison Visiting Committee; Coillte Teoranta; Coimisiún Logainmneacha; Coiste an Asgard; Combat Poverty Agency; Comhair Chathair Chorcaí; Comhairle na Nimheanna; Comhairle na nOspidéal; Comhairle na Tuaithe; Comhairle; Comhar, the Sustainable Development Council; Commission for Aviation Regulation; Commission for Charitable Donations and Bequests; Commission for Communications Regulation; Commission for Electricity Regulation; Commission for Energy Regulation; Commission for Taxi Regulation; Commission for the Support of Victims of Crime; Commissioners of Charitable Donations and Bequests for Ireland; Commissioners of Public Works; Committee for Performance Awards; Companies Registration Office; Competition Authority; Competition Law Review Group; Comptroller and Auditor General; Consumer Liaison Panel; Cork Airport Authority; Council of National Cultural Institutions; County Cavan Partnership; County Leitrim Partnership Board; County Wexford Partnership; Courts Service; Crafts Council of Ireland; Crawford Gallery Cork; Credit Union Advisory Committee; Criminal Injuries Compensation Tribunal; Crisis Pregnancy Agency; Culture Ireland; Data Protection Commissioner; Decentralisation Implementation Group; Defence Forces Canteen Board; Dental Council; Development Education Advisory Committee; Digital Hub Development Agency; Digital Media Development; Director of Consumer Affairs; Director of Public Prosecutions; District Registrars of Marriages; Donegal Local

Development; Dormant Accounts Board; Drogheda Partnership Company; Drug Treatment Centre Board; DTT Network Company; Dublin Airport Authority; Dublin Dental Hospital Board; Dublin Docklands Development Authority; Dublin Inner City Partnership; Dublin Institute for Advanced Studies; Dublin Transportation Office; Dundalk Employment Partnership; Eastern Regional Fisheries Board; Economic and Social Research Institute; Education Finance Board; Eirgrid; Electricity Supply Board; Employment Appeals Tribunal; Energy Advisory Board; Enterprise Ireland; Environmental Protection Agency; Equality Authority; European Regional Development Fund Financial Control Unit; Fáilte Ireland; Family Support Agency; Farm Animal Welfare Advisory Council; Fás; Fás International Consultancy; Finance Civil Service Arbitration Board; Financial Services Consultative Consumer Panel; Financial Services Consultative Industry Panel; Financial Services Ombudsman Council; Finglas/Cabra Partnership; Fire Services Council; Food Safety Authority of Ireland; Food Safety Consultative Council; Food Safety Promotion Board; Fóram na Gaeilge; Foras na Gaeilge; Forfás; Foyle, Carlingford and Irish Lights Commission; Further Education and Training Awards Council; Galway City Partnership; Galway Rural Development Company; Garda Síochána; Garda Síochána Complaints Appeals Board; Garda Síochána Complaints Board; Garda Síochána Inspectorate; Garda Síochána Ombudsman Commission; General Medical Services Payment Board; General Register Office; Government Information Services; Grangegorman Development Agency; Health & Safety Authority; Health & Social Care Professionals Council; Health Insurance Authority; Health Repayment Scheme Appeals Office; Health Research Board; Health Service Employers Agency; Health Service Executive; Heritage Council; High Level Group on Business Regulation; Higher Education and Training Awards Council; HIQA; Horse Racing Ireland; Hospital Bodies Administrative Bureau; Hospitals Trust Board; Housing Finance Agency; Human Rights Commission; Hunger Task Force; IDA Ireland; Implementation Body established under the British-Irish Agreement; Independent Commission for the Location of Victims Remains; Independent Monitoring Commission; Independent Monitoring Committee for Refugee Legal Services; Information Commissioner; Information Society Commission; Inishowen Partnership Board; Institiúid Teangeolaíochta Éireann; Institute of Public Administration; Institute of Public Health; Integrated Ireland Language and Training; Integrated Ticketing Project Board; International Development Ireland; Internet Advisory Board; InterTrade Ireland; Ireland Newfoundland Partnership Board; Ireland-United States Commission for Educational Exchange; Ireland-US Commission for Educational Exchange; Irish Aid Advisory Committee; Irish Auditing & Accounting Supervisory Authority; Irish Aviation Authority; Irish Blood Transfusion Service; Irish Council for Bioethics; Irish Council for Science, Technology and Innovation; Irish Expert Body on Fluorides and Health; Irish Fertiliser Industries; Irish Film Board; Irish Financial Services Appeals Tribunal; Irish Financial Services Regulatory Authority; Irish Manuscripts Commission; Irish Medicines Board; Irish Museum of Modern Art; Irish National Petroleum Corporation; Irish National Stud Company; Irish Prison Service; Irish Productivity Centre; Irish Red Cross Society; Irish Research Council for Science, Engineering and technology; Irish Research Council for the Humanities and Social Sciences; Irish Sports Council; Irish Telecommunications Investments plc; Irish Water Safety Association; Kimmage/Walkinstown/Crumlin/Drimnagh Partnership; Labour Court; Labour Relations Commission; Land Registry; Law Reform Commission; Legal Aid Board; Leopardstown Park Hospital Board; Levy Appeals Tribunal; Limerick Northside Regeneration Agency; Local Appointments Commissioners; Local Government Computer

Services Board; Local Registration of Deeds and Title Rules Committee; Local Employment Service Boards; Local Government Computer Services Board; Local Government Management Services Board; Longford Community Resources; Marine Casualty Investigation Board; Marine Institute; Medical Bureau of Road Safety; Medical Council; Meitheal Mhaigh Eo; Mental Health Commission; Mental Health Criminal Law Review Board; Midlands Prison Visiting Committee; Mining Board; Monaghan Partnership Board; National Adult Learning Council; National Advisory Committee on Drugs; National Archives; National Archives Advisory Council; National Authority for Occupational Safety and Health; National Building Agency; National Cancer Registry Board; National Cancer Screening Services Board; National Centre for Guidance in Education; National Centre For Partnership and Performance; National Childcare Coordinating Committee; National Children's Advisory Council; National Committee for Development Education; National Competitiveness Council; National Concert Hall; National Consultative Committee on Racism and Interculturalism; National Consumer Agency; National Council for Curriculum & Assessment; National Council for Forest Research and Development; National Council for Professional Development of Nursing and Midwifery; National Council for Special Education; National Council for the Professional Development of Nursing and Midwifery; National Council for Vocational Awards; National Council on Ageing and Older People; National Crime Council; National Development Agency; National Disability Authority; National Drugs Strategy Team; National Economic and Social Council; National Economic and Social Development Office; National Economic and Social Fourm; National Education Welfare Board; National Employment Rights Authority; National Forum on Europe; National Framework Committee for Work/Life Balance; National Gallery of Ireland; National Haemophilia Council; National Library of Ireland; National Lottery; National Microelectronics Applications Centre.; National Milk Agency; National Monitoring Committee Overseeing the Operation of Rapid Programme; National Museum of Ireland; National Oil Reserves Agency; National Paediatric Hospital Development Board; National Pensions Reserve Commission; National Property Services Regulatory Authority; National Qualifications Authority of Ireland; National Rehabilitation Board; National Roads Authority; National Safety Council; National Salmon Commission; National Social Work Qualifications Board; National Sports Campus Development Authority; National Standards Authority of Ireland; National Statistics Board; National Technology Park Plassey; National Theatre Society; National Traveller Accommodation Committee; National Treasury Management Agency; National Treatment Purchase Fund; National Youth Work Advisory Council; NDP – CSF Evaluation Unit; NDP – CSF Information Office; NDP – CSF Information Technology Unit; Nítrigin Éireann Teoranta; North West Kildare & North Offaly Partnership; North Western Regional Fisheries Board; Northern Regional Fisheries Board; Northside Partnership; Office for Health Management; Office for Tobacco Control; Office of Public Works; Office of the Appeal Commissioners for the purposes of the Tax Acts; Office of the Chief Medical Officer for the Civil Service; Office of the Director of Corporate Enforcement; Office of the Director of Equality Investigations; Office of the Director of Telecommunications Regulation; Office of the Houses of the Oireachtas; Office of the Information Commissioner; Office of the Inspector of Prisons; Office of the Ombudsman; Office of the Paymaster General; Office of the Pensions Ombudsman; Office of the Refugee Applications Commissioner; Office of the Registrar of Friendly Societies; Office of Tobacco Control; Official Censor of Films; Oifig Choimisinéir na d'Teangacha Oifigiúla; Ombudsman; Ordnance Survey; Outside Appointments Board; Páirtíocht Chonamara; Páirtíocht Gaeltacht Thír Chonaill; Parole Board; Partnership Trá Lí; Patents Office; PAUL Partnership Limerick; Pensions Board; Personal Injuries Assessment Board; Pharmaceutical Society of Ireland; Pobal; Postgraduate Medical and Dental Board; Pre Hospital Emergency Care Council; Prisons Authority Interim Board; Private Residential Tenancies Board; Private Security Appeals Board; Private Security Authority; Probation and Welfare Service; Property Registration Authority; Public Services Benchmarking Body; Public Voluntary Hospitals; Radiological Protection Institute of Ireland; Raidió na Gaeltachta; Railway Procurement Agency; Railway Safety Advisory Council; Railway Safety Commission; Referendum Commission; Refugee Agency; Refugee Appeals Tribunal; Registrar of Friendly Societies; Registrars of Births, Deaths and Roman Catholic Marriages; Registration Council for Secondary Teachers; Registry of Deeds; RELAY; Remembrance Commission; Rent Tribunal; Revenue Commissioners; Rights Commissioners; Roscommon Partnership Company; Science Foundation Ireland; Scientific Committee of the Food Safety Authority; Sea Fisheries Protection Authority; Shannon Airport Authority; Shannon Free Airport Development Company; Shannon Free Airport Development; Shannon Regional Fisheries Board; Skillsnet; Sligo LEADER Partnership Company; Small Business

Forum Implementation Group; Social Welfare Appeals Office; Social Welfare Tribunal; South Kerry Development Partnership; South Western Regional Fisheries Board; Southern Regional Fisheries Board; Southside Partnership; Special EU Programmes Body; St Luke's Hospital Board; Standards in Public Office Commission; State Claims Agency Policy Committee; State Examinations Commission; State Laboratory; Sustainable Energy Ireland; Tallaght Partnership; Teaching Council; Teagasc; Teastas; Temple Bar Properties; Temple Bar Renewal; Tipperary Institute; Tourism Ireland; Údarás na Gaeltachta; Údarás um Ard-Oideachas; Valuation Office; Valuation Tribunal; Veterinary Council; Victim Support; Waterford Area Partnership; Waterford Leader Partnership; Waterways Ireland; West Limerick Resources; Western Development Commission; Western Regional Fisheries Board; Westmeath Community Development; Wexford Area Partnership and last but by no means least, the Women's Health Council.

Apologies to anyone omitted.

Do we really need a Railway Safety Advisory Council as well as a Railway Safety Commission? An Advisory Council to the Commission for Taxi Regulation as well as a Commission for Taxi Regulation? Many of these quangos have significant numbers of staff, their own offices, administrators, websites, boards that must have board meetings, annual reports and usually well-paid chief executives. Some of these quangos have a record of monumental incompetence, such as the Integrated Ticketing Project Board and the Irish Financial Services Regulatory Authority. Some are just unknowable; the Defence Forces Canteen Board seems clear, if pointless, but what does the National Framework Committee for Work/Life Balance actually do?

To be fair, many of the quangos, such as the Taxi Regulator, are dramatically more competent than the national or local government departments that did their work before they took over, although that bar is not set very high. This gives us a clue why we have so many quangos. They are vehicles for ministers trying to make progress. The civil service is so ridden with sloth that the only route to progress is to take the job away from them and give it to a green-field organisation.

This is not an unreasonable way to try to force progress, but it results in us having more and more civil servants, with less and less to do. An astonishing example of this is the 561 staff remaining in the grim Department of Health headquarters, Hawkins House, despite 1,800 newly recruited management and administration staff performing their functions for the newly formed HSE. They have absolutely nothing to do, but the Hawkins House staff are paid an average salary of €66,000 each.[445]

It is correct that when new technology, more efficient working practices or challenging established practices demands it, the government should reorganise responsibilities; however, two guiding principles should govern this. First, new agencies should normally be sited within government departments and use their resources, rather than being established as their own little empires. Second, when such a reorganisation takes place, as would happen in private industry, the people whose jobs are disappearing should be moved to other functions appropriate to their skills if that is required. They should be made redundant if it is not.

New Alliances

France calls itself "America's oldest ally". The British like to talk of their "special relationship" with the US. Israel says it is America's closest ally. Power has always attracted hangers-on who want to bask in reflected glory. If we imagine that Ireland can call on any emotional link to extract favourable treatment from the superpower, we will be disappointed. The US will follow their own interests and no others. Ireland should pursue an enlightened self-interested policy of maintaining good relations with the US, but we should be realistic about the benefits, and we should orient our foreign policy to take account of the fact that the balance of world power is likely to shift.

BRIC is the name given to the emerging economic superpowers – Brazil, Russia, India and China, and Ireland can do nothing to influence their size and resources, which will make them hugely important in the coming century. There is also little enough that we can do about how they treat Ireland. Ireland is so small as to simply not register with these four countries that have close to half the planet's population.

Large Countries

As well as bilateral relations, we should consider a strategy by which Ireland pursues relationships with selected local administrative units in these countries. Ireland should, in effect, establish relationships with key county councils in the BRIC countries. This is logical, in particular since such units are frequently larger than our country. It is likely that Irish diplomats would stand a far greater chance of getting in the door of regional administrations. Ireland should target a manageable number of such regions in the BRIC countries, chosen on the basis of their economic potential, and forge diplomatic and economic ties with them.

Enterprises in these countries, particularly the ones that trade internationally, typically have a high degree of state involvement, and large contracts often cross the desks of political leaders before they are approved. The aim of these relations would be to promote economic ties and make sure that Irish businesses have a fighting chance of getting the contract. As well as having an increased chance of success at lower levels, there is also the chance that, since regional leaders often become national leaders, we could get lucky and have leaders already on good terms with Ireland promoted to a more senior position.

Small Countries

Ireland's diplomatic service is more likely to gain access to the national-level decision-makers in smaller countries, but we don't seem to have realised the full potential of this. Small countries have equal voting powers with large ones in many international arenas and have, at least, power disproportionate to their size in other ones, notably the EU. In addition, Ireland has a cultural image that seems to have cachet with many smaller countries, perhaps because many of them see parallels in their historic domination by a larger neighbour. At a political level, it makes sense for Irish ministers to maintain close links with their counterparts in the Baltic republics and the other new entrants to the EU, particularly in central and Eastern Europe. Ireland's traditional alliances with the UK, France and Germany are not necessarily a wise path to continue, particularly as the interests of small and large states diverge.

Soft Alliances

Aside from diplomatic and governmental relations, softer cultural connections are very valuable. In this we have the great advantage of speaking English, a language that everyone else wants to learn. We should teach them. Firstly, the business of teaching English itself is a huge business, particularly important in China.[446] Secondly, the experience of having spent time abroad, particularly in one's youth, is likely to leave a person with very positive memories of that country; at the very least they would be aware of us, which many people are not. We should not over-estimate our international standing.

Passport Control

Ireland should aggressively promote itself as a place to come and study English. We seem to be doing the reverse. Arbitrary and unchecked power is a bad thing any time, and no state official should be able to make decisions without being having coherent reasons behind them.

Ireland refuses 38 per cent of visa applicants from China, but the UK refused only 7 per cent. Ireland refuses 46 per cent of Turkish applications, but the UK only refuses 11 per cent.[447] Even once an applicant gets a visa, they are not in the clear. There is no shortage of stories of casual racism and utterly irrational decisions by immigration officers to refuse people entry to Ireland, even when they have already been vetted and issued with visas by Irish embassies in their home countries. One such person was the unfortunate winner of a trip to Ireland sponsored by Tourism Ireland in Mumbai, India, to promote Ireland as a holiday destination. He arrived at Dublin Airport with his passport, visa and other documents in order, where an immigration officer decided that he didn't like the look of him and sent him packing on the next plane home.[448]

There is something seriously wrong with the immigration section at Dublin Airport. It could be boredom. An unbelievable 121 immigration officers are employed there,[449] a shocking figure for anyone who has waited in the queue for one of the three or four windows that are typically open.

- The Department of Foreign Affairs, with Ireland's embassies, should create a student visa application process that is integrated with the admission services of universities and commercial English-teaching schools, linked to the payment of fees.

- The visa should bear the name and contact number of a responsible person at the educational institution.

- When an immigration officer proposes to deny entry to any person with a valid student visa, they should not be permitted to do so without giving the responsible person access both to the student and a senior officer.

- The people processed by each immigration officer should be recorded, including their race, age, gender, country of origin and whether they were admitted, any reason for refusal and the identity of the officer responsible.

- This information should be available to management and should be published on a scrapable website, with unique numbers rather than names to identify individual officers.

New Europe

Despite historic rivalries between Britain, France and Germany, it is inevitable that the interests of large countries will converge in the EU, and while it may have been profitable for puny Ireland to hang around with the biggest kids on the block when the EU was smaller, we will need new allies, and the smaller countries of eastern Europe are obvious candidates, not least because so many of their citizens came to work here during the boom. Ireland should forge alliances with them, on a cultural as well as political level.

- Ministers and diplomats should have regular bilateral meetings with their opposite numbers.

- The government should aggressively promote Ireland as a place to come and learn English, as well as have a holiday – at least there are no visa problems possible for them.

- Ireland should open university departments for the study of their languages, culture and politics, bunched in universities by language groups – Baltic languages in one university, Slavic languages in another and so on.

- The government should encourage exchange of expertise at political and administrative level, whereby a country that achieves success in one area of government should send the people responsible on secondment to other states to help them replicate their success.

Spreading Democracy

Democracy is not something everyone can rely on. Although it has made huge strides since 1945, notably in 1989, and half the world's population now live in a democracy of some type,[450] half don't. There is precious little that Ireland can do about this, but democracy is so valuable that whatever we can do, we should. Democracies almost never have famines and almost never go to war with each other. In the half of the world that does not enjoy democracy, there are brave people who risk the imprisonment, torture and murder of themselves and their families to promote democracy. Sometimes, their huge personal risks pay off. Nelson Mandela and Václav Havel spent long years in prison before leading their countries to liberation. Morgan Tsvangirai seems to be on the cusp. Today there are many activists for freedom around the world who play cat-and-mouse with their dictatorial governments, risking everything and going as far as they think they can get away with in demanding reform. Ireland can help:

- Irish embassies should be instructed to compile a list of democratic activists who are at risk of reprisals from their governments.

- These people should be quietly contacted and given a phone number to call, or some other method of getting in touch with an Irish diplomat.

- They should be told that, if they ever feel that they are in imminent danger, they should make contact.

- The embassies should rehearse arrangements to get the activists safely to Ireland.

- They should be told that, if ever the need arises, they and their families will be guaranteed political asylum and resettlement in Ireland.

Aside from saving people's lives, the purpose of this is to embolden activists for democracy, who can continue their campaigns in the knowledge that their personal safety has been slightly improved. Also, today's prisoners of conscience are, like Havel and Mandela, tomorrow's world leaders. Ireland's international relations will be assisted by this scheme.

The Health of the Nation

Ireland's health service is an awkward mix of the socialised healthcare systems of continental Europe and the wildly expensive, profit-driven US system. While Ireland spends more than the OECD average on healthcare, has a higher-than-average contribution from the taxpayer and had the highest rate of increase in spending until the financial crisis,[451] there is a strong perception that access to healthcare is very unequal and that the quality of services is poor. Statistics seem to bear this out. The life expectancy for a of cystic fibrosis patient in the Republic of Ireland is 21. In Northern Ireland it is 33.[452]

People advocating reform either believe in moving towards the private US system or towards the socialised continental system. Without doubt the United States offers the best healthcare in the world, to those who can afford it.

Healthcare seems to have the capacity to absorb almost all of the money thrown at it, and health costs continue to increase far ahead of the rate of general inflation.[453] The US is successful at innovating new treatments for those who can afford it, but this is not correlated to better health for the population, and there is reason to think that this harms public health. In a profit-driven system, the rich can simply outbid the poor for medical care, regardless of need. They can afford to pay surgeons to make them a "virgin" again by inserting a fake hymen,[454] or look muscular by using pectoral silicone implants,[455] but the poor cannot afford life-saving treatments.[456]

A comparison of major western healthcare systems[457] shows that there is no strong correlation between the total health budget and the health outcomes such as life expectancy in a country – quite the reverse. In Japan, $2,358 of healthcare per person results in a life expectancy of 82.1; the US spends $6,402 per person‡ and achieves two years' less life expectancy. Health does not operate like any other market. Even in the most market-driven healthcare system, there is no functioning market. The degree of complexity in medicine means that consumers have no hope of pressurising suppliers to give better value for money, because they have no way of understanding their treatment and therefore comparing suppliers.

Many people don't understand their mobile phone bills either, but some do, and all consumers benefit from the activist minority of mobile phone customers who study their bills and switch supplier accordingly. But, unlike

---

‡ This ignores the fact that 18 per cent of under-65's in the US do not have any health cover. In Japan there is universal coverage.

mobile phones, everybody's healthcare needs are so unique that there is no hope of the majority benefiting from the pressure of a small number of well-informed consumers. Given that only the supplier – the doctor – has any understanding of what is required, it is not surprising that they would decide the best course of action is the one that enriches them most.

Public sector organisations don't have a good record for efficiency, but in healthcare this is not borne out. The state-owned VHI says that it spends 8.5 per cent of its premiums on administration,[458] while Quinn Healthcare, (formerly BUPA) spends 16.4 per cent,[459] but the older clientele of VHI is far more expensive to insure, so the VHI's efficiency doesn't deliver lower premiums. Commercial health insurers such as Quinn and Hibernian are not permitted to charge higher premiums for older customers, but they can still use creative ways to make sure that their customer base is young and healthy. Actually, they don't have to try too hard, because active consumers, more likely to switch supplier – be it health insurance or mobile phone company – tend to be younger anyway. But that doesn't stop insurance companies from trying to push the envelope a bit further, concentrating on internet marketing, offering discounts (the only ones permitted) to "students" under 23 or promoting treatments targeted at young adults such as laser eye surgery.

Risk equalisation is a method of trying to prevent this type of behaviour by ordering insurance companies whose clients have a lower risk profile to pay compensation to those with a higher profile. Although BUPA signed up to this deal when they entered the market, with a three-year payment holiday as they got established, they left the market in a hissy fit when the rule came into operation.[460]

People will do anything for health. Even quacks and charlatans can make a good living from promising cures. This factor, combined with the total control of knowledge that healthcare providers have over their patients, means that a functioning market where suppliers are disciplined by competitive pressure from customers is simply impossible. In addition, since demand for healthcare seems to be infinite, the rich can always price the poor out of the market, creating an inexorable spiral of inflation. This leaves a socialised system as the only realistic alternative, but there are problems with socialised systems too. Producer capture, where the suppliers become so powerful that they run the system for their benefit, seeing patients as an inconvenience at best, is a major risk. Some models suffer from this less than others, but Ireland has managed to combine the worst features of both systems.

Health and Bureaucracy

Easily the greatest disaster that happened to the Irish health service was the ministry of Micheál Martin. In the nine years to 2006, employment in the health services went from 66,000 to 105,000, a 57 per cent increase, the bulk of which were hired under Martin's catastrophic ministry, although the establishment of the Health Service Executive (HSE) in 2005 also led to a bonanza for the bureaucrats. The scale of this is difficult to convey. Almost 20 new staff members were hired for new positions every working day, to say nothing of staff that were hired to replace those leaving.

By far the greatest proportion of those hired were administrators.[461] Paying hordes of pen-pushers from the public purse (and very well paid they are[462]) would be bad enough if it were the case that they simply did no work. But aside from the cost, the increase in administration has its own disastrous effects.

Any HR professional will tell you there is an optimum number of people to get a job done. Too many can be as much of a problem as too few. While the health service had many severe problems before the addition of tens of thousands of bureaucrats, there is no reason to believe that those problems were the result of under-management. The explosion in the number of administrators leads to people featherbedding their jobs, making themselves necessary and justifying their existence.

A natural reaction of a bureaucrat who is coming to the slow realisation that her job is fundamentally pointless is to try to secure her position by creating blocks in the way of people trying to do real work and then highlighting her own role in removing that block, in an attempt to give herself and those around her, the illusion that she is doing useful work. A former public health nurse explains:

> Before, if I needed something, I would just ring up the supplier and order it and tell them to send the invoice in to the accounts office. It would take about a week. Then a whole new purchasing department was established and we were told that we couldn't order anything any more, we had to go through them.

> So I rang them up and asked them to order the new baby scales for me. I knew they didn't know what I wanted because they didn't ask anything about it, didn't take any of the details, they just said 'OK' to get me off the phone.

> A fortnight later they rang me back and asked me if I knew where to get the scales, and I said of course I did, hadn't I dealt with them for years. A fortnight after that the purchasing department rang back again and asked me for the make and model and all that, and I told them.

The whole thing took two months from start to finish and I can't remember how many phone calls I had to make before I got the thing in the end.

A Health Service previously run on spit and promises is being weighed down with people who have no medical knowledge and wish only to make sure nobody gets anything before the correct form is filled in.

Then some lucky firms quoted €9m for the PPARS (Personnel, Payroll and Related Systems) HR software system to manage pay and holiday and sick leave. The health service, with all its new purchasing departments, needed to buy something. They displayed their purchasing skills by eventually paying a total of €220m to various companies for the system. It still doesn't work.[463] The software was intended to manage the payroll for just 30,000 health service staff. It seems that nobody bothered to do the back-of-an-envelope calculation that the system would cost more than €7,300 per staff member served. Their payslips could be delivered by limousine for cheaper. After blowing more than €200m on computers that don't work, ten times that amount went on the fiasco that was the illegal charging of care-home fees to elderly and incapacitated residents. Mostly the charges were reasonable. But they were illegal – they had no basis in law. When the significance of the omission was realised, the law was quickly changed to give a legal basis to continuing the charges, but this could not change the fact that the charges levied up to that point were illegal and had to be refunded, costing the taxpayer more than €2bn.

On 16 December 2003, Micheál Martin attended a meeting in the Gresham Hotel with the chief executives of the health boards. The meeting has since become notorious, because a senior civil servant has said that this was the occasion that the minister was told of the problem with illegally charging medical-card holders for long-term care.[464] Martin says that he was never informed of the wrongful charging issue and that the main thrust of the Gresham meeting was to reassure health board chiefs that they would continue to have high-status, high-paying jobs after the abolition of the health boards. It is outrageously bad management that such a serious issue was not brought to the front and centre of the minister's attention, and the secretary general of the department was rightly ousted from his post.

But almost no commentators questioned why the CEOs of health boards, who had run the health service so poorly that they had to be abolished, were being treated to a day in the Gresham and a meeting with the minister to find them jobs to keep them in the style to which they have become accustomed. Anyone in that position in the private sector would have been fired. So should they.

Socialise Healthcare

"Choice" is the mantra of those who support privatised healthcare. "Patients want choice," they say. Really? Who, given a choice, would not choose the best? Choice is nonsense, because the nature of healthcare means that consumers can never make an informed choice, so there can never be an effective market. The next best thing is to have the government stick up for the consumers. The Health Service should be entirely socialised and paid for by general taxation.

There should be no prohibition of private medicine, but no subsidies for it either, so anyone choosing to use it would pay its full economic cost, with no tax allowances for private health insurance or anything similar. The reasons for not socialising the cost of other services mentioned in this book is to encourage people to use resources wisely, but this point is not valid for healthcare, because customers don't choose what healthcare they use, their doctor does.

Another benefit of a unitary system is that, with the widest possible participation, all citizens would benefit from the political and social pressure to improve the system that is brought when more educated, articulate and well-connected members of society find that it is important to them.

- Each person should register with a GP practice with their PPS number.

- The health service should pay GP practices a fixed annual amount for all the care required by patients on their register, with patients who leave the country, join another practice or die automatically removed from their list.

- Practices should not be permitted to refuse any patient from joining their list, unless they close the list to all newcomers for a minimum of two years.

- Practices would be paid an enhanced amount if they had an above-average caseload of elderly people or others with particular health problems.

- The cost of drugs prescribed to the patient should be funded partly by a contribution from the practice, partly from the patient (up to a fixed monthly ceiling) and partly by the state.

- The portion paid by the GP practice should be adjusted to motivate doctors to keep prescription costs down, without making the incentive so severe that GPs would be tempted to make patients go without necessary medicine.

- Practices would be required to use an online records system, to allow patients' notes to be instantly transferred from one practice to another and to hospitals if necessary.

- The records system would collect statistical data about the clinical outcome of each patient and publish it (without identifying patients) on a scrapable website.

- Access to the records should be controlled via a chip-and-pin system where the health service card of each patient would allow the healthcare professional to access all appropriate data in the system while the patient's card was in a card reader, but would only have access to the data that they had personally entered when it was not.

- All healthcare professionals would also have to input credentials to view or enter data, and each time a record was accessed or changed, the time, location and person would be recorded for audit.

- A detailed cost-management system would be established for all HSE-run hospitals, to allow the cost of each procedure in each hospital to be measured, and this would be published, along with statistical data about all the clinical outcomes in each hospital.

- The Health Information and Quality Authority (HIQA) would continue its role of inspecting hospitals and develop a list of standardised key performance indicators, and publish the information in a scrapable format, to allow comparison of all hospital data.

- Where discrete clinical procedures can be outsourced, their internal cost should be evaluated and private hospitals should be permitted to supply the procedures if they can offer it at a lower cost.

To do all this, deeply entrenched vested interests in the health system must be challenged.

Hospital Consultants

One of the most outrageous abuses are the consultants' contracts, whereby they are allowed to combine a public salary with private practice, with no requirement to do any particular amount of work for their public salary. Regardless of the hours put in, their public work is in competition with their private practices, often in tiny specialist fields. Doing the job for which they get a public salary efficiently can cause a real and immediate reduction of the earning capacity of their private practice, and it is simply unreasonable to imagine that consultants will not respond to such an incentive. The Irish health system permits the most powerful people working for it to create huge waiting lists; the Irish health system motivates the most powerful people working for it to create huge waiting lists; and Irish health system has huge waiting lists. The symptoms and the illness are evident.

Proposed new consultants' contracts that would require consultants to work a 39-hour week have been fiercely opposed by the Irish Hospital Consultants Association. Dr Josh Keaveney described the salary of €205,000 (since raised to €225,000), plus a €40,000 bonus for meeting targets as "Mickey Mouse money",[465] although their relatively mute response to the pay cut in the 2010 budget may have been a reaction to the very poor publicity they suffered following that comment.[466]

Pharmacists

Also creating fierce resistance to change are the pharmacists. They are the beneficiaries of extraordinary anti-competitive rules. If an Irish pharmacist wants to open a pharmacy shop, she is forbidden from doing so if she received her degree from any university outside the country. Even if she does have a degree from an Irish university, she must also prove that her new pharmacy will not impact on the business of an existing one. The pharmacists can control supply in the market and keep prices high.[467] This has enriched the existing operators, making it effectively impossible to enter the market without buying a pharmacy from an existing operator. As with taxi licences, this has hugely inflated their value.[468]

In 2009, Health Minister Mary Harney attempted to reduce the huge cost that these rules impose on the state by unilaterally reducing the wholesale mark-up allowed on pharmaceuticals from 17.66 per cent to 10 per cent and reducing the pharmacists' margins to "only" 25 per cent.[469] Predictably, the pharmacists were horrified and organised an effective resistance, with many refusing to dispense medicines for the HSE at all. Battle lines were drawn with the pharmacists' union deploying PR people on talk radio talking of the harm to patients, and the HSE taking legal action to force pharmacists to honour their contracts[470] and setting up contingency systems to dispense medicine independently.[471] The behaviour of Harney and the HSE was idiotic. For as long as a powerful cartel exists, it will powerfully defend its interests. In December 2009, they lost their court action against Harney in which they claimed that the margin cuts were illegal,[472] but they retain a long list of anti-competitive privileges, and they will keep battling to hang on to them. The pharmacists may be defeated, but it will take a constant input of political energy to keep them defeated, and this is unlikely to be forthcoming because government has other priorities, and its concentration will eventually move on. The pharmacists, it seems, have only one focus – enriching themselves.

The pharmacy cartel should not be battled; it should be liquidated. All of the restrictive rules on owning and opening pharmacies should be wiped away.

Patents and Patients

A patent is a legal protection for an invention. It gives the inventor exclusive rights to use that invention, usually for about 20 years. Drugs are inventions and therefore are covered by patents, and when pharmaceutical firms patent very useful drugs, they can make billions in profits. When the patent runs out, then anyone can formulate the same drug and sell it. Although the profit margins are drastically lower, the companies that make generic drugs have no research and development costs, and they know that there is a proven market for the drugs they will manufacture. The drugs themselves are made to an identical formula, and generic manufacturers are subjected to the same regulations governing the integrity of the manufacturing process as the original makers.

The patent clock starts ticking once the invention is made, and because drugs typically take years to go through testing and approval procedures, the time between the release of the original and the generic can be quite short. Once the patent runs out, there is no benefit to using the version from the original manufacturer. The original manufacturers will use every trick in the book to extend the time they have to sell the high-priced original, and because in Ireland the patient usually pays the cost of the drugs, the patient relies on their pharmacist and doctor to alert them to the fact that the drug they need has a much cheaper generic alternative.

Drug companies have huge marketing budgets aimed at persuading doctors to prescribe their expensive original, rather than the cheaper alternatives. Pharmacists get much higher margins on the more expensive originals, and there is evidence that in some cases they simply refuse to stock the generic drugs at all,[473] probably because the drugs companies are working at persuading them to push their high-priced versions. It seems to work for them. The HSE pays €98 million per year more for drugs than they would pay if they got the generic pricing that the NHS gets in the UK,[474] but this relates only to drugs that the HSE pays for. There is no way of knowing how much over the odds private patients are paying.

- The integrated medical records system proposed under **Socialise Healthcare** on page 209 should include a system to manage all prescriptions.

- Pharmacists should have limited access to the system to view and complete prescriptions for patients.

- This aspect of the system should be reconciled with the records of drugs supplied to pharmacies by wholesalers.

- The system should provide alerts if a patient is prescribed drugs that are known to conflict with each other, or with any condition or allergy that the patient has listed.

- The system should alert doctors to the existence of cheaper generic alternatives to the drugs being prescribed and require the doctor to inform the patient.

- The system should give the patients the option to receive an automated SMS reminder on their mobile phones each time they should take their drugs.

- The prescribing pattern of each GP practice should be included in the data placed online in a scrapable format, to identify GPs with potentially dangerous behaviours, without including data that would personally identify any patients.

Centres of Excellence

Health services are one of the few issues that can bring ordinary people on to the streets to protest. That doesn't make them right. In common with many other areas, medicine has been the subject of extraordinary technological advance in recent years. Much of this has come from well-funded research in the US, a product of their expensive healthcare system. There are real benefits of this – lives are saved. Five-year survival rates from cancer have risen rapidly in developed countries in the last 25 years. Between 1986 and 1999 in England and Wales, five-year survival rates from breast cancer rose by 6 percentage points; for prostate cancer, the improvement was more than 11 percentage points.[475] These are huge advances, literally life-and-death progress for thousands of people. The advances on many other serious illnesses are just as good. Why?

Imagine you are going down a country road, and beside a pretty, if a little unkempt, farmhouse there is a hand-painted sign on rough timber sticking out of the hedgerow at an imperfect angle. It says "Home-made Jam for Sale". Would you be tempted? Now, imagine the same country road, the same farmhouse, the same sign but a different offer: "Home made Laptops for Sale". Would you be as well-disposed? There are some products and services that simply cannot be delivered on a small scale. The changing nature of medicine, moving towards being high-tech, highly specialised and increasingly successful, means that fewer and fewer conditions can be treated at small non-specialised units, because doctors and their teams need practice. It may lead to a boring life for them, but the research indicates that if they specialise in one very specific condition, their success rate improves dramatically.

"Specialising" means very specialist indeed – not just specialising in cancer, not just specialising in breast cancer for example, but specialising in one specific form of breast cancer, reading all the international literature on it, going to the conferences, doing their own study and treating at least one new case a week. This seems to be the threshold for the level of practice needed to keep skill levels up, and that means that their service must cover a population that generates at least 50 cases requiring their specialism every year. The more specialised the treatment gets, the larger the population needed to generate those 50 cases per year.

For medics, working outside their specialism is known as dabbling. When doctors dabble, patients die. This was found to be the case in the inquiry into the Bristol heart-surgery unit in Britain, where for several years surgeons – highly skilled heart surgeons – dabbled in paediatric cardiac surgery (PCS), a slightly different specialism. The report into the scandal concluded:

around one-third of all the children who underwent open-heart surgery receive[d] less than adequate care. More children died than might have been expected in a typical PCS unit. In the period from 1991 to 1995 between 30 and 35 more children under 1 died after open-heart surgery in the Bristol Unit than might be expected had the Unit been typical of other PCS units in England at the time.[476]

Similar effects have been observed in Ireland. In April 2009, the Mid-Western Regional Hospital in Ennis was the subject of a report from HIQA which said that:

It is unsafe to keep the configuration of services at MWRH Ennis as they are and these changes must take place safely and effectively.

The report went on to say that acute, complex and specialist services are "not sustainable" at Ennis.

This is because there are not sufficient numbers of patients presenting with these conditions to enable professional healthcare teams to maintain their clinical skills and expertise.

Continuing these acute services, including acute and complex surgery, cancer surgery, level 2/3 critical care and 24-hour emergency department services, in their current structure, exposes patients to potential harm.[477]

This point does not seem to have any impact on the well-organised and articulate campaigns such as "Save Sligo's Cancer Services"[478] and "Save Monaghan Hospital".[479] While these campaigns make valid points about the long journeys that people who live in thinly populated areas must make to access specialist services, it is difficult to understand why they fail to take on board the point that even if infinite funding were available, it is simply not possible to provide modern medicine in tiny hospitals. Acceding to the demands of these groups would endanger the lives of many people in the areas they claim to represent and also endanger lives in larger centres that would then fall below the critical mass required to keep up the skills of medical teams.

Only one group would benefit from failing to centralise at centres of excellence. These minor hospitals are staffed by medical staff whose skills – as can be seen in Ennis – are simply not good enough. These are people who have leisurely lifestyles, with low workloads and high salaries. They are small fish in very small ponds, and if they were forced to move to large hospitals to keep their jobs, they would lose the local prestige that they enjoy, and their skills might be exposed to an uncomfortable level of scrutiny. It is not surprising that medics take such a leading role in the various campaigns against centres of excellence.[480] [481] The campaigns also frequently include the tone of exaggerated entitlement that is common in demands from areas in rural Ireland that have become accustomed to unrealistic levels of representation. (See **Local Authorities** on page 177.)

The problems cited by campaigns to keep very specialised medical services in small regional hospitals are transport problems, not healthcare problems. The location of medical services should be decided solely on the clinical research that indicates what will give the best outcome for the greatest number of patients.

Organ Donation
In Ireland today there are 1,400 people undergoing kidney dialysis. In 1989, that figure was just 178. Kidney dialysis is an arduous process that is time-consuming and unpleasant; receiving a donor organ is a life-changing operation. However, the reason the number on dialysis is going up is because the number of transplants is going down. In 1990, there were 38 transplants per million people in the country. By 2005, the figure had fallen to 30 transplants per million.[482] The problem is the lack of donors, which has brought calls for presumed consent, which would mean that everyone would be presumed to agree to donate their organs unless they carried a card stating otherwise.[483]

This is not a wise strategy, and it risks undermining public support for the donation system. But the problem remains that, although most people are willing to be donors, few of them bother to carry a donor card. Is there one in your pocket or handbag? The solution to the problem is also in your pocket or handbag – bank cards. After all the bailouts, the banks owe us a favour.

- Banks should be required to alter the design on all plastic ATM, credit and debit cards to include a symbol indicating that the holder has agreed to donate their organs.

- After a short introductory period, banks should be prohibited from issuing or renewing any plastic card without securing an answer from their customer as to whether or not they agreed to be a donor – this could be done online for the many people who use electronic banking.

- Nobody would be required to agree to donate, but they would be required to state their preference before they could receive their plastic card.

- All future cards issued to someone who agreed to be a donor would include the donation symbol unless they requested otherwise.

MRSA and Antibiotics
Antibiotics are unlike any other drugs. Taken properly they are one of the most effective and life-saving medicines known to man. Taken wrongly they

are a serious health risk. Antibiotics are toxic to germs, single-cell organisms which make us sick when they live inside us, although they have no impact on viruses, which are a completely different type of illness. Our body has an immune system that can kill off the unhealthy bacteria that invade our bodies from time to time, but this could take much longer and doesn't always work. A course of antibiotics typically lasts one or two weeks, in order to kill off all the problematic bacteria. The problem begins when you start feeling better.

If somebody doesn't feel so ill any more, they may think that it is not necessary to finish the antibiotic course. This is very dangerous, because when the person feels better it is because most of the bacteria are dead – most, but not all. Even though there may not be enough bacteria to make someone feel ill, the person is likely to still be infectious, passing the bacteria to other people who are then likely to get ill. The danger stems from the fact that bacteria are very simple organisms, which can evolve very quickly, and the bacteria that are passed on are the ones that survived the longest, so they are the ones who have the least susceptibility to the antibiotic that the first victim took.

If this process is repeated, the bacteria can become totally immune to commonly used antibiotics. MRSA is multidrug-resistant staphylococcus aureus, a bacteria that has become immune to many different types of antibiotic, and for this reason is a serious illness and difficult to treat. Prescribing antibiotics when they serve no function, such as for viral illnesses, also reduces the effectiveness of the drugs. People who fail to take antibiotics correctly are putting other members of society at mortal risk. There is a clear correlation between prescribing practices for antibiotics and the prevalence of resistant strains of bacteria, with Spain being a particular problem because antibiotics can be bought in pharmacies without a prescription.[484]

At a minimum, the system of SMS reminders to take your tablets mentioned in **Patents and Patients** above should be configured so that they cannot be disabled by the patient if the reminder is for a drug that has public health implications if it is not taken correctly, and the SMS messages should also contain a text reminding the patient of the dangers of non-compliant use of antibiotics. However, an even more creative method to encourage people to keep taking a TB drug is suggested by Steven Levitt on the *Freakonomics* blog:

> The Innovations in International Health program at MIT ... figured out a simple paper-based test that detects metabolites of the TB drug in urine. So if you take the drug and pee on a special piece of paper, a secret message appears. If you don't take the drug, you can pee on it

all you want, but it will not reveal the secret message. Every time the drug taker texts the secret message to the people in charge, he earns a prize, like cell phone minutes or cash.[485]

Illegal Drugs

The term "war on drugs" is not as common in Ireland as some other countries, but discussion of drug use is terminated by unthinking clichés as much here as anywhere else. In public discussion, the problems caused by drugs, the unintended negative consequences of prohibition and the moral outrage of puritans are often muddled together, with no clear understanding of what either the problem is or the desired solution. Illegal drugs are associated with three sets of problems:

- Depending on the drug, they can cause physical and psychological problems for the drug user.

- People around the drug users can be seriously affected by the taker's behaviour, from neglected children to burgled neighbours.

- Drug users and others suffer criminal penalties imposed by the state for taking and supplying drugs and for the crimes that fund drug habits.

While few would have sympathy for drug barons who get locked up, young people who become addicts in their early teenage years have a miserable existence, and they are at least partly victims, although the victims of the burglaries and handbag snatchings that fund their habits might see it differently. It should be noted that 20 per cent of Irish heroin addicts take the drug for the first time while in prison.[486]

The point is that the third negative effect of drugs is imposed by the state in an effort to ameliorate the first two. The public policy question here is to ensure that the state does as much good and as little harm as possible; but that does not seem to always be the driving motivation of policy. Many people morally disapprove of recreational drug use, and the desire to impose moral standards has become confused with a social policy, so that government action is unclear, unfocused and simply not working.

The smuggler and the border guard need each other to exist. Without the smuggler, the border guard would have no function. And without the border guard, contraband would flow freely in the market, and smuggling would not be profitable. The first issue to be understood is that prohibition reduces the number of people willing to supply drugs, reducing competition and thereby making the market more profitable for the suppliers who remain. These very high profit levels are a motivation to drug dealers to get as many people addicted to drugs as possible.

This increased price must be paid. If the drug is addictive, and particularly if it prevents the addict from retaining employment, then this inevitably leads to the type of crime that can yield quick money – burglaries and muggings. So some of the ill-effects of the drugs are at least partially caused by the prohibition, as opposed to being directly caused by the drug itself.

There is an urgent need to end government policies that reward drug-dealing. A heroin or cocaine addict is a constant source of income for a dealer, so dealers are highly motivated to get and keep people addicted. If that financial reward was broken, there would be no incentive to provide the drugs in the first place.

Drugs can cause real physical and psychological harm, but some drugs are much worse than others. The US government records the cause of almost all deaths. Tobacco is by far the most lethal drug, killing 435,000 people per year. The next drug on the list is alcohol, responsible for 85,000 deaths. All illegal drugs combined, including the associated deaths caused by suicide, homicide, motor-vehicle injury, HIV infection, pneumonia, violence, mental illness and hepatitis are responsible for 17,000 deaths per year. Marijuana‡ is responsible for none.[487]

Ecstasy is not listed separately for the US, but in the UK, where 114,000 people die from tobacco use per year, less than 50 people a year die from using ecstasy,[488] but these comparisons are rejected by prohibitionists because it does not take into account the possible greater prevalence of alcohol and smoking. A detailed academic study of the real risk of drug taking and many other activities was undertaken by the Centre for Applied Psychology at Liverpool John Moores University. This study is adjusted to take account of both the negative outcomes and the prevalence of the activities, to give a true picture of the dangers of each activity.

- Smoking is by far the most dangerous, on a par with space travel or climbing Mount Everest.

- Heroin, morphine, barbiturates and alcohol come next, all about as dangerous as hang gliding, parachuting or working in a mine.

- Lower down the scale is ecstasy, cocaine and the contraceptive pill; they all are about as dangerous as playing soccer or doing DIY.

- The risk from marijuana is extremely low, on a par with the risk of being hit by lightning.[489]

Puritanism has been defined as the haunting fear that somebody, somewhere is having a good time. It is clear that there is no correlation whatsoever between the harm caused by a drug and the likelihood of it being banned, although being banned does significantly expose the user to increased risk

‡   Prohibitionists argue that, since marijuana is often smoked with tobacco, some of the tobacco-related deaths that result should be attributed to marijuana, although this seems like a weak argument for banning marijuana and permitting tobacco.

⸺ illicit markets have no quality control. "You don't know what you are taking," say the prohibitionists, and they are right. And it is because they have put the market in the hands of the criminals.

Simply demonstrating that risk exists is not sufficient grounds to ban a recreational drug. Adults have the right to take risks with their own lives – otherwise mountain climbing, and maybe soccer and DIY, would be banned. Society has no business imposing morals on people who don't accept them. The only valid test is whether allowing a drug poses a risk to other members of society, who have not agreed to accept the risk.‡

It seems clear that some drugs – particularly heroin and cocaine – are so addictive and interfere with a person's earning ability to such a degree that they are always likely to be associated with crime. However, drugs such as marijuana and ecstasy, while they have health risks, have no characteristics that tend to infringe any person's rights. One European country has changed its approach. Portugal decided on 1 July 2001 that possession and use of any drug would not be considered a criminal offence, although supply of drugs is still prohibited. Since then drug consumption has fallen by 10 per cent,[490] and the prevalence of drug taking by teenagers has fallen for all drugs, in some cases dramatically.[491] The policy has been successful in reducing the harm done by drugs.[492]

- Ireland should abandon the criminal prosecution of all drug users.

- Personal cultivation and use of marijuana should be legalised.

- People addicted to drugs should be offered treatment for their addiction.

- People who are diagnosed as addicted to highly addictive drugs, but refuse treatment, should be offered clean, purity-tested drugs and clean needles in a controlled environment at their own risk, for free, with strict controls to ensure that they cannot take any drugs away from the facility.

The last point is certain to meet stern opposition from people who morally disapprove of drug use; however, the state has no business enforcing such moral standards. While this move would make the state complicit in the harm done by long-term use of heroin and possibly other drugs, on balance the amount of harm done to both the addict and society would be significantly reduced:

- Addicts who refuse treatment are those least likely to give up drugs on their own, and sending them to the drug dealers instead does not reduce the harm caused to them.

- Addicts are likely to be far safer taking drugs of consistent purity in a monitored environment.

---

‡ Ireland is, however, constrained by international treaties and other commitments from legalising all drugs.

- Society benefits from the reduction in crime needed to fund drug addiction.

- Drug-dealers' incomes are dramatically cut.

- Drug-dealers' incentives to introduce drugs to new potential addicts disappear, because an addict is no longer a walking cash machine for the dealers.

The last point is the most crucial. People respond to incentives. The state has, at huge expense, put huge barriers in the way of people who respond to the financial incentive to supply drugs to new and existing addicts. Drug dealers have always succeeded in overcoming these barriers, and there is no reason to think that they will not continue to do so. Instead of increasing the barriers, it is sensible to remove the incentives.

Cigarette Taxes

There are excellent public health reasons for taxing cigarettes heavily, particularly to keep them out of the reach of children – it is a good example of taxing the bads instead of the goods. But smuggled cigarettes put a limit on this policy. The higher the tax, the greater the motivation on smugglers to bring in cigarettes illegally. Apart from the loss to the taxpayer, cigarette smuggling causes many other problems. The reduced price encourages more adults to smoke, and to smoke more, with obvious health results. There is no control on the sale of smuggled cigarettes to children, who are the main targets of the tobacco companies who know that a child smoker is most likely a smoker for life, albeit a shortened one.

The scale of the smuggling is caused by the easy portability of the product and Ireland's excellent transport links with locations where untaxed cigarettes are freely available. In 2007, almost every single passenger on a flight from Eastern Europe had their luggage confiscated at Dublin Airport when they were caught with smuggled cigarettes.[493] The attraction for migrants of a couple of hundred euro to bring a suitcase full of cigarettes after their trip home is obvious. Raising the penalties to a point that would deter this activity would be extremely harsh on people at the very bottom of the criminal chain and leave those at the top untouched.

Smuggling was cited as the reason for not increasing the cigarette tax by €2 per packet in April 2009.[494] Our government is literally being held to ransom by criminals. The Revenue improved the situation slightly when they introduced tax stamps on tobacco products; however, these were quickly reproduced by forgers,[495] forcing the adoption of high-tech stamps with holograms.[496] It remains to be seen how long it takes the smugglers to knock them off.

The core of the problem is the system of manufacturing cigarettes in the EU free market, where cigarettes manufactured in any one of 27 countries can be put on a truck, tax free, with only the requirement that a form be stamped acknowledging that they are consigned out of the EU, perhaps having travelled through half-a-dozen countries in the meantime. The stamp could come from any one of hundreds of ports speaking dozens of different languages. It could be a scribbled signature, it could be a smeared or worn rubber stamp, it could be written in one of several alphabets, but once the cigarette companies have it, they are in the clear with the customs authorities in their own country for releasing the cigarettes untaxed.

The Revenue authorities are then left with the task of chasing ships, lorries, migrants with suitcases and petty criminals selling cigarettes door-to-door in working-class estates around Europe hoping to find the untaxed cigarettes that have never actually left the EU. This is a clear example of the problems caused by ignoring principle 10 on page 15 – the wrong person is doing the job. The tobacco industry has been quick off the mark in trying to use this to pressurise the government to reduce cigarette taxes.[497]

The problem could be eliminated if the tobacco companies – huge multinational corporations – would just stop selling their products to smugglers. They claim that they don't supply the smugglers intentionally, but there is ample evidence to the contrary.[498] [499] They have a huge incentive to sell to smugglers, and it is difficult to believe that they would choose to act against their own interests. Apart from immediately increasing the already vast profits that they make,[500] smugglers sell cigarettes to children, who tobacco firms desperately need to take up smoking. Studies show that adults who start to smoke can give up quickly and easily. Children who start smoking are lifelong addicts.[501] The solution is simple – motivate the tobacco companies not to sell to smugglers. Here's how:

- Calculate the total amount of legal tobacco sales from revenue returns.

- Do a survey of the contents of litter bins to compare the ratio of taxed to untaxed product being used in the country from each tobacco company – carefully examining for forged tax stamps.

- Subtract a reasonable amount to account for genuine use by tourists of tobacco bought outside the country for personal use – say 1 per cent of the total amount smoked.

- Calculate the revenue lost on the untaxed tobacco sold in the state and send the tax bill to each tobacco company.

- Prohibit the tobacco companies from trading in the state until they pay the bill.

No doubt they would squeal, maybe even call in the ambassadors of their home countries, but there is no moral reason why tobacco companies should not be stuck with the bill if they have conspired to help smugglers to evade the tax. In reality they would not have to pay much, if anything. They should be given a year's notice of the new policy, time to clear all of their product out of the black market. Motivated by such consequences, their ingenuity would be sure to come up with a way to spot smugglers when they come to buy at their factories and not sell to them.

The benefits to society would be enormous. Apart from the obvious health and child-protection benefits, apart from the benefit to the taxpayer of regaining all that money lost to smugglers – €500 million a year[502] – society would also benefit from regaining all the cost and effort wasted on a fruitless effort by the wrong people to try to enforce the law. The taxpayer would save many more millions from a better use of all the customs officers, courts, prisons and other arms of the state that now try in vain to stop cigarette smuggling.

Gay Rights

Gay rights don't exist; there are only human rights. There is no justification for giving or denying one person rights in a different way from another. Ireland's battle for civil rights is largely won, but that is no reason to soft-pedal the final mile. Official discrimination is largely gone, and what casual prejudice remains will mostly be resolved by time, not legislation. There only remain two areas that are unresolved.

The first is marriage. While it is rooted in ancient property rights, marriage in our society has become the recognition of two people, unrelated by blood, who pledge themselves to each other. The Civil Partnership Bill currently before the Oireachtas[503] will resolve many practical problems such as succession rights, but it fails to address the issue of whether gay people will be seen in the eyes of the state as equal citizens. The public seems to be ahead of the politicians; a Lansdowne Market Research poll in October 2008 found that 62 per cent of Irish people supported gay marriage.[504]

It is likely that the enactment of marriage equality would require a constitutional change. If there is any doubt about this, it is preferable for two reasons to have a constitutional referendum. Firstly, it is not acceptable to run a risk that people's marriages would be challenged in the Supreme Court. Secondly, it is preferable to use a referendum to confirm public support, rather than allow opposing groups to claim that marriage equality does not have a democratic mandate.

Groups who oppose extending marriage rights to gays and lesbians speak in vague terms of how this would undermine traditional marriage. This is the type of argument spoken with such a sense of earnest certainty that nobody bothers to question the complete absence of reasoning. If the gay couple living down the street win the right to marry, how would that undermine the marriage of the heterosexual couple living next door? And even if it did, exactly how would that be the fault of the gay couple to such an extent that it would justify denying them rights available to the rest of society?

The second is an issue used by far-right wing groups to muddy the waters: that is the "right" to adopt children, with dark hints that children adopted by gay couples would either be forcibly "turned" gay, or at risk of sexual assault from their new parents. An objection openly stated is that allowing gays to adopt would leave children open to schoolyard teasing. This argument ignores that there is no prohibition on gays or lesbians from adopting children at the moment, and the sky does not appear to have fallen.

The only issue is that gays cannot adopt as a couple. These issues need to be clearly answered.

There isn't a shred of evidence that gay parents are more likely to abuse children than heterosexual ones, although abuse of all sorts is tragically more common than we would like it to be. There is also no evidence that it is possible to turn anyone gay or straight – as Senator David Norris put it, he has had heterosexuality shoved down his throat all his life, and it hasn't had any impact on him. Blaming schoolyard bullying on difference and not the bullies is a dangerous road to go down, as victim-blaming always is. There are solutions for this under **Bullying in Schools** on page 126, but the notion that bullying is caused by difference, rather than the need of the bully to find difference, is simply wrong.

Adoption has one purpose only – finding a permanent home for some of the most vulnerable children in our society. All adults, gay or straight, married or single, should have equal rights when it comes to adoption: none. The rights are solely with the child. The consideration in selecting adoptive parents, and the only consideration, is what is best for the child. The adults' interests shouldn't come second, because they shouldn't come anywhere.

Decisions should be made on a case-by-case basis, in each case focusing solely on what will give the best possible outcome for the welfare of the child being adopted. Anyone advocating that gay people should be excluded as a group from being considered as adoptive parents is essentially saying that their ideology should take precedence over the welfare of a child.

- The Civil Partnership Bill should include provision for all the social, economic and cultural rights that go with marriage.

- A referendum should quickly follow with the sole purpose of extending the constitutional definition of marriage.

Justice

The Gardaí

Up to independence, Ireland had two police forces – the Royal Irish Constabulary (RIC) and the Dublin Metropolitan Police (DMP) – but from a British point of view, these were just two forces out of many in the United Kingdom. The RUC was formed out of the remnants of the RIC. The Civic Guard was created in 1922, and the DMP was subsumed into it to form the Garda Síochána in 1925, which inherited all the DMP's property and many of its structures and practices. This meant that the Gardaí began life as the only police force in a small state, with structures designed for a force that was one among many in a large country.

Then nothing happened. For the entire rest of the twentieth century, no change or restructuring worth mentioning occurred. Regardless of their position in 1925, it is astonishing that the Gardaí have successfully resisted all attempts at reform for nearly a century. But given that the organisation of the Gardaí was not best suited to its purpose from the outset, problems with the Gardaí were entirely predictable. Also predictable was the fact that those problems would be ignored, covered up and allowed to fester.

The Morris Tribunal, established to investigate Garda malpractice in 2002, concluded that there was widespread corruption, including planting false evidence, forging of signatures on confessions, extreme and unjustified harassment and persecution of innocent people.[505] Morris was highly critical of the Gardaí as a force, finding it in a state of disarray, with low morale, poor discipline, lack of oversight and a culture of silence summed up by one Garda who was not accused of corruption, but failed to report serious crimes that he had witnessed his colleagues committing. He told the tribunal, "We don't hang our own."[506]

More Gardaí

We need more Gardaí; perhaps not more members of the force, but more forces. Crime and the duties of Gardaí have become much more complex in the last century, and it is unrealistic to expect one organisation to handle that level of complexity and competing demands. The recruitment of Gardaí, which has improved in recent years, still does not lend itself to including in the force people suitable for investigating everything from anti-social behaviour to gangland murders to complex banking fraud.

A Garda commissioner trying to decide which of these competing issues should take priority is in an impossible position. Followers of US cop shows will have seen scenes where various police – local, state and federal (the FBI) – dispute jurisdiction in an investigation. This competition is healthy, and it is far better to risk two forces investigating a crime than none.

- The Garda Síochána should be split into several forces, entirely separate from each other with lines of command that do not converge at any point.

- The current Gardaí should be the genesis of a force that retains responsibility for all "ordinary" crime and anything that is not specifically assigned to another force.

- A separate **Garda Tráchta** should be established specifically to police the roads and motoring offences, and report to the minister of transport – see page 256.

- The new body to investigate and prosecute major fraud, tax evasion, cartels and other financial crime, proposed on page 189, should also be designated a Garda force, reporting to the minister of finance.

- The environmental police proposed on page 149 should report to the minister of the environment.

- All Garda forces should share a single integrated computer system.

It is important to distinguish between establishing a new squad or task force within the Gardaí and establishing an entirely new police force. The work culture, procedures and recruitment practices appropriate to one area, such as investigating financial crime, simply don't have anything to gain from those designed to tackle regular crime. They suffer from being seated in the same organisation, because pressure to react to shifts in public mood leads to resources being shifted around in a way that undermines development of specialist investigation skills.

Gardaí recruited into fighting "normal" crime are likely to develop a worldview where the bad guys fit a cliché of being working class, uneducated and violent. If they are then transferred to investigating financial crimes, where crooks look more like the people they previously saw only as victims, it is not surprising that they don't pursue them with the same vigour.

Finally, it is simply not good organisational practice to give one organisation a monopoly on such a powerful position, which is why Ireland is unusual in having a single unitary police force.

Crimes by Gardaí

While crimes by Gardaí should normally be dealt with in the same way as crimes by any other citizen, membership of the force makes some crimes particularly heinous, and the law must reflect this. In particular, Gardaí who manipulate evidence to wrongfully convict someone of a crime, or wrongfully have a criminal acquitted, must be dealt with very severely.

Gardaí who deliberately help a criminal escape conviction are in effect accessories to the crime.

A standard sentencing policy should be established that, if a Garda is convicted of perjury or falsifying evidence, they should receive a sentence equal to what the person on trial received, or would have received if they were convicted.

The Garda Gizmo

In July 2009, Gardaí showed off a new piece of technology that has been fitted to a number of patrol cars. It automatically reads the number plates of passing vehicles, queries a database, and an automatic voice alerts the Gardaí when it passes a car with no record of tax, insurance or which is suspected to be involved in crime.[507] This is an excellent deployment of technology but only scratches the surface of what is possible.

Corruption is a serious issue, but so is routine inefficiency. High-profile cases attract a flurry of activity, but the author has experience of two criminal investigations that simply ground to a halt, and follow-up calls to the Garda station were answered by Gardaí who would not give information or take messages; they would just say when another Garda would be on duty ... "but he might be out on patrol". There is no way of knowing the extent or effect of this type of inefficiency, because the Gardaí don't publish, and don't even seem to record for themselves, a huge proportion of their contacts with the public.

Technology can greatly improve the efficiency and effectiveness of policing and assist Gardaí to greatly improve the service that they give the public. It can also provide information that will allow Garda management to audit in detail the performance of Gardaí – their compliance and the quality of the service they give to the public, giving them the opportunity to replicate best practice throughout the force and address poor performance.

First, every member of the Gardaí needs to get a gizmo. If you have seen the electronic tool that supermarket workers use to check stock levels on shelves, you know the sort of thing. Use of such a device is not novel; similar devices are commonly used by everyone from meter-readers to nurses in hospitals. No member of the Garda should be permitted to be on duty without their gizmo. When a member of the public comes in contact with a Garda, by making a complaint, reporting a crime, being arrested or having their details taken, the details should be noted on the gizmo, replacing the notebooks that Gardaí currently use. It should:

- be hand-held
- be connected to Garda databases via secure mobile broadband

- store no data internally, only reading and writing data from secure computers it is connected to
- include a touchscreen, a bar-code reader, high-resolution camera and a fingerprint reader
- include a GPS receiver to record its location at all times
- have a unique secure login for each Garda, verified by fingerprint
- have software that is transparent to the Gardaí, which can have features added as Garda needs develop.

The gizmo should be able to access and write data to Garda computers; Gardaí already have an extensive database which covers most vehicles registered in the country and extensive information about every person convicted of a crime, along with a large amount of soft information, below the standard of proof that would be acceptable in a court, but useful in investigating crimes. The gizmo should:

- scan car registration plates and instantly report on the tax, insurance and NCT status of the vehicle, and any known criminal associations
- scan the bar-codes on drivers' licences and bring up the licence record, including a photograph of the holder (see page 259)
- allow Gardaí to type in the name and other details of members of the public who they come in contact with, including their mobile phone number and ULI (see **Postcodes** on page 52)
- allow Gardaí to enter a summary of any incident by using picklists to select the category and sub-category
- take photographs of a crime scene
- be the tool with which all crimes reported or noted are first entered into the Garda computer system
- have an emergency button that would automatically direct help to a Garda's location

In addition, all the appropriate features of this system should be available on desktop computers to Gardaí in stations and on the in-car device launched in July 2009. A device similar to this is being trialled in the UK, with impressive results. As well as eliminating paperwork, an officer explained to the BBC how it could be used to send a photograph of a missing child instantly to all officers in the area.[508]

Tracking Incidents

A person making a complaint, reporting a crime or being arrested should be asked for their details, including their mobile phone number. The system should:

- generate a unique record in the Garda computer system, which can later be attached to a larger investigation if appropriate

- record the location of the device at the time the incident is input and record the ULI of where the incident took place, if different

- automatically send by SMS a unique reference number to the mobile phone of the complainant, victim or suspect

- include contact details for the Garda involved in the SMS, including the station that they are attached to

- allow the Garda to assign responsibility for the incident to another Garda and to accept incidents assigned – the incident should remain the responsibility of the original Garda until it is accepted by another member, or until a senior officer enters an instruction to do so

- automatically send an SMS to the member of the public to advise when responsibility for the incident has changed, and advise the contact details of the new Garda

- allow Gardaí to mark an incident as closed and automatically send an SMS to the member of the public to advise them of this, and the reason for closing the case, such as no charges brought, caution issued, or case forwarded to the DPP

- present to each Garda a list of their open cases

- allow Garda management to track the workload of each Garda and Garda station, and manage their resources accordingly.

Garda Ombudsman

The long-overdue Garda Ombudsman was established in May 2007, albeit with a three-person commission rather than an individual ombudsman. They are empowered to:

- directly and independently investigate complaints against members of the Garda Síochána;

- investigate any matter, even where no complaint has been made, where it appears that a Garda may have committed an offence or behaved in a way that would justify disciplinary proceedings included

- investigate any practice, policy or procedure of the Garda Síochána with a view to reducing the incidence of related complaintsinclude.[509]

The data generated in the databases behind the gizmo's computer system would be of enormous use to the Garda Ombudsman in all three of their areas of operation. They should be given unrestricted, live, read-only access to the entire database system and have the capacity in-house to run whatever queries on the data that they see fit to further their investigations.

Public Access to Data

The data in this database is unlike many others proposed in this work; it is vital that much of it remains secret to preserve the privacy of people reporting crime and people wrongly suspected of crimes, and to prevent criminals gaining operational knowledge that would frustrate the detection of crime. Despite this, there would be much information proper to the public domain, which would give journalists and citizens the power to examine the operations and efficiency of the Gardaí and spot inconsistencies in performance.

All statistical data such as number and types of crimes reported and clear-up rates should be made available on the internet, down to a level of Garda station, and the level of ULIs that would not compromise the privacy of victims or witnesses of crime – see **Privacy** on page 55. The Garda Ombudsman should be given the task of supplying the appropriate information on a scrapable website. Decisions on what data to release should be made by the Ombudsman, in consultation with the senior Garda management, and in response to requests from the public. Their guiding principle should be to release as much information as possible without compromising anyone's privacy or security.

Use of the Data

Do not look at DublinCrime.com. The domain has now been taken over by pornographers, but when the website was running, it was a prototype for a very powerful idea. Using a Google map, the website intended to display all crimes committed in a geographical format, with a coloured pin on the map for each type of crime, in the way that property websites show houses for sale.[510]

The website only ever displayed murders, and didn't last, presumably because the workload of collating crime details from the press and entering them was beyond the means of the site's owners. Nevertheless, striking observations could be made. Viewing murders by gender, it was immediately striking that men are murdered in the city, women are murdered in the suburbs.

Imagine the power of a system that would have all reported crimes automatically populated in such a system. It is not a new idea. While mayor of New York, Rudy Giuliani succeeded in reducing crime by a huge proportion. In his book *Leadership*, he wrote about the police computer system CompStat that he introduced in 1993:

> Crime statistics were collected and analysed every single day, to recognize patterns and potential trouble before it spread. At the CompStat meetings, we used that data to hold each borough

command's feet to the fire – a hundred police at a time, from brass to officers, joined by others from throughout the criminal justice system ... every one of that command's statistics faced scrutiny...

Next, any manager who didn't have their heart in the new system was made to understand that it was time to retire or face a demotion. Those on the force who realized that CompStat would not only improve their city but actually make their jobs more rewarding were promoted and entrusted with leadership roles...

We implemented an auditing system ... [which] would flag stations with unrealistic performance, allowing us to dig deeper into its accuracy. There were even commanders removed for tinkering with the numbers...

Before CompStat, it was anyone's guess whether, say, a pattern of three A.M. gas-station robberies was emerging. A sharp-eyed policeman might notice his own activity concentrating in certain areas at certain times, but he would have no way of knowing whether his colleagues were fielding the same type of incident at the same time and place ... Using CompStat, the goal of preventing crime rather than reacting to it was fulfilled. With patterns identified early, the commander deploys officers to probable targets and arrests the criminals before they have robbed the garage, instead of hoping the 911 call arrives in time...

The impact of CompStat was immediate and revolutionary. Major felonies fell 12.3 percent from 1993 to 1994. In two of the most serious categories – murder and robbery – the city's reductions were the largest one-year drops ever – 17.9 percent and 15.5 percent...[511,‡]

As well as in New York, there is evidence from the UK that sophisticated computerised analysis (called data mining) of criminal behaviour can have dramatic results. Cleveland Police say they achieved a 32 per cent reduction in anti-social behaviour, a 70 per cent reduction in criminal damage and an 83 per cent reduction in house burglaries *in one month* by analysing and acting on crime patterns, often with very simple responses such as warning people that there was a spate of burglaries in their area.[512]

The system that Giuliani describes is only a fraction of what is possible with the information technology that is available nearly 20 years later. The data, both for internal Garda use and for the public, should be made available in

---

‡ In addition, Giuliani writes that the fall in crime continued. From 1994 to 2001, crime fell by 57 per cent and shootings by 75 per cent, with nearly 1,200 fewer rapes in 2000 than in 1993, and police shootings fell from 212 to 73. Robbery fell from 85,883 to 32,213. Burglary tumbled from 385,155 to 100,933, while car theft plummeted from 111,611 to 35,673. The crime decline was citywide. In 1993, there were 92 murders in Crown Heights and 35 in Harlem. By 2000, those numbers were 35 and 5.

a format that allows it to be compared easily to an analysis of sentencing data available from the Courts Service, to spot any correlations or inconsistencies – see **Judging the Judges** on page 249.

Minimum Sentences

Since 1999, section four of the Criminal Justice Act provided that any person convicted of possessing drugs to a value of €13,000 or more should receive a mandatory minimum sentence of 10 years or more. It was trumpeted as a strong measure against drug barons, although judges were allowed to impose a lighter sentence in exceptional circumstances. In more than 85 per cent of such cases, a sentence shorter than the "mandatory" minimum is handed down.[513] Exceptional, it would seem, is not all that exceptional.

There are two lessons in this. Judges are paid to hear the evidence and decide an appropriate sentence. If this was not necessary, we would not need to hire them. The Criminal Justice Act mandatory sentence is particularly stupid, and it was clearly designed to catch headlines, not drug barons, because anyone in possession of €13,000 worth of drugs is certain not to be a drug baron. Drug barons never possess any quantity of drugs. They pay pathetic addicts €100 or €200 to stash or move their drugs for them, and a 10-year sentence for such an offence would be grossly disproportionate, and judges are probably correct in adjudicating that the great majority of people charged under this section do not deserve this sentence. So the first lesson is that governments should be exceptionally careful about creating mandatory sentences.

It is possible that mandatory sentences are appropriate sometimes, particularly where there is a problem with society's (and perhaps judges') perception of the severity of a crime. In these circumstances, the message that a mandatory sentence gives is that the judge cannot be trusted, with a get-out clause to say that, in exceptional circumstances, they can be trusted. Judges are human beings, and it would be surprising if they did not conclude that almost every case that came before them was one in which they could be trusted. Secondly, if mandatory sentences are to be used, they should be used sparingly. The appropriate mechanism for exceptional cases where a judge believes that the defendant does not deserve the mandatory sentence should be that the judge may ask a higher court to consider a lower sentence, for stated reasons, rather than making the decision herself.

Bail Hostels

Someone on the brink of becoming a career criminal should be deterred in every way possible from taking that route. A person living on the fringes of crime is unlikely to benefit from prison. Firstly, they will be in the company of criminals, who normalise criminal behaviour for them and educate them in the ways of crime.

Secondly, even if eventually acquitted or given a non-custodial sentence, the time in prison on remand will make them likely to lose their job or place in education and make it harder to regain it. Given the strong association between crime and failure in education and employment, it is critical to do everything to avoid this.

- The state should establish a network of small bail hostels, with 10 to 15 beds each, where a person awaiting trial could be ordered to spend specific hours.

- Bail hostel residents should be encouraged to continue in their employment or education and keep up family commitments.

- The precise hours and conditions for each resident would be ordered by the court, and the hostel would have a small staff who would confirm that they are met, although they would have no role in enforcing them.

- Failure to keep to the conditions would constitute a breach of bail conditions and render the offender liable to committal.

- The hostels should have kitchens for cooking meals, study rooms and visiting facilities, to make sure that residents retain as much control over their lives as possible.

- Provision should be made for locking rooms at night and any other security measures that may be ordered by a court.

- Hostels should be kept as small and numerous as possible, to allow the court the flexibility to send a resident to a hostel close enough to maintain their employment and family connections, but far enough away from temptation to breach conditions.

Ordering a person awaiting trial to a bail hostel at a slight remove would also mean they would not suffer the stigma of being within their immediate community. Locations should be served by good public transport. This would also make it easier to keep residents separate in cases where they may commit crimes together, egg each other on or where it is important for them to give evidence without conferring.

A bail hostel will not be suitable for all people awaiting trial; however, they are likely to be much cheaper to run than prisons, and if only a small proportion of those on remand are suitable for using them, they would be worthwhile.

Bail Hostels and Family Violence
Men's rights groups and others have made a strong case for the injustice of some barring orders, particularly where they have the effect of making

someone homeless. Nevertheless, there remains a need to protect families from violence and oppressive behaviour. Particularly in the cases where a very fast decision is needed, it would be useful to give the courts the power to order a person to reside at a bail hostel, exclusively, or for specified hours. This would provide an extra option which could, in some cases, provide the protection required without escalating a family dispute.

Drugs in Prisons

Prisons, by definition, are the most secure locations in the state, but the prevalence of hard-drug use is shocking. Tests indicate that 75 per cent of all prisoners are taking illegal drugs, with 40,000 positive drug tests in three years,[514] and the problem is getting worse, not better.[515]

This is not entirely down to the type of people sent to prison. More than 20 per cent of heroin addicts began their habit while in prison,[516] so not only are our prisons not the solution; frequently they are the cause of the problem. In March 2009, a prison officer from Limerick was arrested in possession of drugs and 35 mobile phones.[517] Heroin, the most destructive drug, requires equipment to prepare, including candles, spoons, acid and syringes as well as the drug itself. This is difficult to conceal and should be easy for prison officers to detect. A senior researcher on drug use has confirmed to the author that there is no doubt that most prison officers collude in drug use, happy that heroin makes prisoners more docile and compliant, and that a significant number of prison officers profit from dealing drugs to prisoners.

Prisoners will make no progress towards being productive members of society when prisons such as Mountjoy have 80 per cent of their prisoners addicted to heroin.[518] While he may have been going for the wrong target, Michael McDowell proposed in 2004 that contact between prisoners and visitors be stopped if that is what is needed to prevent drugs being passed to prisoners, but he met with determined opposition, with the prison officers complaining about not being "consulted" and the prison governor John Lonergan talking about the "impossibility" of making a prison drug-free. Lonergan also made the valid point that demand for places on detox-programmes far exceeds supply.[519]

Lonergan talks of the harmful effects of denying prisoners contact visits with their families in an attempt to stop drugs coming into prisons. This has to be weighed against the harmful effects of drugs on the prisoners and on society, but in any case, he is wrong to think that this is necessary. Sensitive equipment is now available that can detect traces of drugs without even searching the person carrying them.[520] [521] The sensors detect odour trails, sniffing out any substances they are programmed to find. All prisons should be made entirely drug-free:

- Detoxification programmes should be available to every prisoner who is admitted to a prison.

- A specific offence of smuggling drugs into a prison should be created, with exemplary punishments.

- All entrants to the prison, including prisoners being admitted, visitors and prison officers arriving for work, should be screened for drugs using the latest technology available.

- Screening should be carried out by a separate agency from the prison staff, and people responsible for screening should be rotated in a random pattern.

- Gardaí should be on hand to search anyone found to have traces of drugs and to arrest them and seize the drugs if found.

- Any visitor found to have traces of drugs, but no drugs on them, should be refused admission to the prison.

Recidivism

In theory, prison is meant to deter people from committing crimes and reform those who do. The reality is very different. The Institute of Criminology at University College Dublin studied nearly 20,000 prisoners over an extended period. They found that:

- 25 per cent of prisoners are back in jail within one year of release.

- 50 per cent of prisoners are back in jail within four years of release.

- Most disturbingly, 85 per cent of those imprisoned for non-payment of fines, likely to be very minor offenders, are back in jail within four years.[522]

This is a diabolical record. In addition, the report gives evidence that once someone has begun a life of crime, the prison system does nothing to prevent them from continuing and seems to cause them to continue: 60 per cent of repeat offenders were very likely to return to prison compared to 35 per cent of first time offenders. If you come back, you will keep coming back.

The fact that fine defaulters have such a high rate of recidivism is particularly disturbing, since there is no real reason for them to be in prison in the first place. While there are no statistics for Ireland, in the mid-1990s, 57 per cent of women in English prisons were there because of failing to pay their TV licences.[523] Recognising the destructiveness of this, the British justice minister Jack Straw ordered an end to the practice.[524]

Close All Prisons

Prisons in Ireland should be closed. All of them. And all prison officers should be made redundant. Every single one. Ireland's prison system is hopelessly corrupt. There are some reformers, some idealists, some honest workers in the system, but not enough to make the system worthwhile.

We could look at the fact that in Ireland we have as many prisoner officers as prisoners and still have huge prison overtime bills and a dreadful recidivism rate.

But worst of all, the greatest shame is the rate of drug abuse in Irish prisons. Heroin – the reason so many prisoners are there in the first place – is freely available. The Health Research Board (HRB) has reported that more than half[‡] of all prisoners use drugs.[525]

It is almost beyond belief that, in a country that employs customs officers to try to keep illicit drugs out of the country, the most secure places in the country cannot even begin to contain the availability of drugs. In July 2001, then Justice Minister John O'Donoghue asked the prison service to establish a "drug free" area in each prison, without commenting on whether he was happy for the rest of the prison system to be awash with drugs.

The accepted wisdom is that drugs are smuggled into prisons by being thrown over perimeter walls and during prison visits. While this may be true, it is not credible that such large and reliable amounts of heroin could be in circulation in our prisons without the connivance of many prison officers. A study on British prisons revealed that there were more than 1,000 corrupt prison officers in Britain.[526] It would be deeply naïve to imagine that the situation is any better in Ireland.

Prison officers may be accepting bribes to look away while drugs are being smuggled, distributed, prepared and taken. They may simply be profiteering from dealing in drugs themselves. Or they may just choose to allow the drug trade to continue in the hope of a quieter life. Any or all of these may be true. It doesn't matter. Simply for the fact that almost 60 per cent of all prisoners take drugs, and the prison service fails to prevent it, they deserve to be closed down.

The New Prison Service

An urgent prison building programme should be undertaken. An entirely new agency should be created to establish the prison, hire and train prison officers and then run prisons. It should be based on international best practice, with experts in the field recruited from overseas as required.

As new prisons are built, they should be used to empty an entire existing prison and all the staff of the old prison made redundant. As a prison is vacated, renovations should be done and new facilities added to bring the

---

‡   A figure disturbingly close to the 60 per cent of prisoners who keep coming back.

empty site up to the required standard (see **Escaping from Crime**, below). When it is ready, another old prison can be evacuated into it, to allow the process to continue. The sequencing of this could leave the most decrepit prison until the end, by which time it would, hopefully, be unneeded. The point of this exercise is to effect a revolution in work practices and conditions of Irish prisons. While former prison officers would be as entitled as anyone else to apply to work in the new prison, their applications should be taken purely on merit. Particular care should be taken to ensure that two principles guide the running of the new prison service – rehabilitation of prisoners and value for money for taxpayers.

Crime

There are lots of reasons why someone embarks on a life of crime. Every measure should be taken to prevent young men – it's almost always young men – from falling into a life of crime, by improving education, improving employment opportunities and ensuring that criminal penalties don't inadvertently push people further into a spiral of crime.

Inevitably, sometimes these measures fail. While we should do everything to ensure that they will fail as rarely as possible, it is unrealistic to imagine that they will never fail. When they do, society must choose whether we will enforce the law, or whether out of laziness, sloth, contempt for the victims or some notion that it would be unfair on the criminals, we will fail to do so. The question is how society can coerce people who would otherwise be criminals to uphold the law.

At the moment we are failing. Across generations and geography, there is little correlation between harshness of punishments and levels of crime. If anything there is a reverse correlation, with harsher regimes being associated with higher levels of crime. This is not surprising; when a population suffers from high crime, you can expect a clamour for vengeance.

Vengeance may feel good, but it doesn't get us anywhere. What is needed is a coherent plan to compel young men who take up a life of crime to stop. This is not an alternative to the initiatives to prevent young boys turning into young criminals; they are needed too. It is a plan for when those initiatives fail.

The first issue is empowerment. Criminals typically come from backgrounds where they have very little power over their own lives, and this provides them the psychological space to explain that they are not really to blame for their crimes. Regardless of their pasts, at every turn, any plan to reduce crime must send the signal that the person to blame for a crime is the criminal, and anything that blurs that message is a problem, not a solution.

Training in Prison
Fifty-two per cent of Irish prisoners are illiterate.[527] More than half of them simply cannot read. Without solving this problem, there is no prospect of their leading productive lives. They have almost no chance of employment, and are certain to spend the rest of their lives unemployed at best.

- An intensive, comprehensive education programme should be instituted in prisons.

- Prison education should have stated goals for each prisoner, and the outcomes be carefully measured against those goals.

- Topics should include literacy, numeracy, life skills such as cooking, shopping, budgeting and parenting, and workplace skills.

- All training should be voluntary, but release dates should depend on meeting goals.

Nutrition

Followers of chef Jamie Oliver's campaign to improve school meals in Britain will be familiar with the refrain from teachers and parents that they were amazed at how the more nutritious food led to improvements in children's behaviour and learning. It is hardly surprising that malnourishment would cause problems for children, and that resolving the malnourishment would address these problems.

This may apply to more than children. A study published in 2002 demonstrated that prisoners given supplementary vitamins, minerals and essential fatty acids committed 26 per cent fewer crimes than a control group given placebos in a double-blind study.[528] This is a shocking result. One quarter of all reoffending, spread over the entire criminal population, is an enormous amount of crime, costing society in Ireland alone billions.

Prison food should be analysed for its nutritional content, and any deficiencies should be addressed by improving the food and making supplements available by whatever method gains the greatest acceptance. Even a fraction of the improvement reported in the *British Journal of Psychiatry* would justify a huge investment; but the investment needed is not that much. The rewards of reducing reoffending by one quarter are huge, and the cost would be tiny.

Maintain Good Nutrition

The benefits of good nutrition should persist after the offender has left prison. To achieve this, the prison education should be broadened to include courses on nutrition, cooking and shopping. This may sound basic, but lack of basic life-skills is often what got offenders into prison in the first place, so even a small improvement would offset the modest cost of teaching good shopping, cooking and eating habits.

As well as the practicalities of good nutrition, prisoners should be educated on the reasons for good nutrition and how this can improve their lives, to give them ownership of the process and a sense that they have control over their own lives. While these courses should be hands-on, care would have to be taken not to give prisoners access to a source for potential weapons. This issue would have to be managed, but it is not insurmountable.

Employment and Education

The connection between employment and education – or unemployment and lack of education – and blue-collar crime is too powerful to ignore.[529] Any solution must deliver convicts through an education system straight into employment. The fact that our prison system almost guarantees immunity from employment does nothing to help.

Prison work is problematic for the same reasons as Workfare is (see page 134). Unpaid or very-low paid work by prisoners competes with other minimum-wage employees, and the availability of cheaper labour can displace people in regular employment. This is not a reason to prevent prisoners from taking up employment while in prison, but such employment must pay the going rate for the job and be treated with the same conditions and dignity of any other job. There should be no suggestion of forced labour; the jobs should also be real in the sense that prisoners should be required to apply for the jobs and subject to all the conditions of hiring and firing that are typical of any other job.

Call centres and other jobs suitable for remote working are particularly suitable for being placed within prisons. Call centre jobs can be very low-skill, where agents take hotel bookings or satellite TV subscriptions, and this is dull and repetitive work – although hardly as dull and repetitive as being in prison. More skilled positions require agents to help callers with software problems on their computer, or even talk them through repairs. This variety of skill levels would allow for the different skill and education levels of prisoners and allow prisoners the chance of advancement within the system.

- Businesses suitable for employing prisoners should be encouraged with capital grants to build adjacent to prison sites.

- Workplaces should have secure and non-secure areas.

- Procedures to avoid security problems, such as access to potential weapons or means of escape, should be strictly enforced.

- Employers should have all normal duties and rights.

- Prisoners should be paid the going rate for the job and pay taxes in the normal way.

- The going rate should be adjusted to reflect any loss in productivity from the special circumstances of a prison workplace.

- Wages paid to prisoners should be garnished to reflect the cost of room and board in the prison, and the remainder divided evenly between the prisoner and a fund to compensate the victims of his crime.

- When a court-ordered amount has been repaid, this deduction from the prisoner's wages should end.

- Prisoners' salaries should be paid into a special account.

- Prisoners should have access to an ATM which would inform them of their balance, but not allow withdrawals.

- Prisoners should allow funds be sent to their dependants or save the money for release.

Taking Account

When a criminal comes before the court accused of burglary, car crime and other crimes that have a high rate of reoffending, the judge is frequently asked to have many other crimes "taken into account". Often there are dozens of these, sometimes hundreds. The accused will not be punished for these crimes. He agrees to confess to them in exchange for a promise that he will get a shorter, not a longer sentence. Nobody can ever be charged with those crimes ever again, and nobody ever will get punished for them, but they are recorded as detected (solved) in Garda statistics.

Given that they have a long criminal record anyway, these criminals don't care if it gets a bit longer, especially since it earns them a shorter sentence. The temptation for Gardaí to persuade criminals to confess to crimes that they did not commit is obvious, but some Gardaí don't stop there when manipulating the figures. In 2002, questions were raised about the Waterford/Kilkenny Garda division, which boasted the highest crime detection rates in the state for four consecutive years. For 2000, the division reported a detection rate of 68 per cent.

A memo was leaked to the press that instructed Gardaí to input a crime as detected even when nobody had been accused, charged or convicted of the crime, but when Gardaí were "satisfied" they knew the identity of the perpetrator or when the investigation had "gone as far as it was likely to go".[530] An internal Garda investigation found 114 crimes incorrectly recorded as detected, but helpfully concluded that this was down to human error, not any desire to falsify statistics.[531] There was no report of detected crimes being incorrectly recorded as not detected.[532]

- The system of "taking into account" crimes is corrupt and corrosive; it should be prohibited immediately – see **Escaping from Crime** below.

- All crime and detection statistics should be automatically generated from Garda computer systems in a manner that is immune from interference – see **The Garda Gizmo** above.

Revolving Door

He was 16. He had 230 previous convictions. Burglary, car theft and theft from cars mostly, much like he had smashed the door of my neighbour's car, causing €2,000 worth of damage, to steal about €50 worth of small change and CDs. The Garda said that he was up on a dozen or so charges at the moment and, even though he had been caught red-handed, he would only have this one "taken into account", so what was the point of going through the motions since it wasn't going to make any difference to him anyway?

My neighbour was shocked and outraged and insisted that if there was no punishment then there would be no deterrent. The Garda said that he would probably get a conviction and might go to Saint Patrick's, but this crime wasn't going to give him a longer sentence, and there would be a lot of hassle adding it on to the indictment; if she wanted to press charges, she would have to come down to the station tomorrow and make a formal statement.

My neighbour, slow on the uptake, said that she would have to get off work early but she could come down at about 4pm, would this do? The Garda said if they were to press charges she would have to go to court to be a witness as well and that he wasn't sure that he would be at the station tomorrow, he might be out on patrol, but he'd be able to drop a letter in the post confirming that she'd reported the crime for her insurance company. She got the message. The revolving door is just too convenient for the Gardaí. And for the rest of our criminal justice system. The revolving door cannot be reformed. It is just too lazy, corrupt and incompetent. At a stroke, it should be abolished.

The Criminal Menopause
The term "criminal menopause" refers to the point at which career criminals retire. Almost all crime of this type is committed by males between 15 and 35. A conventional explanation of this is that men mellow once they settle down and get married. This may be a reversal of the cause and effect. As seen above, criminals tend to be extremely low-achieving people; fewer than half of them can even read.

Evolution pushes us all to reproduce, and reproduce with the highest-status partners possible. Clearly the typical criminal is not someone who would be considered a catch by most. Contrary to the popular image of someone living the high life, the authors of *Freakonomics* gained access to detailed data about the finances of drug dealing and discovered that the typical American crack dealer earned less than half of the minimum wage, in a chapter that answered the question in its title, "Why Do Drug Dealers Still Live with Their Moms?"[533]

If young males have no other route to gain the trappings that would attract a mate, it is rational for them to try to enrich themselves through crime and thereby gain female respect. Having criminal convictions makes a man less likely to form a partnership with a female from a well-off family, but that option was probably not very realistic to begin with; criminal convictions do not reduce a man's chances of forming a partnership with a female overall.[534]

It does not matter if this is not a very successful strategy, if the alternative has no prospect of success at all. And once a man does marry, his likelihood of offending immediately reduces.[535] [536] Rather than understanding this as marriage taming a criminal, it may be that crime is the only available route for some low-status males to form relationships. Regardless of whether, or to what extent, this is true, it is vital that criminals have alternatives to financing their lives by crime.

Escaping from Crime
First off, two powers should be removed from judges:

- allowing offences to be taken into account – see above
- passing concurrent sentences

Every crime is a crime, and every criminal deserves to be sentenced for every crime, with the time for each to be served separately. This would leave our 16-year-old one-boy crime wave serving a sentence somewhere into the middle of the next century, so clearly spending that entire sentence in prison wouldn't be realistic – for more on this see below. In fact, the effect would not be quite that dramatic, because the motivation on the part of both the Gardaí and the accused to bring confessions to large numbers of crimes to court would have disappeared. Nevertheless, it could well be typical for criminals to clock up sentences that would consume the rest of their lives before they leave their teenage years.

Serving a Sentence
At present a sentence means exclusively a prison sentence. A system should be devised whereby the criminal serves about the same time in jail that they do now, and that mandatory jail time should be set by the judge at their trial. However, prison would be just the first stage in a sentence. That sentence should be a coherent, realistic plan to return the offender to being a productive member of society. Within a week of arriving in prison, an offender should:

- have an individual parole officer assigned to him
- have his educational level, job skills and life skills assessed
- have his income aspirations and needs assessed, such as need to support a family
- have his drug-dependency issues assessed
- meet his parole officer to discuss the report on all of these issues and be told of the path to freedom that is open to him

- take a week to consider his options

- after this, agree a realistic path with his parole officer which would lead him to being a productive member of society.

The paths that prisoners set out on will differ, but the essential elements for every prisoner should be roughly:

- detox from drugs, and submit to regular drug-testing for the duration of his sentence

- learn to read, write and be numerate

- learn any missing life skills

- decide on a realistic career path and learn the job skills needed for it

- apply for a job with the in-prison employer

- complete the court-ordered prison part of his sentence

- move to a half-way house, similar to a bail hostel, but reserved for convicted prisoners

- agree conditions with his parole officer to continue his job on the non-secure side of the prison employer, and continue to take educational and life-skill classes

- continue to observe conditions of freedom, such as avoiding people and places associated with his previous patterns of offending

- gradually have the conditions relaxed and be permitted to take up a job independent of the prison.

- Finally, the prisoner should be freed on licence and encouraged to live independently in his own accommodation and make his own way in life.

To give offenders the maximum sense of their own agency and control over their own lives, it is important to make it clear to them at the time that they arrive in prison what their path to freedom is, and they should be given a planned release date as soon as possible after they arrive in prison. It is also important to have a clear set of penalties set out for misbehaviour, and these should be communicated to the prisoner in advance, so that they are fully aware of the consequences of any infringement they may consider. For prisoners in literacy training, these rules and penalties should be integrated into the learning material.

The penalties for prisoners should revolve around being set back in the process towards freedom. For prisoners who have been released on licence, any breach of their parole conditions, such as a positive drug test or any participation in crime, should land the prisoner back in prison immediately. As the person is still serving a sentence, they should be open to being recalled at any point if their parole officer believes that it is justified.

Fine or Imprisonment

The power of judges to sentence a convict to a fine *or* imprisonment should be removed – far too many people who have no business in prison are going there for non-payment of fines, and once they go to prison for not paying a fine, there is an 85 per cent chance that they will be sent back to prison within four years.[537] A judge may decide that a sentence includes a fine, or a term of imprisonment or both, but the defendant should not be offered a choice between the two.

- For fines of less than €10,000, the convict should be detained at the court until their PPS number is established to the satisfaction of the bailiff.

- The defendant then would have the option of paying the fine on the spot, or returning to do so within a period set by the court.

- If they did not pay within that time, the defendant would automatically have their tax-free allowance or social welfare payments adjusted by an appropriate amount to cover the fine and the extra cost of collection.

- For fines of €10,000 and greater, the sentence should be considered a court order and failure to pay contempt of court.

- In the event of such contempt, the convict should be imprisoned until the contempt is purged by paying the fine.

- The convict should be made aware from sentencing that any prison term would not be considered as payment of the fine.

Technical Juries

Juries are selected at random from the electoral roll, in a system that we have inherited from the days of British rule. Because middle-class people are more skilled at correctly phrasing their objections to serving, and because all people with legal qualifications are excluded, more working-class people serve on juries than would be justified by their numbers in the population available for selection. This is not a particularly serious imbalance, and it probably is corrected somewhat by a lower-than-average rate of voter registration amongst working-class people. Juries, on average, are ordinary people, which is usually a good thing. But this system falls down where trials are complex.

The trials of Ernest Saunders and the Maxwell brothers in Britain largely failed. Defence lawyers swamped the jury with masses of technical and financial information and achieved their desired result – the juries, unable to understand, could not say that they were convinced of guilt beyond all reasonable doubt and had to acquit.

Ireland has a poor record of even getting white collar criminals to court, let alone convicted; however, proposals elsewhere in this work should improve this situation. This would be for nothing if the courts could not handle the trials, and given the experience in Britain, this is a clear danger. Complex environmental cases should also be referred to courts with technical juries, as mentioned under **Environmental Police** on page 148.

- Juries for complex and technical trials should be recruited to serve professionally.

- They should be chosen at random, like current juries.

- Before their service, they should be given basic training in commerce, economics, accountancy, banking and environmental protection.

- Judges presiding over cases with technical juries should receive the same training.

- The training should not include law, as they should be instructed in this by the trial judge and lawyers.

- Having been assessed to have met a reasonable lay standard of understanding of the topics, they should be offered an attractive salary.

- Professional jurors should serve for a maximum of three years, to avoid the possibility of jurors getting a reputation amongst lawyers for being prone to make a particular decision.

This system would not be without cost, but it is unlikely to cost more than the current jury system. While there are no figures available for Ireland, a UK study found that in 1999 jury trials were found to cost more than €20,000 per day, ten times the cost of non-jury trials.[538]

Pre-Trial Publicity

In the past, problems with publicity influencing juries have been dealt with by cancelling or delaying trials. Charles Haughey was rescued from facing a corruption trial by the comments of Mary Harney, which the judge ruled prejudicial.[539] In an age when international media are beamed into Irish homes with little controls, it is unacceptable that high-profile suspects should avoid trials in this way.

- If defence lawyers believe that their client is at a disadvantage because of pre-trial publicity, they should be able to apply to the judge for a non-jury trial, with the judge deciding guilt or innocence.

- This application should be turned down if the judge held that the publicity was reasonable reporting of the accused's actions.

- The option of dismissing a trial because of publicity should be removed, particularly since in the internet age media coverage is now beyond the control of the courts, and this opens the possibility of the accused generating publicity to escape trial.

Judging the Judges

Judges have made a major contribution to Irish society and democracy. At times, they have shown courage in slapping down unfair and unconstitutional laws made by powerful politicians. Judges have made decisions vital to the well-being of all, such as striking down the law that limited taxi licences to a privileged few operators. When an unemployed man can overthrow the requirement to pay a deposit to stand for election[540] and a beggar can successfully argue that begging passively is protected by his constitutional right to freedom of expression,[541] it demonstrates that the courts can protect the rights all members of society.

However, judges are members of an elite, sharing a very similar educational and career background, and members of a tight-knit social set. It would be surprising if it never happened that such a small, closed world didn't sometimes have a skewed or restricted view of life. The Constitution of Ireland says:

> Justice shall be administered in courts established by law by judges appointed in the manner provided by this Constitution, and, save in such special and limited cases as may be prescribed by law, shall be administered in public.[542]

It is vital that justice is done, and is seen to be done – that is why justice must be done in public. Judges, particularly the most junior ones, district justices, have wide-ranging powers that are not matched by the level of scrutiny they receive. Major decisions attract major publicity and there is evidence that judges respond to public pressure.

Justice Paul Carney freed Adam Keane, who raped a deaf woman in her bed, giving him a suspended sentence of three years.[543] Predictably, there was uproar.[544] It was not the first time Justice Carney was at the centre of a storm. In the notorious Kilkenny incest case, a horrifying life of ritual beatings, rape and unimaginable cruelty ended with the death of Kelly Fitzgerald at the age of 15. Justice Carney sentenced her parents to 18 months' imprisonment for wilful neglect.[545]

After the Keane case, the rapist flicked a cigarette at his victim at Limerick railway station, having shared a train from Dublin with her. For this, he was brought back to court where Justice Carney activated the three-year sentence. The public is left with the impression that rapists walk free, but there is a three-year sentence for flicking a cigarette. The appeal court later increased the sentence for the rape to ten years.

In another case, the left-wing website, Indymedia, accused Justice Mary Fahy of ejecting from her court people taking notes of proceedings.[546] The website, which styles itself as an independent news service, later reported:

> ...the judge ... announced that she had been made aware that there was a stenographer and other people ... taking notes in court!! "And would these people stand up please?" She then went on to make a ruling that no one other than an "accredited journalist" or a "stenographer from a reputable company" was entitled to take notes in court. After much to-do ... the judge finally conceded to Owen's application to allow the stenographer record his case's proceedings. When questioned by Owen Rice and myself on the legality of her assertions of "no entitlement for anyone else in the court to make notes" she refused to give any legal grounding to her decision saying only that she had made her ruling and "any repeats of these type of questions would be treated as contempt of court". [547]

This incident was not reported in the mainstream press, but it would be deeply disturbing if a judge made such an unconstitutional ruling. The case is even more disturbing because notes were being taken because the defendants and their associates believed that the judge was making rulings biased against anti-war protesters at Shannon Airport, and that the absence of a court stenographer prejudiced their chances of a fair trial on charges connected with those protests. Regardless of the truth of the story, the fact that a substantial number of people believe that they cannot obtain justice in court is corrosive of the entire system.

Minor Injustices

Spectacular cases of perceived injustice are likely to attract much press attention; people of means will have the resources to appeal unfair decisions. But if a judge is biased or incompetent, she or he may continue to dispense injustice for years with only a few bad decisions being reversed. Barristers talk of personal injury cases where, when the judge becomes known, the defendants rush to settle because the judge is known to have sympathy with the sort of injury at issue and to award very large damages. Justice should not rest on the luck of the draw.

The best guard against bad decisions is self-correction by judges. Most judges are anxious to be just, but decisions are subjective, and some judges may not notice that their moral compass has deviated from their colleagues and needs to be corrected. There already exists an informal system for this, where judges consult with colleagues, but this system is open to human biases. To make good decisions, judges need good information. The Courts Service should create a detailed database that records:

- the outcome of all cases, criminal and civil

- the judge presiding
- the nationality, gender and age of the defendant, and of any victims
- the charges against the defendant
- any previous convictions of the defendant
- whether the case was appealed, and whether that appeal was successful
- the database should also be used by judges and the courts service to record all aspects of the case, including the ruling

The database should be searchable by any of the criteria, and produce averages and totals. This would allow each judge to compare in detail their sentencing and awarding patterns against the average of their colleagues and contemplate whether deviations from the average were the result of random effect, different type of caseloads such as different circuit with different criminal patterns or whether they represented some form of unconscious bias. As people closest to the system, this bias would be most noticeable to other judges, and a judge who did not self-correct could be invited to have a quiet word with colleagues who could counsel the best course of action.

Public Access
This system could work without any pressure from any quarter; it would raise judges' awareness for fairness in sentencing and other decisions. It would also be a valuable guide to newly appointed judges. It could also work by encouraging senior judges to have a quiet word with their less reliable colleagues who step too far out of line. However the system works, if there was fairness in sentencing, there would be no reason to withhold the information from the public. But if the system does not function, and there are wide and unjustifiable variations in decisions, then it is vital that such shortcomings are exposed.

"Justice shall be administered in public," says the Constitution, and with good reason. That is what will give us the greatest assurance that justice is being done, and there is in nothing there about limiting the public access via new technology. All of the data about every case should be made available on the Courts Service website, in a format that is available to screen scrapers to re-present the information in any way they think may be useful to researchers, journalists and the public. This data should be collected and published in a manner that makes it compatible with information published from Garda computer systems – see **The Garda Gizmo** on page 229.

The only limitation justifiable would be to make sure that judges whose statistics deviated from the mean were not pressured into making knee-jerk judgements in an effort to balance out their numbers. Also, they must not be afraid to hand out extraordinary judgements where merited, for fear that addition of that case would skew their average. So:

- The database should be searchable by every criteria for judges with all available data.

- The database should be made available to the public, directly and via screen scrapers, in batches of six months of data, which become available two months after the final data is added to the batch.

Court Records

Many people have an image of a court with a prim stenographer typing everything that is said into a machine that produces a roll of paper for the record. In fact, most courts in Ireland, particularly district courts, the lowest level, have no systematic record of proceedings and rely on judges' handwritten notes of their decisions. This is particularly problematic when many lower courts don't attract journalists, and a dispute between a judge and any party in the case as to what was said in court is impossible to resolve to everyone's satisfaction. It is understandable that a stenographer in every court would have been a major financial cost in the past, but technology has moved on.

- All courts should be wired for sound recording.

- All cases should be recorded and the recording stored directly on computer in the database of cases and decisions mentioned above.

- All the audio recordings of cases should be made available on the internet in real time, except for cases where reporting restrictions apply.

- The audio recordings should be held securely and should be legally considered a definitive record of the case.

Arcane Practices

Legal dress is based on the style of dress for seventeenth-century gentlemen in London and Paris. The preposterous capes and powdered wigs have not been abandoned in the 400 years since the rest of society moved on.

Black is worn because London lawyers did so in mourning for Charles II in 1685, and they simply never stopped.[548] That Irish lawyers follow such a daft tradition from a foreign legal system shows just how obsequious and sycophantic the entire profession is. The arrogance of a profession that conducts its business dressed in Halloween costumes is both demonstrated and amplified by their insistence that standard business attire should not apply to them.

In 1998, Judge James Paul McDonnell ordered a young woman to be sent to the cells for contempt because she was wearing a top that exposed her belly button in court,[549] but the real contempt is demonstrated by the legal profession. While it is a small point, there can be no hope of reforming the legal profession as long as they can tell themselves, and visually demonstrate to the rest of society, that different rules apply to them. All lawyers and judges should be required to wear conventional business clothes.

Then there are the terms: Michaelmas, Hilary, Easter and Trinity. These legal terms are based on Oxbridge university terms, and between them the courts close down almost completely. It is a simple task to organise cases around the availability of presiding judges. There is no reason why all judges need to take their holidays at the same time. If every other office can remain open for 50 or 52 weeks per year, the courts can do the same.

Secret Societies

The internet is alive with daft conspiracy theories. These stories are usually the product of people with too much time on their hands, but when people come to believe, even wrongly, that they do not have a chance of an equal hearing from our system of justice, this can be corrosive of society. Secret societies frequently form the basis for such conspiracy theories, and care must be taken to avoid even the semblance of injustice. If your opponent in a court case played for the same football team as the judge, you would be justified in asking for a different judge, and judges routinely recuse themselves for far more trivial connections to people involved in a case.

- The Courts Service should maintain a section on its website where judges should declare all the organisations that they are, or have been, a member of.

- On appointment, judges should be required to leave any organisation where membership is not normally disclosed to the public.

Confessions

On 6 March 1997, Sylvia Shields and Mary Callinan were murdered in their Dublin home in a gruesome attack. Shortly afterwards Dean Lyons, a young heroin addict with poor literacy skills and subnormal intelligence, signed a detailed confession while in Garda custody admitting to the crimes, which contained details that had not been released by the investigating Gardaí and would have only been known to them and the murderer. He was sent on remand to Mountjoy prison.[550] The confession was articulate and in educated language that was clearly far beyond Lyons' capability, but the case against him proceeded until long after a second confession from another individual was brought to the attention of the investigating Gardaí.[551]

While the impressionable Lyons had been boasting to friends that he was responsible for the murder, nothing about him made him a credible suspect.

The alternative confession had far more credibility and contained accurate details that Lyons did not have. Lyons could not have committed the murders, because someone else did; he could not have composed the confession he signed because his level of education was far below that exhibited by the text; and he could not have given Gardaí details contained in the confession because he did not know them. It is transparently obvious that, while Gardaí may have been foolish enough to have initially believed Lyons' pathetic boasts, the confession that he signed was a forgery from start to finish.

Many jurisdictions, [552] [553] [554] particularly in the US (not known for leniency on criminals), including US military law,[555] explicitly prohibit conviction on the uncorroborated confession of the accused. There is good reason for this. Investigating crimes is a long, arduous, tedious process far removed from the glamour of TV detectives. It is difficult and frequently ends in failure. A criminal detection system based on confessions powerfully motivates police to seek short-cuts to circumvent the entire detection process.

Frequently, police in all forces say and believe that "of course" they know who all the criminals are and that were it not for the courts and the possibility of acquittal they could lock up all the criminals within a few hours. This assertion has been tested twice in Ireland, admittedly in extraordinary situations. After the 1916 Rising and at the start of the Northern Troubles, British forces were empowered to use internment, and lock up without trial those who they "knew" were guilty. On both occasions they got it disastrously wrong.[556] [557] The system of justice does have a purpose.

Criminals do sometimes confess to crimes, for a variety of reasons. It is entirely proper that Gardaí use this information in their enquiries, but it should be the start of an investigation, and other possible leads should not be ignored. It is not proper that a confession can be considered the end of an investigation, because it creates too great a temptation for Gardaí to extract false confessions or rely on confessions that they know are doubtful.

- The rules of evidence should be changed to prohibit prosecutions based on uncorroborated confessions.

Transport

Two centuries ago, many of our ancestors lived and died in the same parish without ever leaving. Fifty years ago, a summer holiday meant a day trip to Brittas Bay. Now, Irish people of ordinary means holiday in Thailand and Florida, and they show no indication of tiring of travel. Humans like to move. Apart from leisure, transport is the lifeblood of our economy. If you can't deliver your product, there's no point in selling it. The internet economy may be lighter, but you can bet that food, fuel, furniture and fabric conditioner are unlikely to be delivered online any time soon.

There can be no doubt that transport is used badly in Ireland – have a look at the queue of cars on the Stillorgan Dual Carriageway that lasts for about five hours a day now. The average speed of traffic in the Dublin City Council area is 13.6 km/h[558] – slower than a bicycle. Research from the Dublin Transport Office indicates that motor traffic volumes are constant from 7 to 9.30 every morning, while cyclists – unaffected by traffic – mostly travel between 8.30 and 9am.[559]

The conclusion is clear. Commuters who can choose the time of their travel choose to arrive at 9am, but motorists have to plan their entire day around traffic jams. The average commute is 42 minutes,[560] which with 1.8 million workers adds up to 657 million lost hours per year; but that's not all that is lost.

Hundreds die and many thousands are injured on the roads every year. Many Irish people vividly remember the fire in the Stardust disco in Artane on 14 February 1981, which killed 48 people.[561] Its twenty-fifth anniversary brought a series of interviews with survivors and relatives which told the story of how the tragedy is still affecting people's lives; ageing parents still grieving a quarter of a century later, children who grew up never knowing a parent. Since the Stardust Disaster, 250 times more people have died on Irish roads than died that night. Their deaths were no less horrible, their families are no less grieving.[562] Protests against speed limits are common in popular culture, with drivers complaining that there is no harm in driving above the limit.[563] [564] A British Home Office study tells exactly what the harm is:

- A child hit by a car travelling at 30mph has a 95 per cent chance of survival.
- At 35mph, the child has a 50 per cent chance of survival.
- And at 40 mph, the child has a 5 per cent chance of survival.[565]

Irish speed limits were converted to the metric system on 20 January 2005 with a retrograde step. The urban 30mph limit was changed to 50kmh, more than 31 mph. This speed limit (ignored by up to 99 per cent[566] of drivers) is the most crucial. It is now less than four miles an hour below the mean child kill speed – the speed at which more than half the victims die.

Irish drivers pay high insurance costs, and the 19-year-old male insuring his fast car pays more than anyone. Notably, some have called for insurance to be provided by or subsidised by the government.[567] This is wrong. Looking at rule number 1, on page 11, it is sensible to impose the cost of dangerous driving on the dangerous drivers – that is the thing that is most likely to make them drive sensibly.

To a degree this happens already – dangerous drivers kill themselves; that is a real cost to impose on a bad driver. Sadly, this does not work, because the cost is not a continual market response to behaviour; it is a single catastrophic cost, possibly following years of unpunished bad behaviour. By the time that the market sends the signal to the dangerous driver, the damage is done. In addition, the dangerous driver is likely to kill or maim many other road users as they learn their lesson. What is needed is a continual system of feedback that punishes minor breaches of safe driving behaviour, regardless of whether those breaches result in an accident. The point is to curb bad driving before it leads to tragedy.

Garda Tráchta

An entirely new police force, with a separate command structure but the same constitutional powers, should be established to police the nation's roads. We can call it An Garda Tráchta (GT). The GT should report to the Department of Transport and the minister, and not in any way to An Garda Síochána (GS), although it should come within the remit of the Garda Ombudsman. No powers of policing our roads should be removed from the GS, but their focus should be on other crime.

A primary goal of the new force – and a reason for keeping it separate from the GS – would be the focus on using technology for law enforcement. Motor offences are uniquely suitable to automated enforcement. This might sound like a nightmare for the Irish motorist used to regarding rules of the road as optional, but this is a classic case of the Tragedy of the Commons, where individuals are motivated to behave in a way that is against the interests of the group, including themselves.

If all drivers could be persuaded not to stop in yellow boxes or park in bus lanes, then all drivers would benefit more than they would lose; but that isn't the way an individual driver sees it when they are the one to commit the offence.

Technology

Traffic enforcement can be at the leading edge in introducing new technology, but Ireland certainly doesn't have a good record on this so far. Fixed speed cameras are often inoperative because they run out of film.[568] Why is there film in the cameras? The sales of digital cameras exceeded the sales of traditional cameras more than a decade ago[569] – a digital camera could transmit its results without ever having to be serviced, but why stop there? Optical Character Recognition (OCR) is a technology that allows a digital camera to read text (on a page or a car number plate) and transfer it into computerised text.

There is no reason why modernised digital speed cameras could not be connected to a database of vehicle registration numbers, automatically record the speed and the car number plate, print a fine, put it in the post and attach the relevant penalty points to the driver's licence without any manual intervention. The Garda Tráchta should certainly mount patrols to protect and police drivers on the nation's roads, arrest drunken drivers and take on all the other standard traffic police duties. However, this work would be made vastly more efficient by outsourcing the entire process of policing, enforcing and punishing many other traffic offences.

The current Garda Traffic Corps has a chief superintendent, two superintendents, four inspectors, 23 sergeants, 117 gardaí and 11 civilian support staff.[570] It does not take long driving on Irish roads to work out that they are ineffective.

Vehicle Records

The tracking of vehicle records in Ireland is woefully inadequate. Older vehicles in particular are simply not recorded in Garda computers. A record of the registration number may be attached to a record of the chassis number or engine number, but not to a record of who the owner is. This hampers the enforcement of traffic and criminal laws. In previous decades, joyriding was done by stealing cars, but modern sophisticated security systems have made this more difficult, and joyriders typically now buy, or are given, old cars which have failed their NCT tests – this is cheaper for the owners than scrapping the cars. Thousands of these "company cars" are found burnt out each year, and the cost of the clean-up is considerable.[571]

- The ownership of every vehicle should be recorded at the point of sale, including the PPS number or the company registration number of the owner or owners.

- Computer systems should be made available to the motor tax office, NCT centres and insurance companies, and none of these should be permitted to proceed until the PPS number of the owner is recorded.

- After one year, Gardaí should mount a high-profile campaign to seize any vehicles whose details were incomplete (and therefore are untaxed and uninsured).

- A dedicated phone line and website should be established to record vehicle sales, including the identity of buyer and seller and the price, confirming that the buyer has a valid driving licence.

- It should be a criminal offence to sell or supply a vehicle to a person where you have not confirmed that they hold a valid driving licence for that vehicle.

- Companies that own vehicles should be required to assign primary responsibility for that vehicle to a named individual and keep records of who else drives the vehicle, and when.

Penalty Points

People hate losing. [572] This is not an idle observation, it is the object of serious academic study, including by Nobel-winner Daniel Kahneman. He discovered that people value losses much more highly than gains – they will work much harder to avoid losing an amount of money than they will work to earn the same amount.[573] It is totally irrational, but it's human nature. Viewed from a psychological point of view, the penalty points system is deeply flawed.

In particular penalty points are given, rather than taken away, for bad driving; also, the least experienced drivers are most distant from losing their licence by getting penalty points. This is unfortunate, because young drivers are a particular risk on the roads.[574] Also, the all-or-nothing punishment of losing one's licence is capricious.

- Penalty points should be abolished and replaced with a system of driving licence credits.

- All newly qualified drivers should begin with five credits on their licence.

- Drivers should lose credits for each offence that they commit, on the same basis that they gain points now.

- For each year where a driver does not lose any credits, they should be awarded five extra credits, on the anniversary of the issuing of their licence, up to a maximum of 25 credits.

- Drivers losing all their credits would lose their licence and be required to wait one year before being permitted to apply to resit their driving test.

Northern Ireland drivers are required to display R plates[575] and observe a speed limit of 45mph (about 70kh/h) for one year after they pass their driving tests. This is a step to allow inexperienced drivers get used to driving; however, the single limit is a blunt instrument, and driving at 70km/h on a motorway where the general limit is 120km/h is not appropriate. Drivers with less than six credits on their licence should be required to:

- display R plates, indicating that their licence is restricted
- observe a speed limit 10km/h less than the prevailing rate for limits up to 80km/h, and 20km/h less on roads with speed limits of 100km/h or more
- observe a blood-alcohol limit of zero.

This system is designed to appeal to driver psychology to make people proud of gaining credits on their licences and to motivate young drivers to compensate for their lack of experience with extra attention. They have a target to reach – one year driving without losing any credits – and are rewarded if they reach it. If they do miss that target, they will have an opportunity reach it again. Once people establish a pattern of behaviour, such as safe (or unsafe) driving, they are likely to retain that pattern, so it is rational to use every behavioural trick to encourage the youngest, least experienced drivers to establish safe driving behaviour.

Implementation
The management of the penalty points system has been chaotic, to say the least. Some reckless drivers managed to accumulate 12 penalty points without receiving a single notification. Others who were requested to hand in their licence simply didn't do so, and there was no effective method of compelling them. It was not helped by the fact that the computer system used to run it is managed not centrally but by dozens of incompetent local authorities.[576]

- All driving licences should bear a bar-code, and the computer record of the licence should contain the photograph and PPS number of the holder.
- The bar-code should be readable by the Garda Gizmo – see page 229.
- Licence holders should be issued with stickers bearing the same bar-code as their driving licence.
- Drivers could stick these stickers on the dashboard of their car, and as long as the stickers were legible to the Garda Gizmo, they should fulfil the requirement to carry one's licence while driving.
- When scanning a driving licence or sticker, the Garda Gizmo should display the photograph, name and address of the driver, and alert the garda if the driver should be displaying an R plate, is disqualified for any reason or being sought for arrest.
- Licence credits should be run on a single computer system run by the Garda Tráchta, but accessible to all gardaí.
- When a garda detects a driving offence and scans the driver's licence, the driver should have the option to accept the fine and penalty points on the spot.

At this point, drivers must have the option to contest in court the penalty points if they believe that they are unfair, although good judicial practice demands that people should be motivated not to jam the courts with frivolous cases contesting every speeding ticket in the country.

- The notice of a fixed penalty – fines and losing credits from their licence – should be posted to the address of the licensee, as recorded in the PPS computer record.

- The driver should have 14 days to pay the fine, if they accept it, or give notice that they intend to contest the issue in court.

- If the driver fails to respond, that should be considered accepting the loss of credits, and the procedure for recovering fines via tax-free allowances outlined on page 247 should be used.

- The court should have the power, if they believe that penalty points were contested in a vexatious manner, to require the defendant to pay court costs.

Earlier in this book, the efficiency gained by allowing people to pay their motor tax online is mentioned, and it is true that this is a huge improvement over the previous bureaucratic system, but it is still much less efficient than it could be. Once a PPS number is attached to the ownership of a vehicle, it is a simple task to adjust the tax-free allowance or social welfare payments of the owner to collect the amount due. This amount should be listed separately on the tax breakdowns on payslips, but once the system is set up, it can be automated and requires no labour at all by either the taxpayer or the authorities.

An advantage of this would be that it would motivate the seller of a vehicle to make sure that the transaction was recorded properly, because they would continue to pay the motor tax until that happened. Also, vehicle transactions are prone to being used in money laundering, so records of these transactions with PPS numbers are useful to the revenue authorities. Aircraft and powered boats should also be recorded in this system.

Privatised Policing

Private policing is not something that has a positive ring to it. Rightly, many people fear that profit-driven organisations do not have the right public-spirited ethic; profit-driven organisations' main focus is to make profits. This does not mean that services cannot be put to use in such a way as to harness the profit motive to deliver the right result. Many local authorities have given us a good example of what not to do.

Unarguably, clamping illegally parked cars is far more successful than the system that preceded it, where the €19 tickets handed out by traffic wardens often cost less than a day's parking. But there are two crucial flaws with the clamping system. Firstly, just one company has the exclusive right to clamp illegally parked vehicles. Secondly, they are not paid by results – they collect a flat fee regardless of their success rate.

Authorities trumpet the second point as evidence that they have the best interests of motorists at heart; however, the long-term effects of this are not sympathetic to motorists or anyone else. Contracts for clamping, as with automated traffic enforcement, should be given to several competing private companies; and they should be paid by results only. No fine, no fee. Here's why:

Any company will naturally want to extract the most revenue for the longest time. A monopoly enforcer is motivated to pitch the level of enforcement at the point that suits them. The point that suits them is the point that will extract the most revenue from offenders without actually deterring the offence. Set too low, the enforcer is missing revenue. Set too high, the enforcer is prejudicing their future income. This will give exactly the wrong result – the motorist would doubtless resent the fines when they get caught, but they would not benefit from the improved safety and free circulation of traffic.

Multiple competing enforcers will have different pressures. They will be aware that a rival company will quickly pick up the revenue if they don't. They might have a brief bonanza, but very high levels of penalties will end quickly as motorists learn that it pays to play by the rules. Automated enforcement of traffic rules cannot enforce all traffic rules, but where it can it has three distinct advantages:

- Automating enforcement of some rules leaves gardaí free to concentrate on enforcing the rest.

- If done correctly, automated enforcement can succeed without costing the taxpayer a cent.

- A high level of compliance with traffic rules is contagious – people who obey most of the rules of the road (those with automatic enforcement) will be more likely to also obey the others.

Up to recently, there were three fixed speed cameras in Ireland. Three.[577] There are about 20 sites where the cameras can be located, but only three of these sites actually have cameras in them at any one time. This does not seem believable, but it is confirmed to the author by the Garda press office.

Every driver has a list of rules that don't really matter – the ones that they break. It is natural for people to rationalise selfish behaviour, but this is a clear example of the Tragedy of the Commons, where people are motivated to behave against the interests of a group they belong to, because the benefits of their actions go to them personally and the costs are shared by the entire group. When most members of the group behave like this, the costs on each member far outweigh the benefits.

Automation

Automatic enforcement is possible in many areas, and a model of how this could work exists with the barrier-free tolling system on the M50 and other tolled motorways. A series of competing companies offer tags and other systems to automatically bill the toll to the driver for using the toll road.[578] Drivers without tags have their number plates photographed, and a bill is posted out to them, using the address recorded for the vehicle registration.

The entire process requires no human intervention at all, except for number plates that have a record of being misread, which are checked by humans to ensure that the vehicle type and colour matches the registration plate. Since a range of companies already have these systems in place, the capital expense of automating many areas of enforcement would be minimal, and the running costs would be near zero.

The financial savings of freeing the taxpayer from the cost of manual enforcement and all the revenue generated from penalties should be ringfenced and spent on improving transport facilities, and enforcement should concentrate on offences that impact on safety and congestion. Which offences could be enforced automatically?

- Stopping on yellow boxes

There couldn't be a clearer instance of a situation where a tiny advance by one driver can block hundreds of others.

- Compliance with traffic lights

Irish traffic lights are programmed differently from those in other European countries, with no amber signal before green, to compensate for the poor compliance of Irish drivers.

The practice of stopping for a red light several car lengths past the stop line blocks pedestrian crossings and cyclists' advance stop lines and makes the roads more hostile to non-car drivers, encouraging people to abandon other forms of transport and add to traffic jams.

- Parking on footpaths and driving and parking in bus lanes, bus stops and cycle lanes

These also make roads more hostile to non-drivers and delay bus users who are likely to conclude that if they are to be stuck in traffic, they may as well do it in the comfort of their own cars, adding to traffic jams.

- Wandering between lanes without indicating and speeding

These offences make roads more dangerous for drivers, cyclists and pedestrians.

Managing the Enforcers

If Ireland can develop a culture where all the rules are obeyed as a matter of course, everybody's travel can be safer, faster and more convenient – maybe we could even get an amber light to tell us when to get into first gear. Nevertheless, it is important to make sure that the companies responsible for enforcement technology operate fairly:

- Private companies should be licensed and given appropriate access to the database that records the ownership of vehicles.

- Those companies would then install equipment that records the speed and number plate of passing vehicles at any location that they saw fit.

- They would also record vehicles breaking red lights, driving in bus or cycle lanes, stopping on yellow boxes and any other offences that they could buy or develop technology to detect.

- Their systems would be required to send the notification to the offending driver in the post or via email if the driver had an email address registered.

- Notifications should include all relevant evidence, including images of the vehicle showing the number plate.

- Their systems would also send an SMS notification to the driver if they had a mobile number registered.

- Their systems would report to the Garda Tráchta the number plates of passing vehicles that had motor tax, NCT or insurance missing from the databases that record that information.

- For privacy, their systems would be required not to take any record of passing vehicles that were not committing any offence.

- The enforcement company would report evidence of the offence for the deduction of credits to the Garda database and be responsible for collecting the fines themselves.

- Fines would be split, with 50 per cent going to the taxpayer and the rest going to finance the operator.

- Misbehaviour by operators should be punished with large fines, and repeated misbehaviour should lead to them losing their licence.

In addition to installing equipment to monitor areas where there is a high level of traffic offences, it is important also to make sure that high-risk areas that may not generate a large number of fines are policed properly. Gardaí should have the power to require enforcement companies to install equipment at a particular site, with the sites being allocated to operators in proportion to their size in the market.

Insurance

An insurance industry source is stark about the cost of motor claims:

> The dead are cheap. You're usually looking at about 100 grand, maybe a bit more if there are dependants, but it's not big money in the scheme of things. But the thing is, for every three or four dead over the weekend you hear on the news on Monday morning, there are dozens more accidents where nobody is killed – they don't even get on the radio.

> With a broken back, loss of earnings, lifetime nursing care, rehab and so on, you're into the millions. That's the one that costs the real money, and because these are usually young guys, lifetime can be fifty years or more. Even a broken leg can cost half a million if it's bad. Say he played sport, now he can't work and he has big medical bills. It would be a lot cheaper if he was dead.

Motor insurance is expensive for a reason, but that is no reason not to have a competitive market. Technology has made great inroads into solving this problem. Anyone familiar with UK satellite TV channels will know the advertisements for insurance comparison websites, and these have started to enter the Irish market also;[579] however, they are not perfect. Firstly, these websites charge a commission to the insurance companies, so the customer's price may be increased to reflect this. Secondly, larger insurance companies may refuse to supply their data, betting that the loss of business is more than made up for by keeping the market uncompetitive.

- Companies offering motor insurance should be required to place their actuarial criteria on their website in a format accessible to screen-scraping websites.

- Data about driving licence credits should also be made available on a Garda website in a format accessible to screen scraping; however, this information should not contain any data identifying the driver, even a PPS number.

- The record should be accompanied by a unique number, which would be known to its owner, who could then choose to reveal it to an insurer to verify that the driver has the driving licence credits claimed.

The purpose of this is to make the market as competitive as possible, but also to make sure that safer drivers suffer as little of the costs caused by reckless drivers as possible.

Petrol Prices

Because of the temptation to buy fuel when and where it is needed, the market for petrol and diesel may be congested. Since 1997, there have been good regulations in place requiring standardised pricing displays that are visible before the driver enters the filing station,[580] but there are cheap and easy ways to improve the information available to customers.

Petrol wholesalers should be required to establish websites, and petrol retailers should be required to input the price that they charge for each type of petrol, and the websites should make the data available for screen scraping and include the ULI for each filling station. The data could then be displayed on other websites, such as on a dynamic map. The data could also be displayed on satellite navigation devices, which could include a feature to find the cheapest fuel within a certain distance or along a particular route.

Driver Testing

Regardless of whether there is corruption in the driver testing system, there is certainly scope for corruption. Human beings are making subjective decisions with very little oversight, and those decisions have a major impact on people's lives, so it would be surprising if human frailty did not cause either driver or tester to give in to temptation. In addition, there is the possibility that testers will allow unconscious biases to enter their decisions. Monitoring aspects of driver testing is easy, cheap and best practice. One certain problem with the driving test is that it hasn't been updated since its creation and that it does not address the realities of modern motoring, such as motorway driving.

- Every candidate should be asked for statistical information including age, gender, nationality, ethnic background and number of previous tests when they apply online.

- This data should be associated with their test result, tester and the testing centre.

- All the data should be published in a scrapable format, with code numbers to represent individual testers, allowing third-party websites to analyse the data to examine it for patterns that would indicate unusual decisions.

- The key to the code should be available to the management of the driving tester centres.

- The driving test should be updated to include motorway driving, use of roads with cycle lanes and modern driving conditions.

Public Transport

CIÉ (which still exists) is an excellent example of producer capture, where the business is run for its employees. The existence of CIÉ, with board members, meetings to attend and expense accounts, as well as separate boards for Dublin Bus, Bus Éireann and Irish Rail, indicates how jobs for the boys comes higher on the priority list than serving passengers. This chaotic structure has cost the taxpayers millions.[581] With no clear lines of accountability, a difficult issue can just be shunted away to a different board.

The heating systems on Dublin buses blow hot, dry, filthy air into the faces of passengers in the middle of August. A driver asked by the author to turn it off replied that he couldn't. The contempt doesn't stop there. Circle Line, a private bus company, managed to get a licence to run a regular bus service between Lucan-Celbridge and Nutgrove via the City Centre. Dublin Bus responded by flooding their route with unlicensed buses, and Circle Line went out of business. They and another operator, the Swords Express, are pursuing legal action against Dublin Bus. As the near-monopoly provider, steps are needed to prevent Dublin Bus from abusing their position.

The Integrated Ticketing Project Board must be a great gig. It was formally established in 2006, although the project began in 2002 to allow passengers buy integrated tickets that would cover Luas, buses and Dart. Five years behind schedule and €20m over budget, not a single integrated ticket has been sold.[582] In common with not being able to buy an integrated ticket, the information about bus times is hopelessly inadequate. Timetables at bus-stops reference the time that the bus is due to leave the terminus. Even if this data was accurate, it is meaningless to someone waiting 10km of uncertain traffic conditions down the road. Dublin Bus has been piloting a satellite tracking system designed to give real-time information to passengers, since 2002,[583] although progress seems to be at the same pace as the Integrated Ticketing Project.

- All urban buses from all operators should be required to carry satellite tracking equipment which reports their exact position to a centralised computer system.

- The bus ticketing system should automatically report passenger numbers and fares paid on the same system.

- That information should be made available, along with the route of the bus, live on a website in a format accessible to screen scrapers.

- The exact routes and the number and times of buses on those routes currently provided by Dublin Bus should be recorded.

- All operators, including Dublin Bus, should be entitled to apply for licences to operate extra services.

- Dublin Bus should be required to commit to serving the route for a minimum of two years, to prevent them from applying for the route to keep out rivals.

- When a new operator begins a route, Dublin Bus should be prohibited from introducing or increasing services that compete with that service.

- In the event that Dublin Bus runs an unlicensed bus, all fares on that bus should be paid to the company licensed for that route.

- Bus companies should face a standard fine of €1m per instance for running a bus having interfered with the satellite tracking system.

It is also important to assign a ULI code to every bus stop in the country. As well as enforcing competition law, the purpose of making available live data on the position, direction and route of every bus would allow screen scrapers to build websites and mobile phone applications which would tell users exactly how long they would have to wait for a bus and when it was likely to get them to their destination.

Making passenger numbers on each bus available online would allow people to easily spot routes that are being under-served and enable better planning of routes.

Public Transport Security

Once you get on the bus or Luas, the experience can be less than pleasant. Stories of smoke-filled upper buses, with deeply threatening anti-social behaviour on buses[584] and the Luas[585] are common. Drivers are instructed not to leave their cabin, which is wise for their personal security; however, allowing minor infractions to go unchecked creates an atmosphere where more serious trouble is seen as acceptable. Using social disapproval is likely to be a much more effective way to curb such behaviour.

- A new offence of disruptive behaviour on public transport should be created.

- Supported by a public information campaign, bus drivers should be instructed not to tolerate any form of misbehaviour on buses, be it smoking, or threatening language or behaviour, or something more serious.

- When such behaviour is noticed by the driver or brought to their attention, drivers should request the gardaí be called on their radio.

- The control centre should direct gardaí to the bus using the satellite tracking information.

- The driver should stop the bus and announce over the PA system that the stated misbehaviour will not be tolerated, the gardaí are on their way, and if the offending passengers do not leave the bus before they arrive, they will be arrested.

- The bus should not move until the offenders are removed, by the gardaí or of their own accord.

Forcing the offenders, rather than the other passengers, to withdraw is a powerful psychological signal. Offenders would quickly learn that they cannot dominate the shared public space and would be reluctant to begin a contest that they cannot win.

Quality Bus Corridors

Quality Bus Corridors (QBCs) have been an enormous success,[586] despite intense campaigns from motor-industry lobbyists[587] against them. The cost-per-kilometre of QBCs is vastly lower than building Metro or Luas systems. The construction of far more QBCs can provide huge benefits, and not only to bus passengers. Buses move faster – much faster – on QBC routes, if they are not abruptly ended at junctions, and if unauthorised use of them is policed properly. For ease of enforcement, all QBCs should be closed to other traffic around the clock. Even if the buses don't run 24 hours per day, other traffic is unlikely to need the space in off-peak hours.

Buses running faster means that one bus and driver can service the route more times in a day, making the service more profitable for the supplier, and more reliable for the passenger. A double-decker bus can take up to 124 passengers,[588] which is the equivalent of more than 100 cars on the road. If people can rely on a fast and efficient bus service, this will encourage them to leave their car at home, particularly if the bus travels faster than they could driving; in addition, transferring that many passengers from cars to buses also improves journey times for the remaining car drivers. QBCs may look empty because the density of vehicles is low, but the density of passengers is far higher than on a driving lane.

Traffic Message Channel

Traffic Message Channel (TMC) data is broadcast on FM radio stations and picked up by GPS satellite navigation systems, so that they have real-time information about road works, traffic jams and other hold-ups.[589] Except in Ireland, it isn't. TMC has the capacity to be hugely useful to drivers, reducing journey times, saving fuel and emissions, giving better estimates of arrival times and reducing congestions by load-balancing traffic. Austria, Denmark, Germany, Portugal, Switzerland, Belgium, Finland, Italy, Spain, the Netherlands, Czech Republic, France, Norway, Sweden, United Kingdom, Slovenia, Slovakia and Hungary all have systems either planned or, in most cases, up and running for years. Ireland does not.[590] The service is usually provided by national broadcasters.

The phrase "Traffic Message Channel" does not even appear on RTÉ's website,[591] but RTÉ has a different method of giving out traffic information. AA Roadwatch has been broadcast on RTÉ and other stations since the early 1990s, providing valuable branding for the AA, a successful commercial organisation as well as a powerful lobbyist, but the value of the rapid-fire list of five or six streets that are "slow but moving" is of doubtful value to listeners.

TMC can deliver thousands of items of road information to a satellite navigation device, which can then display the ones on the driver's route and automatically recalculate the expected arrival time or plan another route automatically if appropriate. This is not planned future technology; it is currently in widespread use in the UK (including the North) and most countries on the continent. Ironically, the AA Roadwatch website provides a map[‡] which is almost identical to the information that is displayed by TMC on the screen of satellite navigation systems.

RTÉ's relationship with the AA is unhealthy and lacks transparency, so it is unclear whether its failure to provide a TMC service is as a result of pressure to maintain the AA's valuable branding on drivetime radio or just simple sloth on the part of RTÉ. The service costs almost nothing to provide, once data is supplied, and as can be seen from the AA's dynamic map, the data is already available.

Dublin City Council announced in December 2009 that it would begin broadcasting a TMC signal in its area,[592] although since no start date was announced, this may have been an attempt to force some action from RTÉ. It may have worked. A test conducted in March 2010 by the author indicated that RTÉ had, unannounced, enabled TMC transmission on Raidió na Gaeltachta transmitters, although no data was being transmitted.

- RTÉ should be required to provide a TMC service as part of their national broadcasting licence.

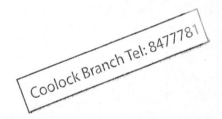

---

‡ www.aaroadwatch.ie/map

Conclusion

Anyone who grew up Irish in the 1970s and 1980s will be familiar with the national inferiority complex that came from the disappointments of independence. Our parents' generation could be told that emigration and social stagnation were worth suffering for the purity of a Gaelic Catholic island, but the advance of travel and communications meant that we were painfully aware of Ireland's humble position in the world.

The Celtic Tiger changed attitudes. Although some of its progress was an illusion, there was much that was real; it also transformed attitudes and expectations. We could succeed, we could be proud of our successes, and we could hold our heads high.

So when it all came crashing down, it is natural to feel that our success was just a brief aberration, and we will now go back to our tradition of failure and disappointment. But one thing is different: we know that we can succeed, because we have done it. If we can succeed once, we can do it again.

> The reasonable man adapts himself to the world; the unreasonable one persists in trying to adapt the world to himself. Therefore all progress depends on the unreasonable man.
>
> *George Bernard Shaw*

Notes

Almost all the references cited in this book are web pages from academic, news and other websites. Rather than wasting paper and printing them here, they are all available in the Reader-only Resources section of the website that accompanies this book, www.HeresHow.ie. If you want to check anything, this will allow you to easily click on the link to find the reference.

If you are interested in the ideas in this book, you can discuss, criticise and add to them on the discussion section at **www.HeresHow.ie/forum**. You can also contact the author, and you will be able to download a free bonus chapter, and view the hundreds of sources of information cited.

ALSO PUBLISHED BY BRANDON

Stephen MacDonogh. *Barack Obama: The Road from Moneygall*

The Irish ancestry of President Obama reveals the hidden history of the Protestant Irish who opened up the frontier west of the Appalachians, and tells the story of the Kearneys who moved out from Maryland in 1801 to be amongst the first settlers of Ohio, later acquiring lands of the Miami in Indiana, settling in Kansas, and participating in the great land rush of Oklahoma.

ISBN HB 9780863224065   PB 9780863224133

Michael Murphy. *At Five in the Afternoon*
My Battle with Male Cancer

'Brave and absorbing.' *Irish Independent*

'Murphy is to be commended for his open, personal and moving account... Each chapter deals with a different aspect of his experience, and Murphy lets us into his mind and heart, telling of the emotional and psychological effect it had on him and also gives us an insight into his relations with other people, three women in particular, which helped him cope.' *Books Ireland*

ISBN 9780863224263

Alan Simpson. *Duplicity and Deception*

Alan Simpson was the senior investigating officer in the case of the controversial killing of Belfast solicitor Pat Finucane. As he writes here, 'from the outset there was suspicion of security forces collusion in the murder.' He reveals for the first time the dramatic secrets behind the kidnapping and murder of Thomas Niedermayer, German Consul to Northern Ireland and manager of the Grundig factory. He reveals, too, the extraordinary degree of collusion between republican and loyalist paramilitaries. This is a unique insight into the murkiest aspects of policing, from an author who was at the heart of events.

ISBN HB 9780863224164   PB 9780863224287

www.brandonbooks.com

THE BOOKS OF MANCHÁN MAGAN

Angels and Rabies: A Journey Through the Americas

'[W]hile exposing the chaotic workings of his own soul, Magan reveals the underbelly of the colourful cultural and sociological jigsaw of these two great continents.' *Sunday Telegraph*

'Frightening, funny and lovable.' *The Sunday Times*

'His writing is intimate and immediate, perceptive and humorous.' *Books Ireland*

ISBN 9780863223495

Manchán's Travels: A Journey Through India

'While the local colour is entertaining, it is the writer's personal journey that makes this book so compelling. It's a funny and occasionally sad, but ultimately satisfying read.' *Sunday Telegraph*

'Magan has a keen eye for the hypocrisies of elite urban India and artfully evokes the "fevered serenity" of the Himalayas.' *Times Literary Supplement*

'Mad, brilliant and often hilarious.' *The Irish Times*

ISBN 9780863223686

Truck Fever: A Journey Through Africa

'Like *Lord of the Flies* meets *Lost* meets *The Amazing Race*, *Truck Fever* is an insightful soap opera that does Africa, its radiant and impenetrable muse, justice.' *Metro Life*

'An excellent writer, has a wonderful talent for transporting the reader into the heart of every experience. He is an intelligent observer of people and places, and his writing is sensitive and engaging. *Truck Fever* is a great read.' *Sunday Tribune*

ISBN 9780863223891

www.brandonbooks.com

Sean O'Callaghan. *To Hell or Barbados: The ethnic cleansing of Ireland*

'An illuminating insight into a neglected episode in Irish history... its main achievement is to situate the story of colonialism in Ireland in the much larger context of world-wide European imperialism.' *Irish World*

ISBN 9780863222870

Larry Kirwan. *Green Suede Shoes*

The sparkling autobiography of the lead singer and songwriter of New York rock band, Black 47.

'Lively and always readable. He has wrought a refined tale of a raw existence, filled with colorful characters and vivid accounts.' *Publishers Weekly*

ISBN 9780863223433

Gerry Adams. *Before the Dawn: An Autobiography*

'One thing about him is certain: Gerry Adams is a gifted writer who, if he were not at the center of the war-and-peace business, could easily make a living as an author, of fiction or fact.' *New York Times*

ISBN 9780863222897

Tom Reilly. *Cromwell: An Honourable Enemy*

'This is an important book. He is scrupulous in his examination of evidence, he has the necessary scepticism, he is assiduous in research and he quotes primary sources extensively.' *Sunday Times*

'A terrific job of research to make a case for Cromwell against the verdict of history.' *Irish Independent*

ISBN 9780863223907

www.brandonbooks.com